Desk Guide to Communication

Desk Guide to Communication

SECOND EDITION

Thomas E. Anastasi, Jr.

CBI Publishing Company, Inc.
51 Sleeper Street
Boston, Massachusetts 02210

Production Editor: Becky Handler
Designer: Bywater Production Services
Compositor: Trade Comp

Portions of this book were previously published in or have been adapted from other books by the author: *Communicating for Results,* © 1972 by Cummings Publishing Company, Menlo Park, Calif.; *Face-to-Face Communications; How to Manage Your Reading; How to Manage Your Speaking; How to Manage Your Writing* (all © 1971 by Thomas E. Anastasi, Jr. and published by General Electric Publishing Operation, Schenectady, N.Y.); and *A Secretary Is a Manager,* © 1970 by Thomas E. Anastasi, Jr. and published by Management Center of Cambridge, Cambridge, Mass.

Library of Congress Cataloging in Publication Data

Anastasi, Thomas E.
    Desk guide to communication.

    Includes index.
    1. Communication in management.   I. Title.
 HF5718.A74   1981   651.7   81-10180
 ISBN 0-8436-0855-2   AACR2

Printed in the United States of America

Printing (last digit): 9 8 7 6 5 4 3 2 1

Sometimes the cobbler fails to fix the holes in his children's shoes.

Sometimes the plumber lets the pipes in his own home go unrepaired.

Sometimes the mechanic straightens every dent but the one in his wife's fender.

Sometimes the dermatologist knows the heartbreak of psoriasis.

Sometimes people who write books about communication . . .

For all of my sometimes, this book is lovingly dedicated to my children, Cathy, Tom, and Nancy, and especially to my wife, Dorothy Devlin Anastasi.

Contents

Preface

I hope that this book will be useful to you. In it, I've tried to provide practical guidance on communication skill, answers to frequently asked questions about communication skill, and a foundation for your personal skill development—all in a reference format. When this book was conceived, it was titled *The Complete Guide to Communication*. Early in its gestation, I realized that the title was not only immodest, but also impossible, and that what I really wanted to write—and what you probably wanted to read—was an *incomplete* guide to communication. Neither you nor I would have the time for completeness.

People in business, industry, and government must communicate—on many occasions and in many forms. They must read, write, speak, listen, attend conferences, and conduct interviews. Sometimes, they're familiar with the most effective approaches to these communication opportunities, and sometimes they're not. This book can reinforce the skills you have and give you brief, practical guidance on the skills you're unsure of. It doesn't tell you everything you need to know about communication, but it should help you to get through any situation that requires a communication skill.

So, in a sense, this two-part book is a first-aid manual. Part I is a series of chapters giving guidance in the several skills of communication. If you want to develop your overall communication skill, you may find it helpful to read all the chapters. Or, you may prefer to use the chapters as reference guides when you must employ the skills discussed. The detailed Contents gives you an outline of the chapters in Part I.

Part II is an alphabetically indexed guide to usage, grammar, punctuation, spelling, pronunciation, and general information about communication. As a developmental exercise, you might want to read a few pages a day. And, of course, it will be ready as a reference when you want to check a point. Either way, this guide will give you up-to-date information on business usage.

As you use either Part I or Part II to help you communicate more effectively, keep in mind that communication is more than words. Communication is people—the men and women with whom you exchange messages—and your skill will be best applied if you keep the people in mind.

T.E.A., Jr

Desk Guide to Communication

Part One
COMMUNICATION SKILLS

1
About Communication

This book is a guide to the most commonly used skills of communication in the business and technical worlds. Part I covers writing in its several forms: letters, reports, and memos; oral communication in its several forms: presentations, meetings and conferences, and interviewing; the receiving skills of listening and reading; as well as other related topics such as grammar, punctuation, audiovisual aids, dictation, editing, and selection of mediums. Part II provides up-to-date guidance on spoken and written usage. It is, I hope, a reasonably complete guide that will help you to communicate more effectively. Stressing as it does the forms and messages that are the heart of your communication activities, this book should not be used without this caution: Communication is not simply a skill with words. Skill with words is mere glibness when it's used without an understanding of the real nature of communication.

The term "communication," most effectively understood, is a word we use to describe all the ways in which people affect one another. It covers not only what we say and write but also what we do. A useful understanding of communication must include the realization that we communicate by what we don't say or don't write or don't do as well as by the circumstances that surround our activity or inactivity in message sending. We communicate with people when we affect them any way. They communicate with us when they affect us in any way. Words are part of communication but only the most obvious part.

This book shows you how to communicate effectively through the various mediums that are part of business and technical life today. This brief introduction suggests that communication is more than words and forms and that communication skill is more than glibness or facility with language. Style is important to communication skill. It's important, too, to have useful ideas to express and to have a reason for listening or reading. It's also important to understand what communication really is and to make use of that understanding in your communication.

The effect we have on people is the standard by which we measure the effectiveness of our communication activities. How, for instance, do we measure the effectiveness of a sales presentation? We ask, don't we, "Did it sell?" We don't ask about the style of the presentation or the esthetic effect of the visuals or samples. If you or I go to a meeting to present an idea or write a report or a letter to stimulate a decision or an action, how do we measure our success, our effectiveness? The answer is, of course, by the response to our idea, by the decision, or by the action. Management literature focuses on *management by objectives* and on *results-oriented management*. Effective communication must have the same focus.

All this means that communication is focused on people and on their needs and responses rather than on words and their order and arrangement. This focus calls our attention to timing. If I expect to get a message from you about a matter which concerns me and if no message comes, then I am affected. You have communicated. Your delay sent me a message—perhaps one which you never intended—which suggests that you are disinterested in me or my problem or that you can't handle the problem. Must we, then, always send messages promptly? Certainly not. There may be many reasons for delay. But in considering the timing of a message, we should weigh the effects of delay. And we should not expect a cleverly worded note to compensate for what, to our receiver, appears to be poor timing.

The effective communicator is aware that messages cannot solve all problems. There seems to be a folk-myth that you can get people to respond as you'd like if you put it to them in the right words. Nonsense. Before one person will respond positively to another and to his or her ideas, the one must first give the other something to respond to. A way with words can't compensate for deficiencies in products, programs, or service.

If you use communication to present useful ideas in a useful way, you'll communicate successfully in most instances. You can't expect to be successful all the time, because you're dealing with people, and people aren't totally predictable.

To communicate effectively, realize the role of words in the communication process. Words are symbols. They stand for things and for concepts; they are not, in themselves, things or concepts. Words have definitions, which can be found in dictionaries. But the meanings of words are to be found in the people who use the words and who respond to them.

If I have an idea, I cannot send it to you. My idea can never leave my head. To communicate, I must try to find a word or some other symbol (a picture, graph, table of figures, gesture, grunt, or nod) which can represent my idea. I can show you a symbol. I cannot show you my idea, so I send you my symbol to represent that idea.

You receive my message, my symbols. Do you respond to them, or do you respond to the idea in my head that prompted that message? The answer is neither. No, you must first decide on the meaning, to *you*, of those symbols at the time at which the message was sent and the meaning to you of me, the sender. You, the receiver, must *add* meaning to my message. Then you will respond—not to my message and its symbols and not to the idea that I started with—but to the meaning *you* add. All this says that if you want to communicate effectively with the people with whom you must deal, you must know not only what you want to say but also as much as you can about the people to whom you will be communicating. When you write or speak, consider the receivers and the meaning they are likely to add to your message, for it is to the meaning they add that they will respond. Conversely, as readers and listeners, we must seek out the meaning the sender intended; otherwise, we find ourselves responding to ourselves rather than to the people whose messages we are trying to read or to listen to.

Effective communicators reach out beyond themselves to the people with whom they communicate. They avoid communicating in a self-centered focus. They realize that communication is far more than an exchange of words or symbols; it is a search for meaning, a process through which we affect others and are, in turn, affected by them. Communication centers on people—not on words. Words are important to a communicator, but people are more important. If there's one fault that characterizes poor speaking, writing, reading, listening, interviewing, counseling, or any other form of communication, it's self-centeredness. Reach out for meaning and for understanding; see communication in the perspective of its social context. Who is writing or saying what to whom? When? Where? Why? Under what circumstances? What is their previous relationship? What is each likely to have in mind? What are each person's goals, needs, and biases? What meaning is each likely to add? How will this affect both parties to the communication transaction? See communication in terms of the people involved, yourself included, and in terms of the effect the exchange of meaning is likely to have on each, and see the words and symbols as one of the vehicles of meaning. If you will see your communication activities in that perspective, then the suggestions in the rest of this book will be useful to you. But if you see your communication activities as the mere manipulation of words and forms, then the most you can hope for is a superficial glibness.

"Communication" describes all the ways people affect each other. When you communicate in any form, make sure that you go beyond the words to the person. Realize that communication is an interaction between you and the people with whom you communicate and that your real message is the total of all the ways you affect those people and of all the ways they affect you.

2
When to Write and When to Speak

Usually, we have several mediums available to us when we must send a message. We can write a letter or memo, make a phone call, call a meeting, arrange a face-to-face interview, send a wire, or choose some other medium. The choice of medium is optional, but important. Let's look at some of the considerations involved in selecting a written or oral medium.

ADVANTAGES OF WRITTEN MEDIUMS

Useful for mass communication.
If you have to get a message to many people at the same time, it's often quicker and cheaper to send copies of a written message than it is to call them all together for a meeting or to talk to them individually.

Useful as a record.
If it's important to have a precise record of the message, writing provides this.

Useful if the message must travel through a chain of receivers.
If your message must travel from person to person along a chain, then writing offers an advantage that speech can't duplicate. Communicating

the message orally risks distorting it. We've all heard of the experiment in which a message is given to one person, who passes it along to others through several links of the chain. When the person who is the last link reports the final version of the message, it usually has little resemblance to the original.

Useful if formality is needed.
A written message usually has more formality and authority than a spoken message. Laws and regulations are written, as are orders and directives. Writing a message gives it authority and formality, but you should also realize that there are many occasions when formality and authority beget resistance. Writers may appear to be throwing their weight around, may appear to be pushing people. Most people, when pushed, push back.

Useful to get your message to places where you can't go.
There are many people to whom you'd like to speak, even though you can't get to see them. Your memo or letter can, however, get their attention. We often use letters and memos to arrange appointments. In this case, the written message is best used to assure the receivers that it would be worth their time to hear our more detailed oral message.

Useful because it is convenient.
You can write when it's convenient for you to do so, and your reader can read it at leisure. There's no need to coordinate your convenience with the reader's, no need to arrange a mutually convenient time for a face-to-face meeting.

ADVANTAGES OF ORAL MEDIUMS

Generally faster.
It usually takes less time to make a phone call or to have a conversation than it does to prepare a document, even one as simple as a letter or memo. People who want to save time have found that they can do so by converting much of their writing to speaking. And, of course, your oral message doesn't have to go through the mails.

Two-way exchange.
Oral communication allows a two-way exchange. Each person can respond or ask questions on the spot. This promotes clarity in novel situations. It permits instant response. Writing, on the other hand, is always one way. I write to you, and you send me a letter in reply. Two-way communication? No, writing is a series of one-way messages. It's instant response that makes communication two-way.

This instant response feature of two-way, oral communication makes it the most useful for negotiating or resolving problems as well as for instructing, coaching, or counseling. Detailed explanation is better delivered orally than in writing, as it permits questions, discussion, and personalized explanation. The two-way, instant response feature of oral communication makes it most useful in situations involving change.

Less expensive.

When we write a letter, it takes writing time, dictating time, transcribing time, and filing time. A face-to-face meeting or phone conversation takes only the speaking time. The same is true for an oral briefing or presentation as compared with a written report. Of course, there are other considerations that make a report the medium of choice on many occasions.

Clearer.

The two-way nature of oral communication promotes clarity with less effort. Written messages, of course, can be clear, but it takes more effort and more skill to make them so.

Less formal.

Oral communication has the informality of conversation. It's often less authoritative and threatening than written communication. Unfortunately, however, many people fail to take advantage of this informality and instead turn their oral messages into imposing orations with the rigidity of poor writing. We'll look more closely at oral presentations in chapter 11.

More persuasive.

It's easier to persuade people through the spoken word than through the written. Telephone talk is more persuasive than a letter, and the most persuasive medium is face-to-face, individual, or small-group talk. Oral communication is a natural, simple, human medium. Many cultures in world history have failed to develop a system of writing, but every culture has developed some form of speech. Writing is an artificial form, an attempt to represent speech on paper. It's the natural, human quality of speech that makes spoken communication so useful for persuasion.

As you plan your communication, consider the various mediums available to you. There are many factors to consider as you choose a medium, among them your own preferences and those of your receivers. The foregoing is presented only to help you in your thinking about your choice of medium. It's your message, your idea, and your choice of how you can best express it.

As we look at the various forms of communication in the rest of this book, we'll explore more of the advantages and limitations of each medium of communication. The brief comparison is given here to start you thinking about the advantages and limitations of mediums and to serve as a general guide for planning communication strategies.

3
Foundations of Effective Writing

A great deal of paper comes to your desk in a year. How much of it is readable? How much of it is simple, clear, and useful? O.K., so much for your "in" basket. Now, what about your "out" basket? What about your writing? How much of it is readable, simple, clear, and useful?

If your answers to the questions are uncomfortably negative, why? You're competent at your job, aren't you? When you write, you have something to say. Why, then, does it come out the way it does? In this chapter, we're going to look at some basics of clear, simple, effective writing. Then, in succeeding chapters, we'll see how these basics can be applied to the various forms of writing that you use in your work.

Let's start with the most important point: *Keep your writing simple*. In fact, if you're looking for a quick guide to better writing, you won't find one more useful than that. There are many books on the subject of business writing, report writing, letter writing, and technical writing. Each of these books stresses that same theme: *Keep it simple*.

Good writing is simple. Although it may not hold true that all simple writing is good, simplicity is still the best place to start if you want to improve your writing. The following are some guides for keeping your writing simple and clear.

GUIDE 1: SAY IT SIMPLY

Consider the words of business writing. Too often, they're stuffy, pompous, and unclear. They're not the words we'd use when speaking. Speaking is a natural form of communication, and writing should be as natural as possible, which is to say that it should use the words and forms of the spoken language instead of the stiff language so common in writing. Take the following paragraph, for instance. Does it sound typical of business writing?

> Efforts should be made to bring about an increase in actual sales over those forecast for future quarters remaining in this fiscal year. In the event that the desired increases cannot be achieved, a cutback in production with its resultant losses in work-force strength will be necessitated.

That's a very complicated way to say:

> Try to increase sales over those forecast for the rest of the fiscal year. If we're not able to increase sales, we may have layoffs in the production crew.

The first version uses heavy, formal phrases seldom used in good conversation. There are many such words and phrases in common use, and it would be impossible to list them all, but here's a sample. Look at the words and phrases in the first column. If you use them in your writing, you'll find that your writing will be simpler and more readable if you'll substitute the words in the second column.

If you usually write	Put it this way
in the event that	if
during which time	while
at which time	when, then
on the occasion of	when
in order to	to
for the purpose of	to
in the month of January	in January
prior to	before
subsequent to	after
enclosed herewith please find XYZ	XYZ is enclosed, I've enclosed XYZ, here is XYZ
attached please find XYZ	I've attached XYZ, here is XYZ
at the present time	now
at this point in time	now
with regard to	about
regarding	about
concerning	about

respecting	about
cognizant	aware
additional	more
solicit	ask, seek
raise the question	ask
with the understanding that	if
contemplate	plan, think
until such time as	until, when
along the lines of	like
in view of the fact that	because
in spite of the fact that	although
promulgate	issue
pursuant to	following
transpire	happen
penultimate	next to last
fabricate	make, build
initiate	begin
commence	begin, start
terminate	end, finish
conclude	end, finish
finalize	end, finish, complete
utilize	use
deem	think, decide
ascertain	learn
afford an opportunity	allow
procure	get
purchase	buy
make inquiry concerning	ask about
give consideration to	consider
definitive	final, complete
maximize	make the most of

And on, and on, and on. It would be impossible to make a complete list. New words and phrases are added every day. Anyway, my list isn't important—yours is. Take a sample of your writing and look it over. Do you have pet words and phrases like those above? If you do, simplify. Your writing will be better for it.

Perhaps we use words and phrases like the preceding (and other treasures like *ramifications, parameters, viable, optimization, per se, interface, feedback, input, vis-à-vis,* and *perspicuous*) because we read them so often in business literature that we think they belong in what we write. They don't. Or perhaps we use them to impress the people to whom we write. What about you? Are you impressed by writing of this sort? Or are you more likely to be impressed by good, useful ideas clearly expressed? Of course we want to impress our readers. The best way to do this is to give them good, useful information expressed so that they can quickly grasp it and use it. Before you can express yourself simply, you must first know what you're talking about. Your readers know this just as you do, and they'll be most impressed with you and with what you say if you do so clearly and simply. Use the words that you would use if you were speaking. Avoid the pompous style of the ineffective business or technical writer.

GUIDE 2: LET THE VERBS LIVE

Verbs are important; they are the souls of sentences. But far too many writers kill them.

Look at this sentence:

An inspection of the site was made by our architect.

The predicate, the verb, of this sentence is "was made." Now, does that sentence have anything to do with "making"? No. What is the central idea of that sentence? Somebody inspected something. There was action; somebody did something, and what the architect did was "inspect."

If that sentence is revised to what it should have been in the first place, we have:

Our architect inspected the site.

This sentence is shorter, simpler, clearer, and far more readable than the first example. Why? Because somebody did something, and this revision says quite clearly that somebody did something. Nothing "was made," and the second sentence doesn't mention "making."

Let's look at another sentence:

An increase in sales was obtained last quarter.

Or perhaps:

We realized an increase in sales last quarter.

Forget the wording of those two sentences for a moment. What is the idea being expressed? What is happening? Something increased last quarter. What increased? Sales. Was there any "obtaining" or "realizing" going on? No. What was going on? Sales were increasing. Doesn't this, therefore, say it better?

Sales increased last quarter.

The examples we've seen commit the same sin. The writers took useful, descriptive verbs *(inspected* and *increased)* and made nouns of them *(inspection* and *increase)*. Then, because all sentences need verbs for their predicates, they brought in weak, nondescriptive verbs *(was made, was obtained,* and *realized)* that had nothing to do with the sentences.

Don't turn verbs into nouns. Let the verb express an important idea in the sentence.

A few more examples may help to make the point. In these examples, the predicate verb in each sentence is italicized. Note how the verb in the revision (which was in noun form in the original) is the focus of what's happening in the sentence.

Weak verb	*Revision*
An improvement in service *has been made.*	Service *has improved.*
A sharp decrease in costs *was noted.*	Costs *decreased* sharply.
Registration of the exhibitors *occurred* at 9:00 A.M.	The exhibitors *registered* at 9:00 A.M.
Adjustment of the clearance *was performed* at the plant.	The clearance *was adjusted* at the plant.
Reorganization of the company *was effected* without delay.	The company *was* quickly *reorganized.*

As you can see, it's not hard to leave the life in your verbs; the result is better, clearer, more effective sentences that get the idea across with crisp emphasis.

As you review your writing, keep a careful watch for nouns with endings like *ion, ing, ment, ence, ance, ency, ent,* and *ant.* These endings change verbs into nouns. Naturally, not all words with these endings indicate a misuse of a verb idea in a noun form, but if you're looking for sentences in which the verb has lost its life, these endings are good clues.

If you'd like to practice before improving the verbs in your own writing, here are a few sentences for you to work with. Rewrite the sentences in Exercise A to put life into the verbs. Make the verb express the central idea of the sentence. As a check, compare your revisions with those suggested at the end of this chapter.

Exercise A.

1. Issuance of the report was achieved without delay.
2. Inspection of the boilers was performed by the resident engineer.
3. The increase in budget is predicated on the assumption that more staff will be necessary.
4. A request for the material has been made by the purchasing office.
5. It is our desire to have the matter settled without delay.
6. Receipt of the subject memorandum is hereby noted.
7. Application for this position should be made as soon as possible.
8. Reference is made in our purchase order #345, dated 25 July.

If you've been able to handle most of those sentences, you should feel confident of your ability to keep the life in the verbs in your own writing. As you look over what you write, pay particular attention to the verbs as well as to the tired, pompous phrases you saw in Guide 1. Try too to keep your verbs *active*, which is the topic of Guide 3.

GUIDE 3: PREFER ACTIVE VERBS

This guide deals with the *voice* of your verbs. If that term seems scary and reminiscent of long-forgotten English classes, don't let it frighten you. There are two *voices* of the verb: *active* and *passive*. Most of your speaking is in the active voice, but if you're like many people, much of your writing is in the passive voice. It's a simple fault to correct, and if you'll give it a little attention, you can easily improve the readability of your writing.

First, let's note that voice has nothing to do with the tense, or time, of the verb. The passive voice can be present tense (The ball is hit by John), past tense (The ball was hit by John), future tense (The ball will be hit by John), or any other tense (The ball will have been hit by John. The ball is being hit by John. The ball was being hit by John.). Time has nothing to do with voice.

The flow of the action in the sentence is what determines the voice of a verb; that is, whether a verb is active or passive. If the action flows *from* the subject, the verb is active; if it flows *to* the subject, the verb is passive. The verb in this sentence is active:

John hit the ball.

The verb in this sentence is passive:

The ball was hit by John.

In the sentence with the active verb, the subject, *John*, is doing something. In the passive sentence, the subject, *ball*, is having something done to it. If the subject is acting, the verb is active; if the subject is being acted upon, the verb is passive. Here are some examples of sentences in both voices:

Active voice	*Passive voice*
The Sales Manager called a meeting.	A meeting was called by the Sales Manager.
Purchasing ordered the new typewriters.	The new typewriters were ordered by Purchasing.
The proposal will specify a payment schedule.	A payment schedule will be specified by the proposal.
The company is maintaining an active market in software.	An active market in software is being maintained by the company.
The shareholders asked many questions at the meeting.	Many questions were asked at the meeting by the shareholders.

The passive voice, as you've probably noticed, always takes more words to express the same idea:

The shareholders asked many questions at the meeting.
Many questions were asked at the meeting by the shareholders.

Thus, it takes more words and more space to state an idea in the passive voice. Wordiness, in itself, reduces readability. But that's not the only objection to the passive voice. The passive voice muffles the action of a verb by turning it inside out. Action normally flows from the person or thing acting. To reverse this flow is to interfere with clarity.

The passive voice is often used to mask the identity of the doer of the action. It emphasizes the receiver of the action, as in this example:

A new procedure was recommended.

Who recommended the new procedure?

An error in the accounts was found.

Who found the error?

If I had to act on the matters discussed in the two examples above, I'd want to know who was recommending and who found the error. The procedure and the error would be of interest, to be sure, but they would mean most to me if I could also know their sources.

Another common use of the passive voice, and one most destructive of readability, usefulness, and clarity is the all-too-common "It is" construction, as in the following examples:

> *It is* assumed that all personnel are qualified to operate the equipment.
> *It is* suggested that steps be taken to minimize access to the proprietary data.
> *It is* recommended that this practice be halted.
> *It is* reported that an investigation will be conducted.
> *It is* well known that he will soon leave the company.

Each of these sentences hides the doer—perhaps intentionally, perhaps unintentionally. But the effect is the same: loss of clarity as well as of impact and emphasis. To restore effectiveness to these sentences, we must change to the active voice and tell the reader who did it.

The passive voice is wordy, weak, often misleading, hard to read, and unnatural in most of its uses. We seldom use the passive voice when we speak. Most of our speech has the emphasis and naturalness of the stronger, active voice. We'd do well to keep the active voice prevalent in our writing, too. If you're like many people, you have the unconscious habit of writing in the passive voice. A little attention can cure that, and until it does, revision can help you to change your passive verbs to active. Exercise B contains a few sentences to touch up if you'd like to practice. Rewrite these sentences to make the passive verbs active. When you've finished, you can compare your results with the revisions suggested at the end of this chapter.

Exercise B.

1. Marketing strategies were considered by the committee.
2. It is suggested that you review the manual from time to time.
3. Appropriate changes to the policy were made by the General Manager.
4. Final estimates of revenue were made by the auditors.
5. Your estimates have been reviewed by the Contracts Officer.
6. Losses are expected to exceed $85 million.

By this time you may be wondering why, if there are no valid uses for the passive voice, there is a passive voice at all. There *are* valid uses for the passive voice. I should stress that it's overuse of the passive voice that is objectionable.

The passive voice is useful:

1.   When the doer is unimportant.

Eighteen test borings were made on the site.
America was discovered in 1492.

2.   When you want to emphasize the receiver, rather than the doer, of the action.

He was sentenced to eighteen months in jail.
The machine was repaired two weeks ago.

3.   When the doer is unknown.

The files were misplaced.
A bomb had been placed in the aircraft.

All the above show valid uses of the passive voice. But, in most instances, if you have a choice between expressing your ideas in either the active or passive voice, your writing will be clearer, simpler, more emphatic, and more readable if you choose the stronger, more vivid active voice. Keep a check on your writing style, and if you're in the habit of using the passive voice, break that habit. As you review your writing, keep a pencil handy to change the passive verbs to active.

GUIDE 4: BE SPECIFIC AND CONCRETE

Effective writing uses words economically. This often means using more precise words. Take the following sentence, for instance:

We plan to construct a long-term storage and distribution facility on this site.

This sentence suggests that we plan to build something someplace. What are we planning to build? According to the sentence, we plan to build a *facility*. That's the noun used to specify the object of our building plans. But, exactly what is a "facility"? An office is a facility. A factory is a facility. So are a laboratory, a refinery, a men's room, a sports stadium, and almost anything else you could think of that could be built. But this sentence doesn't want to say that we're planning to build any of those things; thus, to the general and abstract noun "facility," it adds the explanatory words "long-term storage and distribution" to tell the reader what kind of a facility is planned.

Suppose that the writer had used a more concrete and specific noun to describe the thing to be built:

We plan to build a warehouse on this site.

If he had done that, he would have written a shorter, clearer sentence that would have expressed his idea more effectively. The point of all this is that concrete, specific words are better vehicles for expression than are general, abstract words. Specific expression not only saves words but also does the job better. Which describes a warehouse better: "warehouse" or "long-term storage and distribution facility"?

Choose the right *noun* and *verb* to say what you want to say. Look at this sentence:

The open-topped vehicle went quickly and carelessly down the wide, tree-shaded thoroughfare.

Couldn't that be more efficiently and effectively expressed as:

The convertible careened down the boulevard.

Abstraction, the use of imprecise and general terms where more meaningful words can be used, destroys clarity. In the following, abstract wording makes it difficult for anyone to react as the writer intended:

Recently, cost figures have been seen to increase. We cannot tolerate much more increase and therefore urge all department heads to effect substantial reductions in costs in the near future. Reports on the measures taken to achieve this should be submitted promptly.

This whole paragraph is vague. Sure, you get the idea that the writer is cracking down on cost, but exactly what does he or she want? Let's see if concrete words would be more effective:

Recently. Would it be helpful to know when this started?
Cost figures. What costs? Overhead, direct labor, material, shipping, etc. All of these, or one, or some?
Increase. By how much? How big is the problem?
Much more increase. How much can we tolerate? Will an increase really hurt us?
Substantial reductions. How much should we cut? Is 10 percent substantial? Or 50 percent? Do we eliminate some operations?

Costs. Again, which costs?

In the near future. When? This week? Is next month good enough? What
    about next fiscal year?

Promptly. When? Today? When we've outlined our plans? When we
    have results? When?

People will react to this message from the boss because it's from the
boss, but will they do what the boss wants? All these abstractions can have
one meaning to the writer and another to the reader. The relationship of
abstract words to reality is far more remote than the relationship of concrete
words to reality. The memo above may bring action, but the action could
easily be too much or too little. Less confusion and more positive action
would be likely to come from the same memo worded this way:

Direct labor and material costs have increased by about 13 percent over
the past four months. A 2 percent additional increase in these costs would
seriously affect our ability to bid on future work. I, therefore, urge all
department heads to take a personal interest in cost reduction. I realize
that this cannot be accomplished overnight, but a reduction of 5 percent
per month for the next three months would wipe out the increase and
put us in a more favorable position than we have seen in over two years.

When you choose an abstract word, you raise the likelihood that it
will mean one thing to you and another to your reader. When you use an
imprecise word, you must shore it up with modifiers, and you will probably
still end up with a phrase that falls short of adequate explanation. For
instance, take the use of the imprecise word "device" in this sentence:

The product needs an improved heat-sensing device.

Because "device" is so imprecise, it needs the clarification of "heat-
sensing." But even after this, we're left to wonder what that device may
be. Is it a thermometer, a pyrometer, a bimetallic coil, or a thermocouple?
A better sentence would be:

The product needs an improved thermocouple.

General words are fine when used in a general sense. There's nothing
wrong with a memo that directs that "all company *facilities* should be
checked for fire safety." The writer clearly needed a general word. The
only other choice would have been to have listed every company facility
and that would have been farcical.

Use general words to denote broad categories, but use specific words
for specific things. I would correctly refer to all the rolling stock in my

town as *vehicles*, but I would better refer to my own vehicle as a *sedan* and not as a *vehicle*.

GUIDE 5: USE MODIFIERS EFFECTIVELY

Words conduct meaning. We use them to transmit ideas. They are really semiconductors and can also act as insulators. If five words will express an idea clearly and adequately, the addition of five more words, which do not change the meaning, will make the phrase less clear and less readable. The idea will have to bear the excess weight of five additional words. This is not so if the words added also add or change meaning. We call adverbs and adjectives and the phrases and clauses that do their work *modifiers*. To *modify* is to *change*. Modifiers that don't change aren't doing anything to help the reader understand your message. They just give more words to read. Take this passage, for instance:

> It is absolutely essential that the final and definitive data be entirely complete. Exactly identical carbon copies should be submitted to me and to the General Manager. Several departments may be required to cooperate together to ensure that the necessary requirements are met.

Doesn't this say the same thing?

> The final data must be complete. Submit identical copies to me and to the General Manager. Several departments may have to cooperate to do this.

Isn't it clearer? We eliminated several of the redundant couplets that we see all too often.

Absolutely essential means no more than *essential. Essential* is *absolute. Final* and *definitive* say the same thing. Saying the same thing twice makes a statement no more final or definitive and, in fact, suggests that the words aren't as strong and final as they seem, since one wasn't enough for the job. The same can be said for *entirely complete.* And *cooperate together* suggests that there may be some other type of cooperation. *Requirements* are *necessary,* so no new meaning is added by having one of these words modify the other.

Writers also waste a lot of space with words like:

very	somewhat	basically
rather	considerable	generally
quite	more or less	

These words are usually a waste of time. More often than not, they weaken the sentences in which they are used:

We got very superior results.
His performance has been quite a bit better this quarter.
It is, on the whole, somewhat vague.

I can't say that these words should never be used. Sometimes they are necessary—but seldom. Don't get into the habit of throwing them in as you write, in the mistaken assumption that to do so is to add strength. As you review your writing, question each of these intensives. If you can strike it out while leaving the meaning intact, you'll have improved the sentence. If taking the intensive out means changing the meaning, leave it in.

When we think of modifiers, we think of adverbs and adjectives. Adjectives modify (explain, describe, limit, and point out) nouns and pronouns. Adverbs modify verbs, adjectives, and other adverbs. Phrases and clauses modify too. Often, an adjective or an adverb can substitute for a phrase or clause—with improved readability the result. For instance, the sentence:

The door to his office is open.

could be improved by changing the phrase "to his office" to the adjective "office":

His office door is open.

Suppose the sentence had originally been:

The door that leads to his office is open.

The same result could have been achieved by substituting the one word "office" for the much longer clause "that leads to his office." In either case, the writer would have used fewer words to make a sharper, more readable statement.

You can see this principle in operation in the following sentences:

- The tool that is employed for cutting is not sharp enough.
  Better: The cutting tool is not sharp enough.
  (It might be better still to name the tool and its condition more precisely and say: *The milling head is dull.*)
- The bin used for the storage of bolts was open.
  Better: The bolt bin was open.
- The property of the prisoners was accounted for.
  Better: We accounted for the prisoners' property.

The shorter sentence is not always the better sentence, but if you use words economically, you'll improve your writing. If the shorter sentence leaves out essential information, it will be ineffective; but if it retains the information and leaves out only unnecessary words, it will be a better vehicle for your ideas and information.

IN CONCLUSION

This chapter has described the foundations of an effective writing style. In the chapters that follow, we'll examine the specific forms of writing to give you more guidance in expressing yourself effectively. There is more to know about writing than we have covered in this chapter, but if you'll use the five guides we've looked at, you'll have done much to develop a clear, effective style of writing. These five areas represent the most common weaknesses in style as well as those most easily corrected. Use these guides as you review your rough drafts. Don't try to write and edit at the same time. Write as you always have. Apply these principles when you review your writing. That way you'll develop a better style as you improve your written work. At first, this simpler writing style may be hard for you to acquire because you've probably developed some bad habits, but once you get those habits under control, writing more simply and clearly will take less time, and it will produce better results. Your good ideas and your professional competence will come through to your reader with far greater impact.

Which areas give you the greatest difficulty? Analyze your writing. Take a few samples from your files and compare them with this checklist:

1. *Are your ideas expressed simply?*
   Do you use long or difficult words where shorter, simpler words would do?
   Are the words you use those you would use if speaking?
   Are your readers likely to be familiar with all the words you use, or are you trying to dazzle them with your vocabulary and your mastery of jargon and the current fad words of your field?
   Do you use the tired formula phrases you so often see in other people's writing? Are they necessary to express your ideas?
   If you were speaking, would you have expressed your ideas that way? Can you express yourself more naturally?
2. *Are your verbs alive?*
   Do the predicates of your sentences express important ideas, or are they weak?
   Is the main idea expressed by a noun or an adjective when it should be expressed by a verb?

3. *Are your verbs active?*
    Well, are they? Or, have you slipped into the weak, all-too-common dependence on the passive verb?
    Would an active verb express your ideas with greater clarity or emphasis?
    If you were expressing that idea in conversation, would you use an active verb? (Or to put it in passive form, *Would an active verb be used for expression of that idea in oral form?* Now, aren't you glad that I didn't write this whole book with weak and passive verbs? Do you see what they do to readability? Your readers will be grateful for your active, strong verb forms. Give them and your ideas a break.)
4. *Do you use concrete and specific words?*
5. *Are your modifiers effective?*
    Do you use clauses and phrases where a single word would do?
    Do all your modifiers add to the meaning? Could any be deleted without significantly changing the meaning?
    Do you overuse intensives such as *very, rather, quite, awfully,* and *really?*

If your writing measures up well against this checklist, your style is in the top 10 percent of business and technical writing. If it doesn't, then a little effort can quickly move you to that level. Make the effort. It's well worth it because it produces writing easier to read and more likely to get results. You'll feel more satisfied with your writing if you know that you're doing a good job.

The writing process.
In addition to the question of style, there's also the problem of actually getting the writing on the paper. Many people who know what they want to say and who have a good idea of style find the writing process itself tedious.

The most common complaint of business writers is their inability to get started and to keep the words flowing. Writing seems like drudgery. A letter or a simple report takes an inordinately long time to produce. If this is so for you, it's probably because you are trying to do two jobs at once. As a result, you aren't doing either of them very well. The two jobs are writing and editing, and you can't do them at the same time.

Many writers try to do them at the same time and the result is frustration. Perhaps you're that kind of writer. Let's see. You begin a piece of writing. You're a paragraph or two into the piece when you decide that the introduction is weak, so you go back and rewrite the beginning. You go forward again a few sentences only to be stopped by a grammatical decision. You clear that up and continue—then a punctuation question arises to stop your forward progress. That is no sooner resolved when doubt about the rewriting of the introduction inserts itself into your thoughts. Your mind is constantly led to judge everything you have written. You are caught up in the schizophrenic torment of writing and editing at the same time. You become discontented and discouraged and convinced that you're a rotten writer. You write, you rewrite, you edit, you amend, you blaspheme. You hate writing and you become surer and surer that you'll never be able to write worth a damn. It takes you forever to write something that you feel should take only a few minutes. Is that you?

If it is, you're not alone. Many people write that way. You can avoid all that frustration and you can write better in less time if you'll keep writing and editing as separate functions. Write first. Edit later.

When you have a writing job to do, do it from start to finish. If you find it difficult to begin because you can't think of the proper introduction, add the introduction later. In fact, most introductions are too long and, in large part, unnecessary.

Once you start to write, keep going. Don't stop to correct spelling or punctuation. You can straighten that out later. If you are worried that what you have written is inadequate, don't go back now and rewrite it; you can do that later. Keep your train of thought on the track. Don't concern yourself with the proper choice of words. If you put something down now, you can improve it later; but if you sit in front of your typewriter waiting for inspiration, you will only distract yourself. There is a momentum in writing; idea builds upon idea and phrase upon phrase. If you keep at the job, this momentum will do much to carry you through. You won't write anything so bad that you can't correct it later when you become your own editor.

If you keep the writing and the editing functions separate, you'll write better, find it less frustrating, and spend less time. Write first; let the piece sit awhile if you can; then edit. While the piece is sitting in your desk drawer, the ideas will be congealing in your own mind. When you edit, you won't be editing word by word and sentence by sentence; you'll be doing it the way it should be done. You'll be editing with a view to the whole. It is the impression made by the whole that should concern you. Most good writers don't try to do a perfect writing job. Experienced writers know perfection is impossible; they strive instead to do an adequate job, a job that's good enough. By "good enough" I don't mean mediocre. I mean a job that is truly adequate or *good enough* to achieve the writer's goals.

Hence this tip: Write adequately. When you have a writing job to do, aim for adequacy, for a good job. If you work hard and try your best, you are capable of a good job. When you achieve that good job, you will achieve satisfaction. Writing won't seem such a chore. You'll be more confident in your ability. You'll be able to find satisfaction in writing.

Strive for adequacy. You can achieve it, and adequate writing can achieve your goals for you. If you have confidence in your writing ability, you'll write more; you won't run away from writing tasks, and with practice, your writing will develop and improve.

ANSWERS TO EXERCISE A

The verbs in Exercise A could be improved this way:

1. We issued the report immediately.
2. The resident engineer inspected the boilers.
3. The budget increase assumes a need for more staff.
4. The purchasing office requested the material.
5. We'd like to settle the matter now.
6. We received the memorandum.
7. You should apply for this position as soon as possible.
8. We refer to our purchase order #345, dated 25 July.

It's not important that your revisions be in these exact words. It is important, however, that you have the main idea in the verb.

ANSWERS TO EXERCISE B

These revisions make the passive verbs active:

1. The committee considered marketing strategies.
2. We suggest that you review the manual from time to time.
   or
   Review the manual from time to time.
3. The General Manager made appropriate changes to the policy.
   or better still
   The General Manager changed the policy.
4. The auditors made final estimates of revenue.
   or
   The auditors estimated revenue.
5. The Contracts Officer reviewed your estimates.
6. I *(or some other person named as the subject)* expect losses to exceed $85 million.

4

How to Write a Letter

We write letters to inform, to inquire, to persuade, to record, and to be polite. We'll look specifically at each of these types, but first let's look at how to make letters in general effective. A letter is a substitute for talk. Effective letters are written in a style that is simple and conversational to preserve that person-to-person feeling of conversation. When you read a well-written letter, you can "hear" the writer talking to you. Our first consideration, then, should be the language of a letter. In Chapter 3, you looked at the elements of an effective writing style. These apply nowhere more than in letter writing.

Avoid the standard vocabulary of the uncreative letter writer, with its profusion of phrases such as:

Enclosed herewith please find . . .
Attached is . . .
With reference to your letter of . . .
Please do not hesitate to call upon us if we may be of further service.
I wish to take this opportunity to . . .
I am happy to inform you that . . .
In response to your request . . .
Thank you for your interest in . . .

These bits of archaic Americana, which show up in thousands of letters every day, will make your letter look just like every other letter in the reader's in basket. They are routine phrases suggesting that your letter and its ideas deserve only routine attention.

Be creative. Each letter is unique. You want a specific response from a specific reader. Write for that response; write simply and readably. Write for your readers. You have something you want to say; you have a point to make. That's fine. Remember, however, that readers are more interested in themselves and their own benefit than they are in you and your benefit. Take advantage of that.

Letters are a chance to give something to your readers. That's why they're reading them. They are motivated by their own needs. They may be interested in you and what they can do for you, but your letters will be more readable and more effective if readers feel that they have gained something by reading them. This gain doesn't have to be material. They may gain knowledge or understanding. They may profit from having a new viewpoint. Your letters may show them how to solve a problem.

This way of writing is especially important if a threat is involved in the letter. Threat should be avoided where possible, for it cannot help but generate hostility. But there are situations that call for an ultimatum. Even in these situations, more positive statements will do a better job.

Assume, for instance, that you are dealing with a contractor who is late in completing a job. You could write:

> Your attention is called to the agreement that you signed with us. In this agreement you undertook to perform this work by a certain date. It appears now that this will not be done. We, therefore, will withhold payment until you have completed your portion of the agreement.
>
> Be further advised, that if steps are not taken to bring this work to early completion, then our legal department will institute litigation to compel performance or to obtain adequate redress.

This is a strong letter. It oozes threat. Will it get action? It may but it certainly won't encourage the contractor's best work. It will probably motivate the contractor to do the least possible while avoiding legal action. You aren't likely to get the best he or she can give you, and the possibility for good relations in the future has all but disappeared.

Is this likely to produce better results?

> Our accounting department is ready to process your check for $17,000. This will be mailed to you as soon as the work is completed. I know you must be just as eager to get payment as we are to have this job completed.
>
> Please have your foreman notify me as soon as the work is finished so that I can see that the inspection is completed as soon as possible and have your check on its way to you.

This letter talks in terms of what the contractor *will* get rather than in terms of what he *won't* get. Which would be more likely to motivate you?

In their listings of writing courses, most university catalogs list one or two courses as Creative Writing; these are the fiction-writing courses. No other courses, including those in business writing, are advertised as creative writing. Good writing, all good writing, is creative—and that certainly includes business writing.

Indeed, many people are kept from writing well in organizations because they assume business writing must be prepared according to traditional formulas. Often, when a man or woman takes over a new job and is faced with a writing chore, he or she will go first to the files to see how the predecessors wrote a similar piece.

Now, there's nothing wrong with learning from others, and it's probably a good idea to get the historical perspective of correspondence, but to expect to find a model in the files is to expect the impossible. You may hold the same job as your predecessor, and you may write to many of the same people about similar things, but each communication situation is unique and should be given your creative attention to produce a document aimed at achieving *your* goals at *this time* with *this reader*.

Searching the files for a model results in the perpetuation of errors. The same result is obtained by using models from business-writing texts or from correspondence manuals. When you must write, you must achieve a specific purpose with a unique reader under circumstances that will never again be the same. This calls for your creative effort to compose a letter designed to do just the job at hand.

When we write at work, we write as an agent of our organization. When we write to our cousins, we write solely for ourselves and our cousins. There is a difference between social and organizational writing, but that does not mean that organizational writing is impersonal. When you, as an agent of your organization, write to a reader who is an agent of an organization, neither of you ceases to be a human being. Yet much business writing seems dedicated to creating this fiction. It never uses "I" or "we"; it assiduously avoids contractions; it says everything possible in the passive voice. The result? Dull, dead writing.

Contrast this with face-to-face communication in business. We strive to be human, warm, personally acceptable. We don't turn stilted phrases to express business messages through the spoken word. Why, then, express ourselves that way in writing? Why, indeed? We'll be more effective if we stop it and start to put some life in our letters—to put ourselves in our writing. This doesn't mean that business writing should be breezy and chatty. Not at all. It can be dignified and businesslike and yet be human and person-to-person rather than impersonally station-to-station. Organizations don't write letters to each other. People in organizations write letters to people in other organizations.

The station-to-station, impersonal, passive voice, third-person business letter fools no one. Your reader knows that it was written by a human being. Why not let your humanity show in your writing? Your correspondence will be warmer, more persuasive, and infinitely more effective because of it. You should be you, writing for your organization with its goals and image in mind—but through it all still you. Your readers would rather hear you talking to them through the written medium than they would read a cold, impersonal document that seems as though it came from a stone and steel building. Your writing will be easier, and your organization will seem a more desirable one to relate to and to do business with.

Much writing does no more than provide a vehicle for the writer's expression. The readers are only a passive audience, an ultimate destination for the message. These kinds of writers are more conservative versions of starving poets in garrets, unconcerned with the reader, so taken are they with what their message means to them. Perhaps that's an extreme comparison unfair to both poets and business writers, but it remains that effective writing, whether sonnet or memorandum, begins and ends with the readers. It begins with the readers, as the writers think of them and their needs and as the writers direct the style, organization, and content of the piece to the interests and attitudes of the readers. It ends with the readers, for the effectiveness of a piece of business writing is judged, not by its style, but by the readers' response.

Of course, writers must be concerned with their own goals, but they can reach those goals only if they take into account the receiver's response, for the goals of any message must be stated in terms of the receiver's response.

What does the reader know of the subject, of the writer, of the group which the writer represents? What are the reader's attitudes toward the writer, the subject, or the group the writer represents? What are the reader's interests, background, affiliations, needs, and goals?

The following letter is typical of routine, formula-oriented business correspondence.

Dear Miss Walsh:

Thank you very much for your letter of August 24 in which you requested information relative to the price and availability of our Program for Computer Design of Wastewater Collection Systems. You also inquired about field availability of consultative services in connection with possible adoption of this program.

It is a pleasure to provide the information requested. Please find enclosed herewith our current Catalog, as well as descriptive literature that will answer your questions.

I hope that you will find this information suitable to your needs. Please do not hesitate to contact the undersigned if we may provide any further information.

Yours very truly,

That's a poor letter. Yet, unfortunately, it's not unlike many written every day. The language suggests pomposity, coldness, and a complete lack of creativity; furthermore, the letter is unresponsive to the reader's request. The entire first paragraph is wasted on a recapitulation of the reader's request. The reader knows what she wrote. The reader's questions were simple and direct; they should have been answered simply and directly, not by a reference to a stack of literature.

The wording is archaic. "Enclosed herewith please find" is an invitation to a search. Did the writer hide the catalog? The catalog is not just "enclosed"; it's enclosed "herewith." If it's enclosed, of course it's here—but *herewith*? Where else?

Wouldn't the following letter have been clearer to the reader, and wouldn't the writer have better represented himself and his company if he had written more simply and in a natural style—and wouldn't he have taken less time to write it this way:

Miss Sheila Walsh
Walsh Associates
Cambridge, MA

Reference: Your letter of August 24

Our Program for Computer Design of Wastewater Collection Systems is currently available, Miss Walsh, at a monthly lease fee of $1200. This all-inclusive fee includes up to four hours of field consultation. Additional consultation is billed at $40 an hour plus expenses. As we have a Software Support Office in Arlington, Massachusetts, there would be no charge for service to you performed at your Cambridge office.

I'm enclosing some descriptive literature on this program and on our other related products and services. We'd be happy to meet with you or to answer any questions. Dale Regan of our Arlington office will call you next week, or you can call me collect at 987-555-0052 if you'd like any information before then.

Thanks for writing, Miss Walsh. You'll find the low cost and flexibility of our program useful in your design work.

This letter is simple, clear, human, and responsive to the reader's request. It uses the first paragraph to capture the reader's attention by giving a direct response to her question. A reference to previous correspondence is given in the line between the inside address and the first paragraph. The use of a reference line gives the reader (and her secretary) all the information needed to relate this letter to files. A reference line is by no means always necessary, but when you have to refer to correspondence, a file code, a purchase order, or anything else, it's better to use it than to waste the opening paragraph with a summary.

This letter has another innovative feature. It omits the salutation and the complimentary close. The salutation is in the first sentence as a form of direct address rather than in a "Dear" line, and the complimentary close ("Yours very truly") is left out entirely. This is one of several forms of a letter, and one which I prefer because of its simplicity, cleanness, and directness. But form is a matter of choice and taste. The Appendix presents a collection of acceptable forms in current use.

The revised letter involves the local representative and makes the writer more personal as well. He refers to himself in the first, rather than in the third, person. The original letter refers the reader to impersonal sales literature; the revision makes the writer and his company look human rather than institutional. Instead of asking the reader not to hesitate to call if she has any questions, the revision tells how contact can easily be made.

The final paragraph of the revision calls the reader's attention to the important features of the product that the writer wants to stress. It leaves the reader with her attention focused on economy and flexibility as she prepares to look at the product literature that the writer sent to amplify his letter. In language, tone, style, and organization, the revision is clearly superior. It shows the easy, natural way to write. As you read it, it's not hard to think of the writer speaking to you.

BEGINNING A LETTER

The beginning of a letter is your chance to get the reader's attention and interest. Though very important, this space is frequently wasted in letters. Many writers have the idea that the ideal first paragraph is one that leads up to the subject. A letter is too short to waste space on merely introductory material. The introduction should not be used as a warmup for the writer. Don't waste words; get to the subject. Be direct and to the point in an interesting, vital first paragraph. If you are unsure of how to start, start in the middle. You can add an introduction later if one is necessary, which it probably won't be.

A letter should begin by pointing to the reader's interest rather than to the writer's. This opening, for instance, is writer-centered:

> We're proud and delighted to announce the opening of our New England Service Center in Boston and its branches in . . . .

The same point would be more effective if it were directed at the reader's interest:

> You can now have immediate, local service for all your office equipment. We've just opened our . . . .

The readers, while they may be willing to share your joy and pride in your new center, would be more likely to be concerned about their office machines and with getting service for them. If your opening pointed to their needs, they'd be more receptive as they read on. Indeed, they'd be more likely to read on.

You might choose to take advantage of their curiosity and use a question to get them thinking about their needs and your solutions to their problems:

> How long does it take you to get your office equipment repaired? And where is it sent for a complete overhaul? Our New England Service Center, recently opened in Boston, can give overnight service on most machines . . .

Of course, if the reader has asked for information, the best opening is usually one that provides that information. If you can't provide the information, you might want to open with the reason before you spring the negative reply, but it's best to keep this reason brief and uncomplicated.

A letter can open effectively by getting right to the point:

> I'm going to be in Hartford next week, Norm, and I hope we'll be able to get together to discuss. . . .
> Please send me a copy of your. . . .
> Recently, we've been having difficulty with our Midwestern shipments. In the last month, for instance, we've had complaints from customers on at least seven occasions.
> Your service has been excellent. . . .

And you seldom go wrong in thanking someone. But, to make those thanks effective, be sure that you're thanking for something that really deserves gratitude:

> Thanks, Sally, for your help last week. I was really in a bind . . .
> I appreciate your arranging accommodations for me at the last minute—especially since it was convention week.

A "thanks" opening that seems patronizing, subservient, or obsequious is a poor beginning and sets a poor tone for the rest of the letter. Avoid that kind of opening.

However you begin, focus on the reader's interest and avoid the trite formularies of traditional correspondence. Begin directly and sincerely; doing so shows the reader that the rest of the letter is likely to be worth attention. Follow through by keeping the rest of the letter simple, direct, sincere, and whenever possible, focused on the benefit to the reader.

ENDING A LETTER

As important as the beginning of a letter is, the ending, the last paragraph, is of equal importance. It's the last impression that your readers have of you and your idea, and it should leave them with your main idea uppermost in their minds.

If you want action from your readers, ask for it in the last paragraph; don't assume that what you want will be obvious. Of course, your request for action should be polite and tactful, but it should be direct and specific. If you are to get the action you want, the last paragraph alone won't do the job; you must prepare your reader to respond favorably in the preceding paragraphs.

Don't use the last paragraph as a catchall for forgotten details; it's no place for afterthoughts. If you forget something important, rewrite and put it where it will be most effective. The same for postscripts; they are best used to highlight important ideas, not to remedy oversights.

To end a letter most effectively, break away from the formula ending and try one of the following:

1. If you have been building a chain of reasoning, put your most compelling point last. Then stop; avoid anticlimax.
2. If your purpose is to get action and you have been building the reader up to it, close with a request for action.
3. If you have been discussing a problem, put the solution in the last paragraph, or if you are seeking a solution from the reader, ask for help.
4. Restate, emphatically, the main point of the letter.

Before looking at the specific types of letters common in business correspondence, let's sum up the common elements of all effective letters. To keep your letters effective:

- Avoid formula phrases. Use the simple, direct language you would use if speaking.
- Be creative. Write each letter for the reader. Learn from past experience, but don't rely on standard expression and form.

- Stress benefit to your reader. Where possible, focus the letter on the reader's needs and interests.
- Keep your expression natural and human.
- Let the beginning point to the reader's interest. Don't waste time with summaries of history.
- Use the last paragraph to focus the reader's attention on your main idea.

5
Types of Letters

This chapter presents some of the principles and techniques useful in writing common types of letters. Keep in mind that your letters should be creatively written to do the jobs you have in mind. You'll find here no models of letters suitable for all occasions. Models assume that business situations and needs can be reduced to a small number of types, each typical of its class. Reality, on the other hand, reminds us daily that each letter-writing situation is unique and that the best letters come from writers who consider their purposes and how those purposes can best be achieved with the readers for whom they write. Beyond that, it's important that letter writers develop their own style reflecting their personalities and points of view. Your letters should speak for you. When your letter-writing style contradicts or varies from your face-to-face style of communication, you present a confusing image to the people with whom you deal. So please note the suggestions in this chapter, and then write letters that truly reflect you and what you want to say.

COURTESY LETTERS

Courtesy letters are the routine letters we write to say thank you, to acknowledge a favor or courtesy, to congratulate, to invite, or to request a favor or assistance. For the thanks or congratulation letters, what we say isn't as important as is the fact that we wrote the letter. These might almost be called ritual letters. When we have done something for someone, we expect to be thanked; when something felicitous happens to us, we expect our friends and associates to congratulate us. When they do, we make note of it and consider that they have discharged their obligations to us. We make less note of what they said or how they said it. For that reason, it's hard to write a poor letter of this type. Of course, face-to-face, or telephonic thanks or congratulations are quite in order too, and they are, to many people, preferable. It is seldom necessary to offer both personal and letter thanks or congratulations.

If clients or colleagues extend courtesies to you while you're visiting and if you thank them before you leave, it isn't necessary to write a special letter of thanks upon returning to your office. Of course, if you have occasion to write for some other purpose in the days following your return, you could quite effectively include a sentence or two to say "Thanks again for . . ."

In any case, courtesy letters should be brief and sincere. Don't get flowery. Florid letters, though they may express sincere feelings, can easily become saccharine. Don't struggle for the right way to say it; say it as you would if you were speaking to your reader. A brief note of this type might well read:

> Thanks, Al, to you and Marge for your warm hospitality last week. It was good to see you both again, and I hope you'll soon give us a chance to reciprocate on one of your trips to Boston.

Many people seeing this note on their letterheads might feel that it should be puffed out and lengthened, but that isn't so. If you've said what you sincerely feel, stop. Don't add a lot of words that you have to struggle for. Struggled-for words seldom sound sincere.

In any courtesy letter, don't worry about an introduction. One isn't necessary. Get to the point; be concrete and specific. A letter of congratulation, for instance, should mention in specific terms what you're congratulating the reader for. This letter, for example, is too general:

> Congratulations, Anne, on your recent good fortune. All of us who've known you over the years rejoice with you on this happy occasion.
>
> It couldn't happen to anyone more deserving of the good things of life. I know that I speak for all of your many friends when I say that I know that the future holds for you many more occasions for all of us to extend to you further congratulations.

In addition to being close to unbearably flowery, this letter is so unspecific as to look as though it came from the "Congratulations, General" section of a greeting-card rack. A less florid and more specific letter might have been:

Congratulations, Anne, on your promotion to District Manager. It's a well-deserved promotion that you've earned through your fine work in Fort Worth. Best wishes for continuing success at your new desk.

This letter seems more sincere. The first version was so overdone as to seem patronizing. When writing letters of thanks or congratulation, say what you really mean, and you'll never risk the offensiveness of a patronizing tone.

For letters of request or invitation, be specific in the details and guide the reader to how and when to respond. Unless you're dealing with a situation in which you must invite many people or one in which you cannot easily reach your receiver by phone or in person, a phone call or a face-to-face meeting is likely to do a better job. It lets you ask for details and negotiate alternatives if the terms of the original invitation or request can't be met. In general, for all courtesy letters follow the rules of common courtesy and general etiquette, and you'll not go wrong.

LETTERS THAT ASK FOR INFORMATION

Unfortunately, our knowledge has its limitations, and often we don't have information which we need. Perhaps we can turn to the person next to us to get that information. Often a phone call will bring the needed data, but sometimes a letter is called for. Letter writing is a poor substitute for personal contact in the information-gathering situation. Whenever possible, personal contact should be used, but time and distance make the letter the only possible medium in many situations.

The letter that asks for information should tell what information you want, how much detail you want, and why you need the information. This is not only courteous, but also gives the receiver an indication of what information will be most helpful. Background on the problem or the situation which prompts the request will illustrate your request and help to insure a meaningful reply. Where possible, tell of other sources which you have consulted, again with a view to giving the receiver as much background as possible. If it's not obvious, tell why you have chosen the reader as a source. Assure credit for whatever use is made of the information.

None of us likes to have our ideas pirated, and we may hesitate to give our ideas when we feel that someone else is going to use them as his or her own. It is helpful to promise that the receiver will be notified of the results of the project that will make use of the information. This, of course, is not always possible or necessary. Still, it puts the receiver in a more cooperative frame of mind.

LETTERS THAT GIVE INFORMATION

Before you can answer a request for information, you will want to know three things:

1. Who is requesting the information?
2. What does he or she want?
3. Why does he or she want it?

1. Who is requesting the information?

The signature on the requesting letter will tell you name and title. You can get this information in person if the request comes from personal contact. So now you know name and job, but you still don't know who the reader is. You don't know if he or she has the technical background to appreciate the information that you can supply or if you have to spell it out in fine detail. You don't know how deeply the reader has gone into the problem indicated by the request.

Of course, if your correspondent had followed the guide in "Letters That Ask for Information," you would know this and a great deal more. If the process of giving the information is complicated or laborious, ask your correspondent for further detail. If you explain that you would like this information to give a meaningful reply, then you should not only get the information that you ask for, but the reader should appreciate your having that much interest.

2. What does the reader want?

It's easy to see what someone has asked, but it doesn't always tell us what he or she wants to know. Knowing why a person wants to know will help us to know what he or she wants. Until we know what he or she wants, we can't give it, and our communication and the time spent preparing it may have been wasted.

Communication transfers ideas. Like electricity, communication must have a completed circuit to function. When you write or speak or even nod your head, you are generating a potential communication. You are sending out an idea. The communication circuit is effectively completed only when the receiver gets *that idea*. I emphasize *that idea* because if the receiver gets some other meaning, some other idea, from your message, you haven't communicated effectively.

3. Why does the reader want the information?

This point, of course, is tied in with *What does the reader want?* This is, in fact, the whole key to success in writing letters that give information. The person requesting the information should have told you why he or she wants it. If not, you should find out why. If this isn't possible, then guess on the basis of title and the company or the agency he represents. It would be better to err in giving more rather than not enough information. Giving too much information is generally to be avoided, but in this case you don't have much choice. The receiver can always boil down too much to enough but can't always build up too little to enough.

When people write to ask for information, that is just what they want, but often our replies seem to forget this. A paint manufacturer received the following letter from a building contractor:

The Barnes Paint Company
466 North Willow Drive
Spokane, Washington

Gentlemen:

Our firm has recently been awarded a contract to construct docks at a seaside harbor near Boston, Massachusetts. There will be a number of wooden buildings on the docks. Paints which we have used in similar jobs have not been satisfactory because of peeling due to the salt water spray.

I understand from other contractors that your firm manufactures a "Marcote" paint designed to ward off the blistering effects of salt water. Could you please send me information on whether or not this paint is still being manufactured, the colors available, the cost, and the earliest date you could deliver 1000 gallons to Boston.

Very truly yours,
J. Almond Brewester
Purchasing Agent

This is the reply:

Mr. J. Almond Brewester
Purchasing Agent
J.P. Murphy & Sons
987 Lond Boulevard
Medford, Massachusetts

Dear Mr. Brewester:

Thank you very much for your letter of 24 July in which you asked about our "Marcote" line. Barnes Paint has a long history of manufacturing special paints for special jobs, and I am happy to provide the information that you requested.

Marcote was developed to meet the needs of the U.S. Navy's Bureau of Yards and Docks and has proved itself in countless trials. We are always happy to receive an inquiry about this fine paint from a new customer, because we are proud of the Marcote record and know that it can do the job for you as it has for hundreds of other outstanding contractors.

Marcote is available in a wide range of colors as you can see from the enclosed color guide. The cost and the detailed specifications can be found in the enclosed catalog. We can deliver to Boston within 14 days of receipt of your purchase order.

Thank you very much for your interest in Marcote. Please do not hesitate to call on me if I may be of service.

Yours very truly
Lois Downing
Sales Manager

The writer of this reply believes in her product, but she forgot her reader. Her reader wrote with specific questions for which he wants answers. She had an opportunity to sell some paint by answering those questions. But, let's look at what she did.

She began by telling the reader what he already knew. The reader did not have to be told that he wrote a letter asking about Marcote paint. She told the reader about Barnes' fine history and that she is happy to provide the information. The reader still doesn't know what information he is going to get, and it's that information that he's interested in. She told the reader about Marcote's history, and again she was happy, and proud, and confident. She still hasn't given the information. At last, in the third paragraph, the Sales Manager is able to contain her happiness, pride, and confidence long enough to give the information that is, after all, the reason for the letter.

A reply like the following would have given the information more clearly and directly and would have represented the paint manufacturer as a responsive and eager supplier:

Yes, Mr. Brewester, Barnes still makes Marcote, and you can have the thousand gallons that you'll need delivered to you in Boston no later than 14 days after we get your order. Marcote comes in a wide range of colors; they're all listed in the catalog I'm enclosing. The catalog also shows the prices for various colors and quantities.

Barnes developed Marcote to meet U.S. Navy specifications for a marine paint that would take the worst in weather, and both the Navy and hundreds of commercial users have found that it does the job.

If you'll send your purchase order to my attention, I'll see that it's taken care of immediately. Or, if you prefer, call me collect at the number above, and I'll see that your order is rushed to you.

This letter begins by giving the reader a favorable answer to his inquiry. There's no better way to put a correspondent in a receptive frame of mind than by giving the asked-for information.

In the first letter, the first two paragraphs were about the writer and her product. The reader and his interests weren't even mentioned until paragraph three. The revision is centered on the reader and his interest. It gives a stronger impression of the Barnes Company, not by extolling the virtues of the firm, but by giving straightforward, businesslike answers to the problem.

The revision closes by suggesting action to the reader. He's given a choice of sending the purchase order to a specific person in the company (and it's always easier to do business with a name than with an entire organization) or calling collect. The writer made herself personal—someone to do business with, someone cooperative and ready to help with special attention.

We expect or hope for action from our letters but sometimes seem too bashful to ask for it. Don't hesitate to tell readers what you want them to do, assuming that they'll get the idea themselves. Ask for action. It may be just the stimulus they need to get them moving, especially if you make the action an easy and desirable one.

In the revision, the writer tried to think of her reader and his needs. She promised personal attention and tried to make it as easy as picking up the phone to get action. Compare the original with the revision. Do you think the revision is more likely to sell paint?

Don't miss an opportunity to analyze a letter that impresses you favorably. Always ask why and apply what you learn to your own writing. The same is no less true of letters that annoy you or leave you with a poor impression. Again, ask why and learn.

LETTERS THAT SAY NO

Letters that say *no* almost always involve long-range goals in addition to the obvious short-range purpose of transmitting a refusal. While we must, for instance, tell customers that we are unable to fill an order, we must also keep the future in mind, for we want to keep them as customers. We may have to refuse to extend a line of credit to newly established merchants, but we want to keep in mind that they may prosper. When they do, we will want them to think kindly of our company.

No letters are difficult to write and, paradoxically, the apparently best-written ones often are the most ineffective. That is to say that the ones that seem to be the smoothest, the most professionally prepared, often fail to achieve the desired result. They ooze. They are too pluperfect, and this pluperfection seems unreal and insincere. They evidence just the proper amount of concern for the reader's interest; they are phrased to temper the refusal with assurances of good will and a willingness to do anything to maintain the custom and affection of the reader.

A good *no* letter should say *no*. The reader should not be left wondering what the letter said. Many of the smoothest *no* letters, those obviously well-written, surround the negative with so much psychology and positive thinking that they leave the reader wondering whether the writer said yes, no, or maybe.

This letter, for example, tries so hard to be inoffensive that it never gets around to saying *no*.

Dear Ms. Miller:

We have completed the selection process for this year's appointment of a Personnel Management Intern. We were most fortunate in having a large number of highly qualified applicants for the single vacancy that we can fill.

The choice was a most difficult one, but we have selected the applicant who appears to be the most highly qualified.

Thank you very much for your interest in our program and for coming for an interview. And best of luck in the future.

If I got a letter like that, I'd show up ready for work. If they selected the most highly qualified applicant, I would assume that they had selected me.

Among the apocrypha of the writing trade, there is the story of the Chinese rejection letter. When a Chinese publishing house rejected an author's manuscript, they allegedly accompanied it with a face-saving letter:

Thank you for sending us your excellent manuscript. It is among the finest we have ever been privileged to read, but we regret that we will be unable to publish it. For if we were to do so, we would set such a high standard of excellence for our humble house, that never again would we be able to equal it.

It is, of course, harder to say *no* than it is to say *yes*. Writing a letter that avoids saying *no* in a *no* situation is not the answer. A good *no* letter should tell the positive side of the story, if there really is one. The readers will be interested in what you can do for them. It might be well to begin the letter with this. Tell the positive aspects to the reader as soon as possible. Does this seem to contradict the point of the last paragraph, that *no* letters should say *no* and not leave the reader in doubt as to what was said? It needn't as long as the *yes* and the *no* are kept distinct and are not allowed to merge in a *maybe* message.

The *no* portion should say *no* clearly and directly. The *yes* portion should be just as explicit and direct. The overall effect of the letter should make it clear to the reader that the writer said, "No, we cannot do ABC, but yes, we can do DEF, which is related to ABC, and may, therefore, be of benefit to you. Of course, Reader, it's up to you to choose. We want to help you if we can. We're waiting for your instructions."

This last point of leaving the option to the reader is extremely important. Many of us have been offended by a refusal letter that suggested an alternative and implemented that alternative. These writers were, of course, ". . . sure that this will meet with your satisfaction and approval." Perhaps they gave us an alternative of cancelling the action by notifying them or by returning the merchandise. In any case, those writers made a decision that we may have felt was ours to make. We can't, of course, state that writers must never implement an alternative for the reader. But, it is something to consider carefully in light of the conditions of the situation, and not something which should be done as a matter of course.

A good *no* letter should indicate why the reply is negative, if this will make the reply more meaningful. *Why* should generally be eliminated when it would offend the reader. *Why* should sometimes be eliminated when it would put the writer or the writer's company in an unfavorable light or if the *why* is overdetailed or argumentative. The reader is interested in getting a response from you. The reader wants a clear, direct reply. Knowing the *why* of the response may promote this clarity.

The reader isn't interested in your letters that go into great detail about materials shortages being caused by the failure of a vendor to deliver on time because of a flood in the warehouse "caused by the breaking of a dam that had been weakened by the worst spring floods since '08, with all of this further complicated by the derailment of a freight car. . . ." All of this is of no interest to your reader. So, leave it out or, if it's important, boil it down to the essentials.

Let's look at a letter sent by a bank to Charlie Baxter. Charlie wanted to add a new room to his house. He figured that it would cost about $6500, and applied to a local bank for a loan. The bank looked at Charlie's salary and his debts and decided that they could not go $6500, but that they could lend him $4000 toward the project.

Dear Mr. Baxter:

Our loan committee has reviewed your request for a loan in the amount of $6500.00, and we regret that we will be unable to comply with your request for this amount.

The stated amount of your income and your current outstanding obligations make it impossible for us to honor your application, much as we would like to. I am sure that you realize that our first obligation must be to our depositors and the protection of their interests. We are, in addition to this, regulated by the banking laws of the Commonwealth and the regulations imposed by the State Banking Commission. For all of these reasons, with which I am sure you will agree, we cannot oblige you in the amount requested.

We can, however, loan you the sum of $4,000.00 toward your project. If this would be of assistance to you, please do not hesitate to notify me or one of our loan officers at your earliest convenience. The rate of interest for this amount, and under these circumstances, will be nominally higher than that requested in your application.

Please do not hesitate to call on us if we may be of any further service to you.

Yours very truly,

Assistant Treasurer

On the good side, this letter is clearly negative. Charlie won't be wondering whether his loan was granted or not. So much for the good point.

The letter begins negatively, not a terrible thing in itself, but undesirable because it could have started with the $4000 the bank was willing to offer.

Charlie was told why the loan couldn't be granted but in terms that implied that he was a menace to the community, represented by the depositors who had to be protected from him. His loyalty to nation and Commonwealth were also impugned; it also seems that the body politic had to be protected from him. And, yet, to all of this, the Assistant Treasurer is blandly certain that Charlie will agree.

An alternative was offered, but not until the last paragraph. By this time, Charlie, unless he was in dire need, was probably ready to tell the bank and its bland official to do something rude. The $4000 would have been more appealing if it had preceded the refusal and if the reasons for the refusal had been eliminated or reworked in a more palatable form.

The alternative is conditional. A new rate of interest has been added, but Charlie has not been given the percentage. He has only been told that the addition will be nominal. That is an abstract word that doesn't fool anyone anymore.

The concluding paragraph would be extremely offensive if it weren't so typical. "Further service" indicates that they have done something for him. They have only insulted and refused him unless we consider the offer of the $4000 at the nominal increase in interest as a service. Considering the frequency with which this closing is offered, it really says nothing. And nothing is no way to end a letter.

Some things to be considered in writing a *no* letter include:

- *No* letters should say *no*. Their meaning should be clear and direct.
- *No* letters should consider both the short-range and long-range effects of the message.
- *No* letters should give the reader any reasonable positive statements as early as possible.
- If alternatives are offered, the reader should be allowed to choose whether to accept the alternative or not.
- *No* letters should add a dimension to their meaning by telling the reader why the response had to be negative when the *why* is compatible with the purposes and tone of the letter.

No letters, then, should be written with the reader in mind and with the writer's purpose in mind. They should be clear, simple, direct, and, where possible, helpful to the reader.

PERSUASIVE LETTERS

A persuasive letter calls for careful planning. First, set your objective: Who do you want to persuade to do what? Be specific in your definition of purpose and don't settle for a statement like: *I want to persuade Jane Smith to cooperate in our Job Opportunities program.* That's too vague. What do you mean by cooperation? How do you want it shown? When? Until you have your objective specifically clear in your own mind, you can't write an effective persuasive letter.

Once you've defined your objective, examine it from the reader's point of view. Is what you propose reasonable to the reader? Does it benefit her, her family, her organization? Does it meet her needs? Is she aware of the needs that it meets? Does it solve her problems? Can you show her how it meets her needs, solves her problems, or benefits her?

Who is your reader? What does she know? What does she need to know? Your letter may want to mention some things that both you and she know and can agree upon; it's usually pleasant to have someone say something that we agree with or that reinforces our own point of view. The main force of your letter should be directed to giving information that she doesn't have but which she needs to make a rational decision in your favor. The tone and approach of your letter, your "selling," may make her well disposed to you, but to get positive action you have to make that action a reasonable thing for her to do. You've got to show her why it's a wise move for someone in her position to make.

How does she feel about you, your organization, your idea, or product? You aren't likely to change her attitudes, but you should know what they are, if that's at all possible. Take advantage of positive attitudes and avoid confronting hostile feelings. Though it's tempting to try to change attitudes that we don't like, doing so doesn't work. Concentrate your efforts on your reader's behavior. What do you want her to do? Never mind how you want her to feel.

Emphasize the "you" aspects in your letter. Don't tell your readers what acceptance of your ideas or course of action will do for you; tell them what it will do for them. How will it promote their survival or safety if those aspects of life concern them? How will it promote their sense of belonging in their organization or in their community? How will it contribute to their prestige? What will it let them accomplish? How will it help them to grow personally or professionally? How will it relate to their self-fulfillment?

These last several paragraphs have raised many questions. Persuasive writing calls for all these questions. The answers are to be found in your analysis of your readers and their situations. All good writing is reader-centered. This is especially true of persuasive writing. Know your readers and know what you want of them.

Open your letter by pointing to the reader's interest.

Develop your letter by showing the relevance of your proposal to their needs, problems, or benefit.

Close your letter with a specific request for action. In sales terms, "ask for the order." Don't assume that readers will know what you want of them and that they will do it. Ask them to do it. Many persuasive messages, from sales calls to persuasive letters, have failed because they forgot this last step. Build your case; make the desired course of action a reasonable one for your reader; then ask for action.

This approach doesn't guarantee action. When you're dealing with people, nothing can offer a guarantee. But this approach does make it most likely that your persuasive letter will persuade. Try it.

6

How to Write Reports

A report is a business document designed to inform, influence, or record. Most reports go "up" to higher management or "out" to clients or customers. Many go "across" to our colleagues. Some go "down" to help others perform their functions more effectively. Some go into the files as records to help an unknown future reader to know what was done today. Some reports are required by contract or statute. Others are required by the demands of sound business practice. Others have their origins in tradition and the unreasonable fear of what might happen if the reports didn't exist.

In itself, a report is worth only a few cents as scrap paper. Its value comes from the usefulness to the people for whom it is prepared. What the report tells them and how they can use it are the only true measures of its value. If it tells them nothing which they didn't already know or if they have no use for it, the report is without value regardless of the cost of its preparation.

Reports, to be of value in decision making or as records, should be concrete and objective. This doesn't mean that the writer should be only a computer or transmitter of facts. No, the writer may interpret the factual data without affecting the objectivity of the piece as long as interpretations and opinions are clearly labeled as such. The report containing subjective data should be organized so that the subjective aspects of the report are physically separated from the objective. Readers can thus have the facts for their own interpretation as well as having the benefit of the writer's experience.

The writer should be objective in gathering and selecting the matter for the report. Each of us is biased, and our biases are our own business. In writing an essay, we can allow our bias to have free rein, but report readers have the right to assume that they are getting the best and most objective picture possible under the circumstances.

Reports for the decision maker should not provide decisions already made. Reports for the record should allow the future reader as complete and unbiased a picture as possible. Valuable report writers present their messages as completely and objectively as possible, with knowledge of their readers and their needs in mind.

Reports to management are a vital part of business. Management's function is to make sound decisions. In almost any business larger than a corner store, it is impossible for management to have first-hand experience of all that is going on in the business. Managers can't be everywhere at once. Managers can't be qualified in every technical aspect of the business.

Rarely is one person qualified in accounting, engineering, law, design, production, personnel, public relations, sales, research, materials handling and warehousing, security, training, contracts administration, and all the other skills that combine to produce a product or service. Even if managers could be everywhere at once, they couldn't possibly understand the details of all that is going on in the company. Yet, management must make the basic decisions and set the overall policy for a business, which includes all the areas mentioned and more. Any sound decision must be based on sound knowledge. Reports, written and oral, give managers the information they need. They tell them what is going on and, where necessary, they interpret technical information. Reports "up" are the raw material for management decisions.

Reports "across" help us to link our activities in a business enterprise, which must be coordinated and cooperative to be profitable. Reports "down" inform our subordinates. Reports "out" to clients and customers inform, influence, motivate, and sometimes instruct or record.

THE FORMAT OF A REPORT

The information in a report can be presented in a variety of formats. The one suggested below is useful because it gives all the information required to set the report in the proper context and because it eliminates the letter of transmittal. This form calls for:

Date of the report
Title
Prepared for:

Prepared by:
Reason for the report
Summary (including a summary of conclusions and recommenda-
     tions)
Table of contents
Body of the report
Conclusions (in detail)
Recommendations (in detail)
Appendixes

The *date* identifies the time for a future reader. Obviously many of the statements in the report are based on the time at which it was written, and the date clarifies these statements.

The *title* line, quite obviously, gives the title. I would like to say something more profound, but what can you say about the function of a title line? Well, there is one thing. Have you ever seen the several-line titles of some technical reports? A title should simply identify the general and specific area to be covered. The report itself should be presented in the body of the report, not crammed into the title.

The *prepared for* line is a step to eliminating the letter of transmittal and tells anyone who may read the report the context in which it should be understood.

The *prepared by* line identifies the writer and is another step to eliminating the letter of transmittal. It helps any reader to a fuller understanding of the report.

The *reason for the report* is the final step in the elimination of the letter of transmittal and further qualifies the report. When we read something, it is helpful to know as much about the piece and the circumstances surrounding it as possible.

The *summary* comes last in many reports. But it should come first. To see why, let's look at the techniques of effective reading. Almost every course and textbook on the improvement of reading skills advises the student to preread the material quickly before studying it in detail. There are two reasons for this. First, we can tell whether we should read the report or whether we should delegate this to someone else more likely to understand or to use it. Second, prereading gives us an appreciation of the main theme, and as we read we do so by relating to the main idea.

Writers get two benefits from putting the summary at the beginning. First, we are more likely to get a reader who can understand and appreciate our material. Second, by giving readers the main ideas and an indication of how we will develop them, we give them a guide to better comprehension and understanding. We give them a theme to which they can relate the whole body of the report. It is through perceiving relationships that we comprehend and retain what we read.

The *table of contents* lists the major portions of the report. Other than its obvious general value, it serves as a skimming guide for the reader interested in only a portion of the document.

The *body of the report* presents the data. This section is supported by the rest of the report. To be of maximum value, it must be well organized. Headings and subheadings will allow this to happen easily and naturally and will make the problem of transition simpler. Transitions are the bridges between ideas. Transitions facilitate the flow from sentence to sentence, from paragraph to paragraph, and from section to section.

A good piece of writing will have unity; it will be about one thing. But it will concern itself with different aspects of that one thing. That is where transitions come in. Good transitions ensure a smooth flow of ideas and link the various parts of the report into a unified whole.

The body of a report should have unity, coherence, and authority. It should be united, about one thing, with no unnecessary side trips. If you feel that your writing is going off in several directions at the same time, you should look for the concept that unifies all these things that take your interest. If found, that thing should become the subject of the report, the main trunk to which all the other things can attach themselves as the branches, twigs, and leaves of subtopic and detail.

Sometimes as we read the rough draft, we have the feeling that something is wrong: The piece just doesn't hang together the way it should. It's difficult to make the transition from idea to idea. Oh, the structural transitions are easy enough, but there isn't the right feeling about the piece. When this happens, take another look. Maybe it isn't the transitions at all. It may have nothing to do with the style. It may be that you have several subjects competing for primary attention. If they are related, then you need a new subject that will encompass all of them—a real subject that can unify all the competing items by making them topics and subtopics of a new and broader subject.

Of course, this isn't always the case. Sometimes we have this feeling and can find no *real* unifying subject. Then, it may be possible that we have several subjects. That means that we are trying to write several reports at the same time. If this seems to be the case, stop. Establish the scope of the report you are working on. Write about that subject. If it still seems that the other subjects should be reported on when you have finished, then make each of them the subject of its own report. We'll discuss this further when we cover Step 2 of the report-writing process: defining the scope.

The report should flow smoothly. There should be no sudden, hard-to-follow changes in subject. The use of headings and subheadings makes transition easier, but it doesn't work miracles. The heads and subheads signal topic changes and mark the main divisions of the paper. They help the reader to see overall structure. They prevent that state of affairs in which the reader has to wonder, "What is this about now, and when did we get on that subject?"

Conclusions and recommendations follow the body of the report. These items should be presented separately and not mixed together, for conclusions should be objective and recommendations subjective. Conclusions are the results of the reasoning from the objective evidence presented in the body of the report. Conclusions are directly related to the material in the body. They are the natural outgrowth of the matter presented there; each item under "Conclusions" should be directly supported by data in the body of the report.

Recommendations are those things that, in the writer's opinion, should be done as a result of the conclusions. They are often of greater value than conclusions. It is not because their subjective nature makes them of less value than the objective conclusions that I suggest they be segregated from the conclusions. It is because they are of a different order. Recommendations are often the most valuable part of a report, and it is in the recommendations that a skilled report writer can be of most value to the reader. Recommendations, soundly reasoned and clearly and effectively presented, are in constant demand.

Appendixes come at the end of the report and contain the detailed data that the report must present. Appendixes are one of the best devices for making a report readable and useful to a diverse readership. The more people for whom a report is prepared, the more useful is the appendix. Even in a report prepared for one person, however, the appendix promotes the readability and usefulness of the report.

Appendixes present, completely and in as much detail as may be required, details that would weigh down the body of the report. For instance, a report on a possible new plant site may be prepared for the top executives of a company. Such a report should be complete, for each reader will want to have an overview of the whole situation. But, it is unlikely that each will have the same interests and background or that each will want the same degree of detail. Some will want only a general picture. Others will want this too but with a little more detail. Others will want all the detail; still others will be looking for the details of a particular aspect only.

How can the report writer satisfy all these varying interests? Three alternatives suggest themselves: (1) Prepare a separate report for each of the executives concerned. (2) Make up a detailed report and allow each reader to dig out the parts of interest to him or her. (3) Prepare a report that gives the whole general story in the body of the report and that refers to the supporting and amplifying details in appendixes at the end of the report.

The first alternative is expensive. It might, of course, be worth the expense, but why bother. This plan offers no advantage over the report with appendixes; it is, in fact, less complete, and each executive will probably want to feel that he is getting the same degree of completeness as his colleagues. The second could waste a great deal of executive time or the time of executive staff personnel who would have to prepare abstracts of the data that are of interest to the boss. The third, the report with the appendixes, provides each leader with what he or she wants, in whatever degree of detail he or she may want it.

Appendixes are useful in reports prepared for one reader too. They ensure that the body of the piece will be readable and that any amount of desirable detail can be included. Appendixes, then, give any report the flexibility that both reader and writer need.

WRITING THE REPORT

Failures in communication can often be traced to improper planning. Successes are often the result of careful planning. This is especially true in the case of written communication, for we have no immediate opportunity to correct failure or to clear up confusion. In fact, we may not be aware of the failure or confusion until long after the communication is sent, for written communication goes only one way at a time. The one-way nature of written communication makes planning for clarity and effectiveness important. When we are communicating through the spoken word, we have immediate personal contact with our receivers. We can tell whether or not our message got across. They can question us on unclear or confusing points. We can, if we handle the situation correctly, get instant response on the clarity and effectiveness of our spoken communication.

The pressure that causes haste in business writing is, as often as not, from external causes such as a deadline from the boss or other equally imperative source. While deadlines often fail to leave a reasonable time for planning, the writer interested in communicating clearly and effectively, and in preserving a reputation for judgment and discretion, will take the time to go through the planning stages of the report-writing process.

The report-writing process can be divided into eight steps. These steps take writers from the point at which they realize the need for a report, or are assigned to write one, to the finished smooth copy. The eight steps serve as a guide in the manner of an aircraft pilot's checklists. In themselves they do nothing. They are not magical. Their value is that they give the writer help in careful and complete report writing.

The eight steps:

1.   Define the purpose of the report
2.   Define the scope of the report
3.   Gather the facts

4.   Prepare an outline
5.   Hold a preapproval conference
6.   Expand the outline
7.   Prepare a rough draft
8.   Prepare the final copy

Step 1. Define the purpose.

It is impossible to state the purpose of any report without mentioning the reader. We must therefore define our purpose in terms of our reader or readers. What do we want them to do?

Is our purpose reasonable to the readers? Can they understand what we want? Consider their background. Can they do what is necessary to accomplish the purpose?

Have we asked too much of them? If the report recommends some immediate and all-or-nothing-at-all goal, we may want to consider a less drastic goal.

If a report to the head of a large machining department recommended that he eliminate industrial accidents from his department, he would probably dismiss the whole thing. His experience would indicate that it's impossible to eliminate *all* accidents from this type of heavy industrial work, and he would likely regard the writer of such recommendations as someone who doesn't know much about a machine shop. This attitude could carry over to the whole report and everything in it. Thus, because of this *unreasonable* purpose, a good report might become useless.

If the report writer had realized the unreasonableness of this recommendation to stop all accidents and had instead suggested a plan to reduce accidents by a significant percentage each month, the writer would be more likely to meet with success. The department head could see the possibility of a reasonable reduction in accidents and could accept a report recommending this goal.

In planning, consider whether the report should be a one-time communication or whether it is part of a long-term communication strategy that calls for a series of documents and other types of messages and actions. Do you want to tell the whole story at once, or would you be better able to achieve your purpose with your reader by giving the message in pieces, with each piece preparing the reader to accept the next, and the whole series being planned for an overall effect? Is it, in other words, reasonable for us to expect readers to react positively to what we are giving them, or would another communication strategy be more likely to achieve that effect? Only knowledge of the situation and of the intended audience can provide that answer. This writer should consider the other available mediums. The oral medium should always be considered because of its ability to provide instant response. Oral mediums may often be better when several points of view will have to be reconciled or when it seems that there will be many objections to be met and that these cannot be effectively anticipated and dealt with in a report.

Step 2. Define the scope of the report.

Knowing our purpose, we should next define the scope of the report. There are two elements to the scope: the breadth, how much of the subject we will cover, and the depth, the specific detail and background we shall incorporate. Length is determined by the breadth and the depth. The report should be long enough to do the job adequately, but no longer. It is easy to go beyond the point of diminishing returns in writing, and this is a common error: to write impelled by fear of doing an inadequate job. Length can't compensate for value and clarity. The readability and value of the piece are destroyed by the insulating effect of words. Any good ideas in the piece are so imbedded in the excess words that they are lost to all but the most persistent reader who must dig out the insulated ideas.

Many reports deal with a scope too broad for a single report. A report with the subject "Working Conditions in the Electronics Industry" is doomed to failure before it begins. No report is going to give that subject adequate treatment—nor any book. It's too much subject for any piece of writing. This is not to say that an effective report cannot be written with that title. But, subject isn't title. A title is an indication of the subject. A realistic *subject* might be "Working Conditions for Electronics Technicians in Three Major Companies in the Greater Boston Area." This subject has a chance. It's sufficiently restricted to allow proper coverage. The first subject is so broad that no writer could do it justice in an encyclopedic tome, much less in a report. It would, perhaps, be well if the title reflected the subject. But, in any case, effective writers will limit the subject to one they can handle.

Step 3. Gather the facts.

When you have defined the purpose and scope of your report, you are ready to begin gathering data. Data gathering is a process that continues until the report is issued, for you should remain sensitive to the continuing need for new or amplifying data.

Many writers have found it best to begin building the substantive content of the report by taking inventory. In this inventory the writer, knowing the subject and scope, takes stock of what will be needed in the report. The writer compares these specifications with the data on hand and makes a list of the information needed. This "Data Needed List" is usually in two columns: the first lists the information needed; the second lists, opposite the needed data, the most likely sources of the information.

Once this list is started, the writer can begin to take the necessary steps to obtain the data. If there is any lag time, the writer can start to process the data on hand. As information gathering is often one of the most time-consuming steps in report writing, it is best to begin it as soon as possible. Certainly, as the approach is organized and the outline written, additional data will be called for. It may then be added to the list.

The question of which should come first, the gathering or the outline, is best decided by the writer of the report. The outline will certainly raise needs for additional information. But, at the same time, the listing of facts will suggest the outline.

If you have always preceded your gathering by an outline, try it the other way around once or twice. Many successful report writers have found this way works best for them.

Step 4. Prepare an outline.

In order to be clear and effective, a report will have to be well organized. Approach your readers in a logical fashion, constantly preparing them to accept your next point and ultimately your conclusions and recommendations. If you fail to do the work of organizing your presentation, you can't assume that the readers will do the work. They may discard it, or they may remain inactive out of confusion—or they may impose their own organizations on it and from them get an impression other than that which you intended.

Many writers fail to organize their ideas because organizing is work. This is especially true of very capable specialists who feel, rightly so in many cases, that what they have to say is the important thing. They may at the same time feel, quite wrongly, that how they say it is of little consequence. There is nothing as useless as an uncommunicated idea. True, the value of the idea being communicated is the most important ingredient of the message, but if the message fails to get the idea across—nothing.

Your outline should help you to see that your ideas are well organized and presented logically and are understandable and acceptable to your readers. An outline is a working schematic of your report. If an outline is a restrictive device, it's not doing an effective job. An outline should be a flexible guide you can change any time you see a good reason for change.

Many of us feel that we can outline a report in our heads. This may be so, but for anything longer than a page or two we will probably find the written outline most helpful. Putting ideas into words helps to concretize some of the abstract notions that run around our heads. Reducing these notions to the more disciplined form of an organized outline lets us visualize the organization and ultimate form of the piece more clearly than can be done through the internal pictures and diagrams of imagination.

One of the most valuable and flexible outline devices is a set of index cards. Write a point or topic on each card and, when all of the topics are listed, organize by arranging them in order as topics and subtopics. Arrange and rearrange as often as necessary. Each rearrangement takes no more effort than shifting a few cards around. Outline cards work better than the same outline on a sheet of paper because they're more flexible and cater to our inherent laziness. Our laziness makes us hesitate to change a fixed written outline because of the work involved. We may make a few changes, but once the paper becomes crowded with scratchings, arrows, and insertions, we are more likely to decide that what-the-heck-it's-good-enough sooner than if we had only to shift or add a card or two. The copy on the cards should be triple-spaced to allow for corrections.

When we have the index cards arranged to our satisfaction, we can copy this outline on paper, again double- or triple-spaced. This will give us a working outline. This outline is not final. An outline, to repeat a point, is a working document. It is the writer's personal property. It exists for the writer's benefit, though the readers will be the ultimate beneficiaries of the careful planning and thoughtful organization. An outline can and should be changed in the face of a better idea.

But, a word of caution. While you can and should change an outline for good reason, it is not always sufficient to change just one point. In a well-organized presentation, the points are related to each other and to the main idea. Changing one point may mean that other points are thrown out of sequence or out of context; thus consider the relationship of a changed point to the rest of the piece and, where necessary, change the other parts of the outline.

The next step, the preapproval conference, is optional. It is sometimes not possible and at other times not necessary. When writing must be approved, it is helpful in many cases to have a preapproval conference after the outline is completed.

Step 5. Have a preapproval conference.

Often a writer must have the report approved before it can be issued. The writer usually takes the rough draft, or final copy, to the person or persons who must approve the work. These approvers often make sweeping corrections, deletions, and additions to the report. Many times the whole piece is scrapped, and a great deal of work goes down the drain or is, by an optimist, chalked up to experience. The approvers themselves are sometimes in disagreement, leaving the writer to apply patience and wisdom to the mutually exclusive editorial comments of those in authority. This kind of disagreement is expensive and frustrating, and it produces an inferior report designed to keep a host of approvers smug if not satisfied, quiet if not happy. The reader's needs are often forgotten in the writer's anxiety to relieve the pressure from the top.

The preapproval conference, while it cannot possibly relieve all these frustrations, treats them in a better way. It brings together, at the outline stage, the writer and all potential approvers. The time-consuming work of the rough draft, revision, and smooth draft have not yet been done. These steps follow the conference and will be guided by its results.

The writer submits the purpose, scope, approach, facts, and outline of the report. The approvers review these and make whatever recommendations they wish. As all the approvers are present, they can work out any conflict of opinion among themselves. At the end of the conference, the writer has a mandate and can continue writing with tentative approval of the basic material and logic of the report.

The writing process continues more smoothly than if the conference had not been held. There will be other changes, but the writer reduced the probability that there will be catastrophic change and also received the benefit of other opinions on the project.

Though one preapproval conference with all approvers together is the most convenient for the writer, a series of conferences, each with one approver, is also effective. However you do it, it is important to get tentative approval for your basic structure before you begin to write. A 10 or 15 minute chat about your outline can save you hours of writing and rewriting.

Step 6. Develop an expanded outline.

This is an optional step and one that most people can omit without prejudice to their final product. It's useful in two, possibly three, situations to develop an expanded outline:

1. If you have trouble getting started with your rough draft.
2. If you are having trouble putting your ideas into separate paragraphs.
3. If you need a more understandable document to take to the preapproval conference.

The expanded outline takes the words and phrases in your initial outline and expands them into sentences. The sentences of the expanded outline become the topic sentences of the paragraphs in the report. To write the report from the expanded outline, flesh out each sentence to a paragraph by adding supporting, clarifying, or illustrative sentences that complete the paragraph.

By turning words and phrases into sentences at one step, and by rounding those sentences into paragraphs in another, the problem of getting started is simplified. Because you write topic sentences first, your paragraphs have topic focus. It may be necessary to add paragraphs for transition or clarity, but the substance of the report can be written from the expanded outline. Because the expanded outline is in sentence form, it may be clearer to others and may be a more useful document for the preapproval conference.

A section of your initial outline, for instance, may look like this:

Marketing problem
    Poor market definition
    Overcrowded market
    Strong consumer loyalty to competition
Reasons
    We're new to market
    Product in current great demand
    Competition well established
Solutions
    Concentrate on institutional market
        Better suited to our sales structure
        Equal to consumer market
        Largely untapped
    Develop new packaging to suit this market

Like most outlines, this one is a collection of words and phrases. An expanded outline would take each line of the outline and change it to a complete sentence. Thus, for the initial outline, the expanded outline would be:

In spite of our general success with marketing convenience foods, we have failed to exploit successfully our freeze-dried dinners.
    Our market has been ill-defined.
    The market is overcrowded.
    Our chief competitor has earned strong consumer loyalty for its other convenience foods, and this loyalty has been transferred to freeze-dried dinners.
There are three main reasons for this problem.
    We entered this market only last January, though others have been exploiting it actively for over two years.
    Many competitors have been attracted to this market because of strong consumer acceptance and demand.
    Our chief competitor has thus had over two years to capture a commanding share of the market.
Our research has uncovered a solution in two parts.
    The most profitable strategy for us would be to concentrate on the institutional market.
        Our sales force is used to selling in this market, and our advertising and distribution is keyed to it.
        This market has a potential for $350 million in the next year, and this easily equals the consumer market potential.
        As our competitors have left this market virtually untapped, it offers us a unique opportunity to gain primary acceptance.

This market will call for the development of institutional packaging to replace the consumer packages.

The expanded outline gives you and your reviewer or approver a clearer picture of the report. Strengths become stronger, and structural weaknesses become more obvious. Those weaknesses should be obvious now when we can most effectively deal with them. If weaknesses don't show up until the rough or smooth draft, they will be harder to deal with and will probably result in much wasted time.

The expanded outline seems like an extra step that will take more of your valuable time. But try it. You may find it, in the long run, a valuable time saver.

Step 7. Prepare the rough draft.

Up to now you have been aware that you were writing a whole report, but your attention has been upon points one at a time. Now you must consciously unite all these points into a coherent whole. As you go from point to point, make sure that the movement will be clear to the reader. Transitions should be smooth. Relate point to point, and show the readers that they are reading something that hangs together. Each paragraph deals with an aspect of the same subject. They are separate parts, to be sure, but they combine. Put yourself in your reader's place. Will the movement seem jerky to the reader? Will the development of the report be clear?

When you have finished the rough draft, consider it carefully and revise it if necessary. Have you made your points clearly? Have you said everything necessary for clarity? Will the piece be effective in achieving your purpose *with your intended reader*? Are there more words than necessary?

All of that is the work of revision. The job now is to get words on paper. Working from your outline or your expanded outline, get the words down. Don't write and edit at the same time (see the tip on pp. 23–24); this is the time to write, not the time to edit. Don't worry if your words are the right words or if they're in the right order—just get the ideas on the paper. You'll revise the rough draft when you've finished it. That's the time to polish the report into its final form.

Step 8. Prepare the final copy.

Your job is almost complete. You have only to revise the rough draft and supervise the preparation of the final copy.

Revision should be a careful process. Revise with purpose and the reader in mind. Have you accomplished your purpose? Have you given the reader a useful, readable document? Have you done a good job? Not a perfect job, but a good job?

Many reports are ruined in this stage by a desire to write a perfect report. There are good reports—some excellent. But none is perfect. The writer who aims for perfection is doomed to failure and frustration. Revision will be frantic. Ashtrays will fill and reservoirs of confidence empty. Writers who aim for good, useful reports can see progress toward the goal throughout the revision. "That's good," they can say. They can feel reinforced. But colleagues who write toward perfection will feel only that something is wrong. Frantic revision will cut all life out of the report. Only the lifeless, sterile, and noncontroversial report can mock perfection—and this is the usual output of the perfectionist.

As you revise, you may cut. We generally write too much. But the cutting should not be done for its own sake, and when you cut, be sure that you aren't cutting out important meaning. Confine the cutting to words that detract or say nothing.

Some revision is not cutting, but rewriting. A similar danger exists here. Rewrite to eliminate confusion and wordiness but be careful not to eliminate meaning in the process. As you look at a piece that seems to call for rewriting, ask yourself what it means. Rewrite. Then look at the revision. Does it retain the essential meaning? Have you edited out an important part of the report?

The mechanics of revision will be simpler if report writer, approvers, and typists use the same revision marks to indicate corrections. These standard revision marks help to avoid confusion. If the work has been done double- or triple-spaced, with wide margins all around, there will be ample room for the revision marks to be placed clearly. The revision marks in Table 6–1 are commonly used. They are based on standard proofreader's marks.

Table 6–1   Revision marks

Mark	Meaning	Example
∧	Add element	in ∧ final stages the valve ∧ that control opening
℮	Delete letter or punctuation	the valve℮ which controls opening. There are several℮ steps in the
——	Delete word(s)	in ~~several~~ many instances
• • •	Retain crossed out words	there are ~~several~~ ways to

Table 6–1   *(continued)*

Mark	Meaning	Example
♌	Reverse letters	afthenna housings should
↶⟳	Move to place indicated	the accounts are different seen
λ	Change to letter shown	horizon
¶	Start new paragraph	The last account should be used to charge over- head expenses in stat- ics projects. Direct labor costs are ac- counted separately as provided in the basic policy.
no ¶	Don't start new paragraph	There are four ways to seat the participants. no ¶ The first is in schoolroom style. The second is in groups
/	Change to lower case	the four Plants are in
=	Change to upper case	is in framingham, massachusetts
|	Separate words	the best procedure has been

When the rough draft is completed and revised to your satisfaction, you can have it typed into the final smooth copy, or if you have to have it approved by others, you're ready to do so. When all the approval comments have been received and when you have reviewed them and assured yourself that you understand them and that the reader will benefit by them, you're ready to have the final copy prepared.

A purposeful and planned approach is the key to clear and effective writing. Planning gives understandable form to your writing. It saves you from the hurried, random scribbling that characterizes so much writing. It's effective because it makes you consider the elements that contribute to reader acceptance. You haven't left the whole matter to chance, inspiration, and the assumed cooperativeness of the reader. The report is prepared in a businesslike way. Each step in the process has a job to do. Costly repetition is avoided. Your cost of report writing should be reduced, and the quality should be improved. The final report should be good. Not perfect. Not just "good enough." But genuinely good.

7

A Brief Guide to Editing and Being Edited

Writer and editor are often assumed (by writers and editors) to be natural enemies. But without a writer, an editor would have nothing to edit, and without an editor, a writer would have no critical or creative intermediary between the writing and the reading. A good editor is the best friend a writer has, and a good editor is an important part of the creative process. This applies to all editors—those without, as well as those with, portfolio. Some organizations provide writers with skilled, professional editors. In other organizations, managers and technical specialists must function as editors for the persons whom they supervise.

The suggestions in this chapter are intended more for the latter, the person who is not, by profession, an editor. They are directed, too, to all writers who must have their writing edited or approved by others in their organizations. And, in addition, they are offered to men and women who must serve as their own editors, who must review and revise unaided.

There are three distinct functions that are often called the editing process. The first is proofreading, the minute examination of copy to make sure that spelling, alignment, grammar, and punctuation are correct. This is a painstaking skill and one that requires a special kind of reading. One who proofreads must read not for thought or idea alone, but must read word for word, letter for letter to see what is on the page. It's hard for a writer to do this, because a writer is tempted to see what should be there rather than what is actually there. Then, too, a writer who wrote "preceed" for "precede" the first time, likely hasn't learned the correct spelling by the time he proofreads his own work. An outside viewpoint, often provided by a skilled secretary, is a very useful thing to have. Proofreaders make corrections and clean up copy.

The second, what I call approving, is sometimes referred to as editing. An approver looks over a manuscript to make sure the content is valid or in conformity with organization policy. A scientist might have a report read by a superior or colleague to make sure that the content represents valid data validly presented. A manager might look over a report to make sure that nothing in the report contradicts the organization's policies or to ensure that the organization's viewpoint is effectively presented in accordance with executive guidelines.

An approver represents the organization. Approvers should not, in my view, make corrections or changes to the pieces they are assigned to approve. Rather, they should note areas where they feel that change should be made and should discuss those areas and those changes with the writer, whose job it should be to make changes. This isn't due to any feelings that writers have a proprietorship over what they write and should guard that proprietorship with a temperamental petulance. I suggest this because I feel that a piece should have one logic and one style to it. You and I have seen many reports that have been "edited" by one or more people other than the writer. As each person makes changes, each infuses a different personality into the piece, and smoothness and coherence disappear. Unity, that principle of writing that dictates that a piece should be about one thing, is often destroyed by too many cooks salting the broth.

I don't wish, however, to undermine the approvers' authority. Theirs, indeed, may be the final authority in determining what goes out of the organization. Fine. The writer should accept this. But, to return to my earlier point: to preserve the integrity of the report, the writer should make any necessary changes.

Someone once observed that a camel is a horse designed by a committee. The same distortion happens to a piece of writing written or rewritten by a committee. Approvers should approve. Writers should write.

Finally, we come to editing. The editor, in a sense, represents the reader. An editor looks at the writer's product as the reader might and is the reader's advocate or *ombudsman* for clarity, usefulness, and readability. The editor is, in another sense, a teacher or a coach. And just as it's not necessary that a track coach be able to outrun and outjump the team members, so, too, it is unnecessary that an editor be able to outwrite the writer. But the coach must be a competent coach, and the editor must be a competent editor. So, then, I offer these tips to make your editing easier, and more effective—and your being edited easier to accept.

Good editing should be done in three steps:

1.   Read through the entire piece once without a pencil in your hand. Read it for content, for organization, and for a sense of

its wholeness. That way, when you do edit, you'll edit the piece as a whole, just as the reader will read it as a whole. You won't be as likely to edit words and sentences as things in themselves. Your reader and your writer will both benefit from this approach to the wholeness of the piece.

2.   Edit on the second reading. Make or suggest changes as they would seem to benefit the piece.

3.   Read the whole corrected piece again to see how the editing blends with the original writing. This third reading can also serve as a final check before the piece is returned to the writer for his revision.

IF YOU EDIT OTHER PEOPLE'S WRITING

Keep in mind that it's the writer's piece. Let the writer and his or her personality be part of the piece. Writing is far more credible if we can sense a person and an intelligence behind the words. Don't edit the person out of the piece; otherwise, you may find that you are left with a piece which, although technically perfect and stylistically flawless, is dull as dishwater and looks as though it had been turned out by some highly qualified, perfectly programmed writing machine.

Make changes only if they are necessary, and never make changes if you can, instead, suggest them to the writer. When possible, the writer, and not the editor, should make all but the most minor changes.

Editors, particularly those in a business or public organization, should have two goals in mind as they approach a piece. Certainly, they should work to improve the piece, but they should also work to improve the writer's writing skills. That's the reason for the stress on letting the writer make changes. If you make the changes, the piece may be improved, but the writer won't have learned anything. Next time the person writes, he or she is likely to make the same error. However, if you point out the weakness to the writer and suggest a remedy and then leave it to him or her to think through and write the improvement, the piece will improve and so will the writer. Guided by this kind of editing, the writer will develop writing skills, and writing will continue to be a developmental and productive activity.

This kind of editing means that you must know what you're talking about when you ask for corrections and improvements. Your comments to the writer must be direct and concrete. It won't do to say something like "I don't like the way this reads. Fix it up." Your comments will have to be specific and relevant to the material being written and edited. You'll have to tell the writer what the fault is. For example:

The illustration predominates in this section. It's a good illustration, but when your readers finish reading it, they'll remember only the illustration and not the main point you're trying to make. That's because you devote four pages to the illustration and only one brief paragraph to the statement of the main point. Moreover, the connection between the illustration and the main point is never clearly stated.

Or, you may want to suggest a remedy:

Cut down the illustration to its essentials. Leave out the narrative details and link the illustration to the main point with a strong, explicit statement.

Editorial comment like that gives the writer a clear picture of the editor's view of the problem and the solution. The writer and editor can then discuss the validity of the editor's point of view, but even that discussion will be clarified by a clear statement of the point under discussion.

Be just as specific with positive, reinforcing comments. If writers have done good jobs, let them know that their writing was good and let them know why. Doing this makes it more likely that they'll repeat the good performance. A comment like "good report, well written" makes writers feel good, but it doesn't tell them anything useful. A far better comment would be:

Good report. Your use of examples should make the problem clear to the customer. The appendixes will promote clarity and readability and will let the whole decision team understand both in general and in detail each of their specialties.

That pat on the back reinforces the writer's good performance and makes it likely that he or she will want to repeat it and that he or she will be able to repeat it. It also shows you know what you're talking about. If you can't comment concretely and specifically on the piece, then perhaps you need to learn more about writing and the writing process.

As you edit, remember to let each writer develop his or her style. Leave the piece alone if its only vice is that you would have said it differently. As a writing teacher, I've seen and corrected many students' papers. I've often made corrections, as well as suggestions for corrections and revisions. And often as I've sat with colored pencil in hand, I've been tempted to change a word, phrase, sentence, or paragraph. When I've tried to give the student a reason for the suggestion, I've been stuck. The only thing that I could say was, "I wouldn't have put it that way." If that's the best I can do, I leave it alone. Indeed, I may not have put it that way, but it's not my piece. If I can give the student a concrete, specific reason for my comment or suggestion, I'm on solid ground. But if my only reason is that his style doesn't agree with mine, then I'm on very shaky ground.

A teacher's function and an editor's function are to help writers develop their own styles, not to impose a style on them. Cookie-cutter teaching and editing, with their goals of producing writers who are clones of the teacher or editor, are neither good teaching nor good editing.

Criticize the writing, not the writer. Don't attack the writer's personality, motivations, or supposed neuroses. If writer and editor can mutually discuss the work and not each other, their relationship is far more likely to be productive than is a relationship of mutual name calling, backbiting, and distrust. And that's just the sort of unfortunate and unproductive relationship that will come from concentration on personalities instead of on the writing itself.

Don't use your blue pencil as a scepter. Edit to improve the piece or to develop the writer's skill. Don't edit to reinforce your place in the organization's power structure. In other words, don't throw your weight around just to prove that you can do it and that the writer must accept it. And while we're on the subject of colored pencils, try to use one that's blue or green. Those colors show up nicely. Red also shows up nicely but avoid red pencils. A red-penciled piece looks too much like something that comes back from a teacher. One almost expects to see a grade circled at the top. A red-penciled report looks like it's bleeding, and this suggests to writers that their work has been badly cut up, if not butchered.

Try to work with the writer through the process of writing. Don't come in just at the end, when all of the work is done. In Chapter 6 we discussed the preapproval conference. Use preapproval or pre-editorial conferences as often as necessary to ensure a productive writer-editor relationship.

And, finally, as you edit, edit toward adequacy rather than perfection. Perfection is an impossible goal, and its pursuit can only frustrate you and your writer. But you can work together to develop a piece and a style which are truly and fully adequate to your opportunities to communicate through the written word.

IF SOMEONE EDITS YOUR WRITING

Work with, not against, the editor. It's more productive. The editor represents your readers, and that gives him or her a point of view valuable to you. Your piece may be clear to you, but if it's not clear to someone else—whether editor or reader—it's simply not a good piece of writing. Writing is all about readers, not writers, and your editor can be a helpful intermediate reader for you. If the editor says that your piece is not clear, in whole or in part, the editor's right and you're wrong. If your piece isn't sufficiently clear to have its meaning obvious to anyone who reads it, then it needs rework until it is clear. *Clear to you* is no criterion. *Clear to someone else* is a valid criterion. So don't fight your editor, whether your boss, your secretary, or a professional editor—use what the editor contributes.

Do your best work the first time, then read it over to make sure that it says what you want to say as you want to say it. Don't give your editor a half-done piece of work on the theory that it offers something to change. Many editors and managers approach their editorial work with a less than open mind because their experience with writers leads them to believe that they get second-rate stuff as a first draft. Show your editor that that isn't so with your work by giving your best work.

Your best work won't, however, be perfect. Accept that fact, and don't let yourself be defensive in your reply to each comment, criticism, or suggestion. Your work can be improved, and your editor may be able to show you how to improve it. Let's face it, writers are a cocky lot. Each of us, whether report writer or poet, thinks we are possessed of inspiration in the turn of a phrase; and each of us thinks, in unguarded moments, that our lines cannot be improved. There's a marvelous passage in a great play, *Cyrano de Bergerac*, which says it for us all. De Guiche suggests to Cyrano that he should let his uncle, the Cardinal, become his literary patron: "Let him rewrite a few lines here and there, and he'll approve the rest."

Cyrano replies, "Impossible. My blood curdles to think of altering one comma."

De Guiche continues, "Ah, but when he likes a thing, he pays well."

Cyrano closes the door on being edited by declaiming:

Yes—but not so well as I—
When I have made a line that sings itself
So that I love the sound of it—I pay
Myself a hundred times.

And Cyrano, that most romantic character in all poetry or prose, persists, his white plume of honor unbesmirched in all eternity. I'm afraid that there's a little Cyrano in each writer.

Such a position, romantic as it is, is unrealistic. Our lines can be improved; we are never likely to achieve perfection. When we can see that and admit it, we can work effectively with an editor or manager to make our writing not perfect, but as good as it can be.

If you don't understand what the editor or the boss wants, ask specific questions. Get the kind of concrete, specific suggestions that will let you understand the situation and improve the writing.

Finally, don't be a fussbudget. Temperamental posings represent you poorly and show a writer at his or her most insecure, defensive worst. And it usually means that your writing isn't as good as it should be—and that you know it.

WHETHER YOU EDIT OR ARE EDITED

Most writers read their work over at least once before submitting it, but this reading is often no more than a final check for grammar and spelling. A more effective final check would focus on the content and organization of the piece as well as its accuracy and correctness and would act to control the overall quality of the piece. This specific checking not only will improve the piece being checked but also will indicate patterns of weakness in style. You can check your own writing in this way, and you can also do it as you edit others' writing. Such a check will deliver concrete response to the writer rather than just a blue-penciled draft. Each writer or editor should develop a checklist for help in editing. Such a checklist might well include the questions in Table 7–1.

Table 7–1   Writers' and editors' checklist

	Ade-quate	Needs work
Organization:		
1. Does the thought flow smoothly?	☐	☐
2. Are there any hard-to-follow breaks in content or organization?	☐	☐
Style:		
1. Are there any long or difficult words that could be more simply expressed?	☐	☐
2. Will all technical and specialized words and abbreviations be clear to the reader?	☐	☐
3. Can this piece be shortened without loss of effectiveness?	☐	☐
4. Is it long enough to represent the fullness of the writer's thought?	☐	☐
5. Is the piece direct and sincere or will it seem evasive and misleading to the reader?	☐	☐
6. Is it sufficiently creative or does it place undue reliance on a "formula"?	☐	☐

Table 7–1   (*continued*)

	Ade-quate	Needs work
7. Is the ending emphatic?	☐	☐
8. Are all modifiers necessary? Do they add to meaning?	☐	☐
9. Are there any passive verbs that can be made active?	☐	☐
10. Are any sentences involved and confusing?	☐	☐
Reader Orientation:		
1. Has the reader been considered?	☐	☐
2. Does the beginning point to the reader's interest?	☐	☐
3. Knowing what you do about the reader, will the piece appeal to the reader's interest?	☐	☐
4. Will the purpose seem clear to the reader?	☐	☐
Tone:		
1. Is the tone suitable to the relationship of *this* writer and *this* reader?	☐	☐
2. Is the tone courteous and human?	☐	☐
Accuracy:		
1. Are facts adequately substantiated?	☐	☐
2. Is opinion justified?	☐	☐
3. Are assumptions stated as such or are they represented as facts?	☐	☐
4. Are recommendations and conclusions justified by the content of the piece?	☐	☐
5. Are punctuation, spelling, and layout correct?	☐	☐
Overall:		
1. Is the piece seen as a whole adequate?	☐	☐

8
How to Dictate

Dictation is a simple skill, and it's done best if it's kept simple. It takes just a little planning to let dictation save time for you and your typist. The first principle of effective dictation is: Talk talking; don't talk writing. Avoid the conventional formulas and heavy phrases of standard, ineffective writing. Keep your wording simple and natural; talk to your reader, not to your secretary or dictating machine.

Machine dictation is cheaper and more efficient than dictation to a secretary. A machine has nothing to do but await your dictation. Dictation never interrupts your machine's work, and the time cost for one hour of dictation is one hour of your work.

A secretary, on the other hand, has many things to do in a day. Your dictation may come at a time when the secretary is in the middle of something else, and the time cost per hours of dictation is two work hours (one of yours and one of the secretary's) for each hour of dictation. In either case, transcription time is the same. If you dictate to a machine, your secretary can transcribe it at a time convenient for him or her, or you can send the tape to a typing pool and free a skilled secretary for work more demanding than transcription.

Effective dictation is planned. Organize your thoughts before you start to dictate to machine or to stenographer. Collect any information you may need before dictating. Effective dictators find it a good idea to make notes to guide their dictation. These notes needn't be extensive—perhaps a key word or two for each paragraph. They help you to plan the content and the order of ideas for maximum reader understanding and acceptance.

You can look at a brief set of notes as a blueprint or as a preview of your letter. Do you have all the ideas and information covered? Are the points in the best order for understanding? This advance organization will help you to plan paragraphs effectively too.

If you are replying to a letter, you can use that letter as the basis of your own. Marginal notes on that letter will help you to make sure that your own letter will be responsive, by guiding your dictation point by point in response to the message you're answering.

After you're sure that you know what you want to dictate, you're ready for the dictation itself. A few simple principles can ensure effective dictation:

1. Speak clearly. Without resorting to an artificial "how now, brown cow" elocution, speak distinctly. Pronounce word endings clearly. Speak in normal phrases rather than word by word. Keep your pace and rhythm constant; don't speed up at the ends of thoughts or sentences.
2. Spell out difficult or unfamiliar names, addresses, or technical words. If you are answering a batch of correspondence, number the letters you're answering and begin dictation by announcing the number of the letter you're answering. This practice will allow the typist to get the receiver's name and address from the letterhead.
3. Announce paragraph divisions, but don't insert punctuation. A competent transcriber can add punctuation, particularly if you dictate in a normal rhythm. Of course, if you have special, non-conventional punctuation, mention it.
4. When you begin dictating a letter, give any special handling instructions, such as those for copies or distribution. If you are dictating by machine, you should also note any special instructions on the identifying label or tab that accompanies a tape or record.

Review the transcribed copy when you get it back. There's no need for a rough draft for most letters. Rough drafts just run up cost, unless they are necessary for the final clarity of the writing. For involved or unusually important letters or for reports, proposals, or other longer documents, ask for a rough draft triple-spaced and with wide margins so that you can easily and neatly make corrections and additions.

Review the transcribed copy carefully when you get it back. Be sure that you are reading what has been typed and not what you expect to see. Often, we allow our expectation to contradict what we see and let errors get through to the reader. Proofreading is careful work; give it your fullest attention.

That's all there is to it. Plan your dictation. Dictate clearly with a steady, conversational rhythm. Review carefully. If you'll take these three simple steps, you and your transcriber should be able to work together smoothly as an effective writing team.

9
Grammar in Brief

Most people write grammatically correct sentences without knowing how they do it. The correct form sounds right to them, though they couldn't quote the rule or principle on which the right form is based. If you're one of that fortunate majority, keep your trust in your instincts. If you're not, then you need a more thorough review of grammar than we can present in this book, and you'd be well advised to make a special effort to learn the basics. This chapter will review the highlights of grammar most useful to business and technical writers. Part II of this book, "The Guide," offers, in alphabetical arrangement, specific guidance to problems of grammar and usage. Consult it for answers to specific questions and problems.

Even if your instincts are current and accurate, the highlights of grammar presented below should be a useful review for you.

PROBLEMS WITH PRONOUNS

A pronoun is a word that stands for a noun. Pronouns are used as nouns are, but they require additional consideration. The word for which a pronoun stands is called its *antecedent*.

> We had hoped to arrange an out-of-court settlement with their *lawyer*, but *she* insists on litigation.

In that sentence, the pronoun *she* stands for *lawyer*. Thus, *lawyer* is the antecedent of the pronoun *she*. The relationship between a pronoun and its antecedent is strict and you must follow certain rules in using pronouns.

Agreement of pronouns.

A pronoun must agree with its antecedent in person, number, and gender. Agreement in gender provides little problem. You're not likely to say of your sister that "he is fixing his boat." And unless you harbor ill feelings toward your brother-in-law, you're unlikely to suggest that "it is coming to dinner." In the case of an antecedent of undetermined or unspecific gender, conventional usage has been the masculine. Thus:

A manager should plan *his* work and that of *his* subordinates.

That sentence with its masculine pronouns would be traditionally correct even when the *managers* referred to are both men and women. If all the managers referred to are women, then traditional usage would demand *her* as the pronoun. This use of the masculine pronoun to refer to a mixed or unknown gender is called the *generic masculine form*. The generic masculine came not from a desire to discriminate, but from the inadequacy of the English language: we have no neutral singular pronoun. We have *he, she,* and the neuter *it. It* is neuter but not neutral and is an offensive way to refer to people of any gender. There have been attempts to create neutral pronouns, but they haven't met with much success. So, what do we do?

Many people find the generic masculine offensive, but a sentence like the following is often cumbersome.

A manager should plan *his* or *her* work and that of *his* or *her* subordinates.

One answer may be found in the neutral plural pronoun, *they (them, their, theirs)*. This pronoun may refer to many men, women, things, or combinations of masculine, feminine, and neuter beings. Thus, if we make the antecedent plural and refer to it with the neutral plural pronoun, we avoid the generic masculine and its possible offensiveness as well as a cumbersome sentence:

Managers should plan *their* work and that of *their* subordinates.

Use the *he or she* construction to emphasize that the sense of the sentence applies equally to both sexes. If, for example, you were posting a job opening and you wanted to emphasize that you were soliciting applications from both men and women, you'd be better advised to write:

Anyone interested should submit *his or her* resume.

instead of:

Applicants should submit *their* resumes.

Still another way to handle the pronouns that refer to antecedents of mixed gender is to alternate the masculine and feminine pronouns as in this example:

> A writer should write for a reader. He should know the reader's need for the information. She should see her work in the context of the reader's situation. He should take the time to look into his reader's background. She should not satisfy herself solely with assumptions about her reader.

If this alternation is not carefully done, it may confuse a reader. It's one of the devices used in the first draft of this book. My antecedents are often words like *writer, speaker, reader, listener,* and *interviewer;* and men and women write, speak, read, listen, and interview. I certainly want to address this book to both men and women. Sometimes, to do so, I used a plural antecedent and the neutral plural pronouns, but sometimes that didn't prove a fluent way to make a point; thus I used alternating pronouns when they seemed to fit. The copy editor of this book thought this was confusing and changed all these alternating pronouns to *he or she.* I'm inclined to think the editor was right and that it would be difficult to use alternating genders of pronouns successfully. Still, it is a practice one encounters from time to time and if one could do it without confusing the reader, it might have some value. I obviously can't do it without confusing my editor and, as I noted in Chapter 7, if the editor says your piece isn't clear, the editor is right.

Agreement in person provides few problems. Don't use *you* when the antecedent is in the third person as in:

> Sales representatives must plan *their* work if *you* expect to cover *your* territory.

Sales representatives and the first pronoun, *their,* are in agreement, since both are in the third person. However, *you* and *your,* which also have *sales representatives* as their antecedent, don't agree with their antecedent. Their antecedent is in the third person; they are in the second person. That sentence can be written in either the first, second, or third person; but, to be correct, all the pronouns must be in the same person as their antecedents. Thus you would write either:

> Sales representatives must organize *their* work if *they* expect to cover *their* territories.

Or (if addressing sales representatives)

> You must plan *your* work if *you* expect to cover *your* territories.

If you were one of the sales representatives, you could correctly write the sentence in the first person and say:

We must plan *our* work if *we* expect to cover *our* territories.

Agreement in number of pronoun and antecedent causes some problems, but the following rules should help you avoid them.

1. When a sentence has several nouns and a pronoun, make the pronoun agree with its real antecedent.

    Incorrect: If he wants a *summary* of our findings, I'll send *them* to him.

    Correct: If he wants a *summary* of our findings, I'll send *it* to him.

    Summary, the real antecedent, is singular and calls for the singular pronoun *it* rather than the plural *them;* I have offered to send a summary, not the findings.

2. A pronoun that has a singular antecedent (or one that relates to another singular pronoun) should be singular.

    Incorrect: The *department* has sent us *their* report.
    Correct: The *department* has sent us *its* report.

    Incorrect: Each *branch* must send us *their* budget.
    Correct: Each *branch* must send us *its* budget.

3. A pronoun can have two antecedents joined by *or* or *nor*. If both are plural, the pronoun should be plural:

    Correct: Ask our *lawyers or* our *accountants* for *their* advice.

    If both are singular, the pronoun should be singular:

    Correct: Ask either *Bill or Ray* for *his* advice.

    When one is singular and the other plural, the pronoun agrees with the nearer antecedent:

    Correct: Ask our *accountants or* our *lawyer* for *his* advice.
    Correct: Ask our *lawyer or* our *accountants* for *their* advice.

    Though either of the above is, strictly speaking, correct, the second sentence is preferable. If you have a sentence with a singular and a plural antecedent joined by *or* or *nor*, put the plural antecedent closer to the pronoun and use the plural pronoun. It reads more smoothly.

4. The words *each, every, neither,* and *either* may be pronouns or adjectives. In either use they are singular. Pronouns referring to them must be singular.

> *Incorrect:*   *Each* is responsible for *their* own work.
> *Correct:*   *Each* is responsible for *his* own work.

> *Incorrect:*   *Neither* had written *their* report.
> *Correct:*   *Neither* had written *his* report.

5. The indefinite pronouns *one, anyone, no one, nobody, someone,* and the like are singular. Pronouns referring to these words must be singular.

> *Incorrect:*   *One* must see that *their* work is done on time.
> *Correct:*   *One* must see that *his* work is done on time.

> *Incorrect:*   *Somebody* left *their* notes in the conference room.
> *Correct:*   *Somebody* left *his* notes in the conference room.

Reference of pronouns.

The antecedent of a pronoun should be specific and clear to the reader. Don't leave your reader or listener in doubt about an ambiguous antecedent. This sentence is confusing:

> Fred said that he had called Bill and that *he* still didn't know what the problem was.

Who didn't know what the problem was? Fred? Bill? A better sentence would say:

> Fred said that he'd called Bill, *who* still didn't know what the problem was.

or:

> Fred said that *he* had called Bill and that *Bill* still didn't know what the problem was.

Don't use a pronoun that has no antecedent.

> *They* say that the economy should firm up in the last quarter.

Who are *they?* And in this sentence, who is *it?*

> *It* is generally assumed that the economy will firm up in the last quarter.

Who is generally assuming? Avoid the indefinite passive. These sentences would be clearer if stated as:

Our financial analysts say that . . .
Our financial analysts assume . . .

PROBLEMS WITH VERBS

A verb must agree with its subject in person and number. As with pronouns, person causes few problems. Those problems that do occur are usually the result of words that come between the subject and the verb. You aren't likely to say: *I is going.* With the first-person subject *I*, you would naturally use the first-person verb *am.* But if you aren't careful, you might slip into a sentence like:

I, along with our Executive Vice-President, *is* going to Cleveland.

But that unlikely error isn't likely to survive a rereading.

As with pronouns, the major agreement problems with verbs are problems of agreement in number. A few rules will help you to avoid these problems.

1. Make the verb agree with the subject. Don't be thrown off by words that come between the subject and the verb.

   Incorrect: The *completion* of seven projects *were* reported.
   Correct: The *completion* of seven projects *was* reported.

   Completion, not *projects*, is the subject of the verb, and the verb must be singular to agree with it.

2. Just as 1 + 1 = 2, so two singular subjects joined by *and* call for a plural. The *and* adds the singular subjects to form a plural subject.

   Correct: The *manager and* the *superintendent are* going.

3. If compound subjects are joined by *or* or *nor*, the verb should agree with the closer subject.

   Incorrect: *Neither* the *sales nor* the *profit were* good enough.
   Correct: *Neither* the *sales nor* the *profit was* good enough.
   Better: Neither sales nor profits were good enough.

4. Indefinite pronouns are singular and call for a singular verb.

   Correct: *Each* is useful in its own way.
   Someone wants to see you.
   Either is ready to go.
   Anything is better than that.

5. In American usage, collective nouns, words that name a group considered as a single entity, usually take a singular verb.

> Correct: *Congress has* approved it.
> The *committee is* in session.
> The *company has* a new product.
> The *team is* winning.
> The *jury has read* the transcript.

The phrase *the number* takes a singular verb. *A number* takes a plural verb.

> Correct: *The number* of accidents *was* increasing.
> *A number* of claims *were* filed in Omaha.

6. Nouns expressing a measurement considered as a single unit are singular and take a singular verb.

> Correct: *Four years is* the usual time spent in college.
> *Three quarts is* enough to fill it.
> *Forty hours is* the normal work week.
> *Eighty-four feet* of wire *was* enough to do the job.

Other than problems of agreement, problems of tense are the most common. Regular English verbs add *ed* to the infinitive to produce the past tense and the past participle (the form of the verb used to form certain phrasal verbs). Thus, we say *today I walk; yesterday I walked; in the past I have walked*. Many verbs, however, are irregular in forming their past tenses and past participles. The following lists the more commonly misused irregular verbs and their past tenses and past participles. The most troublesome are marked with an asterisk:

Present	Past	Past participle
am	was	been
awake	awoke (or awaked)	awaked
become	became	become
begin	began	begun
bet	bet	bet
bid (offer)	bid	bid
bid (order or command)	bade	bidden
*burst	burst	burst
cling	clung	clung
cost	cost	cost
*creep	crept	crept

*dive	dived	dived
	(Note that the past tense is *dived*, not *dove*. *Dove* is barely acceptable, but only in the United States.)	
drink	drank	drunk
drive	drove	driven
fling	flung	flung
forget	forgot	forgotten (forgot)
get	got	got (gotten)
*hang (something)	hung	hung
*hang (a person for execution)	hanged	hanged
*lay	laid	laid
*lie	lay	lain
light	lighted (lit)	lighted (lit)
prove	proved	proved (proven)
ride	rode	ridden
seek	sought	sought
set	set	set
slay	slew	slain
sling	slung	slung
sting	stung	stung
stride	strode	stridden
*swim	swam	swum
swing	swung	swung
teach	taught	taught
think	thought	thought
*wake	woke (waked)	waked
write	wrote	written

PROBLEMS WITH ADJECTIVES

The major problems with adjectives are stylistic rather than grammatical. Poor writers use too many adjectives. Remember that an adjective is a modifier. To modify is to change. An adjective should change the meaning of the word it modifies, and it should change it so that the reader will get the meaning the writer wants to convey. If an adjective adds words alone and adds no real change in meaning, then it makes writing wordy and less readable.

Adjectives have three degrees: positive, comparative, and superlative. The comparative degree is normally formed by adding *r* or *er* to the positive degree. The superlative is formed by adding *st* or *est* to the positive. Thus, *fine, finer, finest; loud, louder, loudest.*

Some adjectives compare irregularly, for example, *good, better, best.* Other adjectives compare by using the words *more* and *most.* Usually, adjectives that compare by using more and most have three or more syllables. Thus, *beautiful, more beautiful, most beautiful.*

Use the positive degree to describe a noun or pronoun considered by itself. Use the comparative degree to compare two things and the superlative degree to compare three or more things.

> Use a *large* bolt to fasten the extension arm. (Positive)
> The store in Springfield is *larger* than the one in Worcester. (Comparative)
> This is the *largest* of the dozen boxes we have in stock. (Superlative)

Some adjectives, and their related adverbs, represent absolute qualities and cannot be compared. *Perfect* means without flaw. If something has even a single flaw, it is not *perfect.* A thing is perfect, or it is not; there are no degrees of perfection. *Unique* means one of a kind; a thing is unique or it is not. There can be no notion of *uniquer* or *uniquest;* no notion of *more unique* or *most unique.* To compare the degree to which things approach an absolute quality, use the words *more nearly* to compare two things, and *most nearly* to compare three or more things. Thus:

> This is *more nearly perfect* than that.
> This batch is the *most nearly complete* of all of them.
> This is the *most nearly square* plot of land we have seen.

This pure tradition which holds that absolute adjectives cannot be compared is a good one. It keeps the strength of the words undiluted. If we begin to think and to speak of things as *more perfect* and *most perfect,* then we will say little when we say that something is *perfect,* and trapezoids will become *sort of square.* But no rule of grammar or usage should become dogma; people should be free to use their language creatively. Our Constitution offends few when it speaks of a "more perfect union." If you must embellish an absolute with *more* or *most* to achieve the meaning that you seek, do so. But do so rarely and sparingly if, indeed, at all. The more commonly seen absolutes are:

circular	immortal	superior
complete	impossible	supreme

correct	incorrect	total
dead	infinite	unanimous
endless	perfect	unique
equal	perpendicular	universal
exact	square	vertical
horizontal		

Readers react to all they see. Their reaction to ideas is often colored by their perceptions of how those ideas are expressed. Follow the conventions of grammar and usage. Don't let carelessness distract your readers from your ideas.

Part II of this book, "The Guide," gives a useful presentation of many troublesome areas of grammar, usage, spelling, and pronunciation. Consult it or other sources, such as a dictionary, whenever you are in doubt. Though "The Guide" is intended primarily as a reference source, you may find it profitable to read through it occasionally. A page or two a day should provide you with much useful information to help you in your communication opportunities.

10

A Guide to Punctuation

Punctuation is more than a set of rules designed by sadistic grammarians to torment you. Most of the marks of punctuation represent a form of notation much like musical notation. Speech needs no punctuation. Emphasis, variety, separation, and other subtleties of meaning can come from the pitch, pace, volume, and tone of the voice as well as from gesture and movement. The written word, though, is two-dimensional and lacks the arsenal of expressiveness that speech so naturally has. Marks of punctuation indicate the variety of expression that would be in the written sentences if they were being spoken.

The period indicates a full stop and the abrupt halt of the voice at the end of a sentence. A question mark shows the upward turn in tone of the voice at the end of an interrogative sentence. Comma, semicolon, and colon represent pauses of different durations. Italics show emphasis.

Other marks of punctuation promote clarity. Quotation marks make it clear to the reader that the writer is using words other than his or her own. Brackets identify editorial comment in the midst of a quotation. Parentheses keep clarifying or explanatory comments out of the main stream of the sentence.

There is a purpose for punctuation, and if you punctuate properly, you'll improve your writing. Careless punctuation can be distracting to readers, and you want nothing in your writing that will lead the reader away from the ideas you are trying to communicate. So here, then, is a guide to punctuation. First, we'll look at the punctuation marks in some detail; at the end of the chapter, you'll find a summary for quick reference.

PERIOD

1. Use a period at the end of a sentence that makes a statement (declarative sentence) or gives a command (imperative sentence).

We should be ready to begin next week.
Leave space for the other material.

2. Use a period at the end of a sentence that is phrased as a question but is really a request.

Will you please send it to my attention.
May I suggest that you telephone your order directly to the factory.

3. Use a period to punctuate an indirect question.

I wonder if we'll have it ready by the end of the year.
The question in my mind is what to do about it.
He asked if we'll be able to make the changes within the month.

4. Conventional uses of the period:

Use a period following an abbreviation:
a.m., etc., Inc., Corp.
Many commonly used abbreviations are written without a
period:

FBI	DOD	log
NASA	GNP	rpm
FNMA	LCL	ft
FICA	PERT	mph

If a term is frequently used in a field, it often is written without a period in the literature of that field. But if in doubt, use a period. Periods are usually omitted from abbreviations for the names of companies or government agencies and are always omitted when the abbreviation is an acronym (an abbreviation pronounced as a word). Thus, Performance Evaluation Review Technique is abbreviated PERT and is called PERT. These abbreviations for the names of organizations are written without a period, as are GE, IBM, GM, NATO, CBS, UNICEF, MIT, DEC, ITT.

Use a period to express decimal numbers. If the number is less than 1.0, always put a zero before the decimal point.

1.348965   356.09   0.87654   0.3

QUESTION MARK

1. Use the question mark at the end of a sentence that is a direct question.

Why are you doing that?
What is the purpose of all of this research and study?

2. Use the question mark in parentheses to express doubt or uncertainty.

We processed the order in March (?) and shipped it on June 8.
He was born on September 25, 1935(?) in Cambridge, Massachusetts.

3. If there is a series of questions in one sentence, put a single question mark at the end.

Have you checked the advertising layout, the space cost, and the release date?
Not: Have you checked the advertising layout? the space cost? the release date?

4. If a statement is made into a question by a short phrase at the end, use the question mark as end punctuation.

You're going to go to the meeting, *aren't you?*
It's all settled then, *isn't it?*

EXCLAMATION POINT

Use the exclamation point at the end of a sentence or phrase to signal strong feeling or excitement. That is the traditional role of the exclamation point, but it's often overused. The strength of a sentence comes from the strength of the ideas and the words used to express those ideas. An exclamation point used to end a weak sentence is wasted. Indeed, it highlights the weakness. The exclamation point has a place in dialogue, such as that which a novelist might write. Business and technical writers should avoid using it. Strong ideas, well expressed, don't need it.

COMMA

1. Use a comma to separate two independent clauses connected by a co-ordinating conjunction. An independent clause is a clause that could stand alone as a sentence. The principal coordinating conjunctions are *and, but, for, or, nor,* and *yet.* Of these, *and, but,* and *or* are the most commonly used to connect independent clauses.

> We negotiated the contract, *and* they will start construction in July.
> Harry will go to Cleveland, *and* I'll stay here.

If the two independent clauses are very short and joined by *and,* you may separate them with the conjunction alone:

> We saw it *and* we bought it.
> Jack drove *and* I flew.

2. Use a comma to separate items in a series.

> They have offices in Boston, New York, Philadelphia, and Trenton.
> We have investments in land, commodities, bonds, and common stock.

The use of the comma before the *and* preceding the last item in the series is optional. I suggest that you use it. To do so never causes confusion, but leaving it out can do so, as in the following sentence:

> It comes in several colors: red, orange, yellow, blue and white.

That sentence could leave the reader wondering if *blue and white* is two distinct colors or a two-tone model. Of course, it would be better to recast the entire sentence to make the color distinction clearer if it were a two-tone model, but the comma would insure that confusion would not result from the statement as worded.

3. Use a comma to enclose appositives. An appositive is a word or phrase that renames or supplements a noun.

> Harold Jenkins, *our personnel manager,* will see you on Wednesday.
> The final step, *litigation,* can be avoided by a reasonable settlement now.
> Our main advantage, *knowledge of the market,* should be exploited.

4. Use commas to separate a series of coordinate adjectives that modify the same noun or pronoun.

It came in a *heavy, bulky* carton.
It's a *hot, humid* day.
She's an *articulate, experienced, ambitious, intelligent* woman.

Coordinate adjectives are adjectives that modify a noun in the same way. The ones in the examples you've just read are coordinate adjectives. The adjectives in the following sentence are not coordinate and shouldn't be separated by a comma:

They are discussing a *serious legal* problem.

Serious and *legal* both modify *problem*. They aren't, however, coordinate adjectives. How can you tell? That's simple; their order can't be reversed. You wouldn't say:

They are discussing a *legal serious* problem.

The coordinate adjectives can be reversed. You could say either:

It came in a *heavy, bulky* carton.

Or:

It came in a *bulky, heavy* carton.

You could say:

She's an *articulate, experienced, ambitious, intelligent* woman.

Or:

She's an *experienced, ambitious, articulate, intelligent* woman.

You could also mix those four adjectives in any other order without changing the sense of the sentence.

5. Use commas to set off words in direct address.

It was good to see you again, *my friend,* and I hope to see you again soon.
I've enclosed our application form, *Ms. Miller.*
Mr. Reagan, it's important that we get together soon.

6. Use a comma to separate introductory words, clauses, and phrases from the main clause.

Incidentally, I'm leaving for Europe next month.
Since you haven't finished the drawings, we'll have to delay the bid.
Without the drawings, we can't submit the bid.
Until the drawings are ready, we can't submit the bid.
His dinner still unfinished, he left for the airport.

7. Use commas to set off nonrestrictive modifiers. Modifiers that don't limit the meaning of a noun or verb but that provide descriptive detail are nonrestrictive.

These features, *though they're nice to have,* are not essential.
Four men, *each carrying a sack,* came into the bank.

Don't use commas if the modifier is essential to the meaning of the sentence. In the following sentence, the clause *who has been authorized to sign purchase orders* is essential to the meaning of the sentence:

An employee *who has been authorized to sign purchase orders* may approve changes in specifications.

8. Use commas to set off interrupting or parenthetical elements.

If you have the report ready on time, *and it had better be ready no later than June 1,* we can begin to schedule vacations.
This study, *in his opinion,* will be quite helpful.
We will, *of course,* meet him at the airport.

9. Use a comma when it will improve the clarity of the sentence. That doesn't mean that you should promiscuously proliferate commas, but it does mean that if a comma would make the sentence clearer, you should use one even if you can't think of a rule that covers it. The sentences below would be confusing without the commas:

The soldier dropped, a bullet in his leg.
Not: The soldier dropped a bullet in his leg.
Soon after we left, the plant began production.
Not: Soon after we left the plant . . .

10. Use a comma to set off a tag question. A tag question is a short question at the end of a statement that makes it a question:

We're all going to go, *aren't we?*
It will be ready to go on Monday, *won't it?*

11. Use commas to set off transitional words and phrases except conjunctions.

This, *however,* is the last renewal that we can approve.
His application, *therefore,* is denied.
Staff activities, *for example,* don't produce revenue directly.

12. Conventional uses of the comma:

a.   *In dates:*

June 5, 1937

No comma is necessary if dates are written in the European style, which is becoming more popular in the United States:

5 June 1937.

No comma is necessary if just the month and year are written.

October 1956.

b.   *To separate names and titles or other designations:*

P.D. Cole, M.D.
John J. Leary, Treasurer
Thomas E. Easter, III
Captain Henry G. Barry, USN

c.   *When names are written with the last name first:*

Devlin, Dorothy A.
Washington, George

d.   *In figures:*

4,789,234

SEMICOLON

1. Use a semicolon to separate two independent clauses not joined by a conjunction:

We received your inquiry; we're working on an answer.
He sent letters to 400 potential exhibitors; only 18 replied.

Note: Words like those in the following list are conjunctive adverbs, sometimes called transitional connectives. They are not conjunctions.

Therefore, when they are used to introduce the second of two independent clauses, the clauses must be separated by a semicolon. The most common conjunctive adverbs are:

accordingly	hence	perhaps
also	however	so
anyhow	indeed	still
besides	likewise	then
consequently	moreover	therefore
furthermore	nevertheless	thus

If these words introduce the second of two independent clauses, the clauses must be separated by a semicolon:

We wanted to go to the convention; *however,* we had to work here.
We can find no justification for it; *nevertheless,* we are reluctant to call the account.
Harold couldn't get the loan; *consequently,* he must shut down.

There are three ways to punctuate a compound sentence (a sentence with two or more independent clauses). You can:

a.   Separate the clauses with a comma and a coordinating conjunction:

We studied the problem you sent us, *but* we haven't been able to come up with any useful recommendations.

If, however, the clauses joined by the coordinating conjunction contain, between them, a total of two or more commas, a semicolon must precede the coordinating conjunction. The following sentence is correctly punctuated with a comma before the coordinating conjunction that joins the two independent clauses:

Sarah Phillips will attend the meeting, *and* she will give the main presentation.

But, if that sentence had two commas in the clauses, it would have to have a semicolon before the word *and*. For example:

Sarah Phillips, the new member, will attend the meeting; *and* she will give the main presentation.

Or:

Sarah Phillips will attend the meeting; *and,* following the prelimi nary remarks, she will give the main presentation

b.   Separate the clauses with a semicolon:

We studied the problem you sent us; we haven't been able to come up with any useful recommendations.

c.   Make each of the clauses a sentence and separate them with a period.

We studied the problem you sent us. We haven't been able to come up with any useful recommendations.

2. Use a semicolon to separate elements in a series when the elements contain commas:

They have offices in Dayton, Ohio; Elmira, New York; and Boise, Idaho.

COLON

1. Use a colon to introduce a list or schedule when the word "following" is used or implied:

It comes in the following colors: red, orange, yellow, green, blue, and violet.

Preference shall be given to people in these trades:

shipfitter	test technician
modelmaker	inside machinist
welder	electrician

2. Use a colon to introduce a long quotation. A long quotation is one that takes three lines or more. Use a comma to introduce a shorter quotation. For an example of this use, see the section on quotation marks.

3. Conventional uses of the colon:

a.   After the salutation of a business letter.

Dear Sirs:
Dear Ms. Devlin:

b.   In certain bibliographical, legal, biblical, and other citations.

The Journal of Communication, 18:4
Boston, Mass.: CBI, 1981
Genesis 36: 9–32

DASH

In print, a dash is longer than a hyphen. Most typewriters, however, have no dash. To make a dash in typescript, use two hyphens unspaced as:

The cause--and keep in mind that it was the only cause--was his failure to plan for emergencies.

1. Use dashes to indicate a break or abrupt change in thought:

Dashes are overused by people who would let punctuation substitute for style--but this doesn't mean that dashes are somehow second-class punctuation.

2. Use dashes—but use them sparingly—to emphasize a parenthetical element:

Two factors, motivation and fear--and motivation is by far the more useful--control performance.

3. Use dashes to set off an appositive (see p. 87) that contains a comma or commas:

Three engineers--Jones, Miller, and Clark--will attend the conference.
One executive--Murphy, the Senior Vice President--has resigned.

PARENTHESES

Use parentheses to set off explanatory, amplifying, or classifying words and phrases from the mainstream of the sentence:

The contract (paragraph 7) provides for sequential payment.
Any group larger than a dyad (a two-person group) is likely to be unstable.
FICA (Federal Insurance Contribution Act) deductions are made from each paycheck until the maximum deduction is reached.
They will provide (1) complete plans, (2) material lists, and (3) detailed specifications.

The last example above shows parentheses used to enclose numbers within a sentence. This is not usually a good use of parentheses unless you want to stress the enumeration or call particular attention to the number of factors or elements involved. Unless this emphasis is essential, that sentence would be better written as:

> They will provide complete plans, material lists, and detailed specifications.

BRACKETS

Brackets are used only to insert editorial explanation or comment in a direct quotation. They signal the reader that the words within the brackets are the quoter's words and are not part of the original quotation. They should *never* be used instead of parentheses. They should never be used for parentheses within parentheses. If it's necessary to use parentheses within parentheses, use parentheses.

Most typewriters don't have a bracket key. If yours doesn't, then leave a space where the bracket is to be inserted and put it in with a pen or pencil after you remove the sheet from the typewriter. Don't try to manufacture brackets with underscores and slant signs. The result, $\angle\_\overline{7}$, is crooked brackets and a waste of time. Brackets ought to be squared, and you can do that quite nicely with a pen.

1. Brackets are generally used to correct errors in quoted material. When you quote directly, you shouldn't change anything, including errors, in the original. Make corrections in brackets to show your reader that the error is not yours:

> "Water freezes at 32°C [Water freezes at 32°F or 0°C]."
> "President Nickson [Nixon] resigned."

Sometimes, the word *sic*, Latin for *thus*, is put in brackets after an obvious error, to signal the reader that the error was in the original. Modern style is moving away from Latin expressions, so you'll often see *thus* in brackets after an obvious error. Either *sic* or *thus* is currently acceptable:

> "Please send us fore [*sic*] sets of material."
> "I hope that I may have the opportunity of waking [thus] with your company."
> "Texas Jack Gardner [*sic*] was his Vice-President then."

2. Use brackets to explain a term in a quotation:

> "The process [the final plating process] cannot be attempted until the surface has been cleaned and prepared."

ELLIPSIS

This punctuation mark consists of three spaced periods. It is used chiefly to indicate an incomplete quotation. If a quotation begins in the middle of a sentence, it should begin with an ellipsis. If it ends before the sentence ends, it should end with an ellipsis. If a word or phrase is left out of the sentence or if a sentence or several sentences are left out of the middle of a quotation, the break should be marked with an ellipsis:

> He said that they would never agree ". . . to any arrangement that failed to ensure seniority."
> Bob reported that "the plant can't be ready to start until August . . ."
> The contract provides that "if either party . . . wishes to terminate the agreement, ninety days written notice . . . must be given . . ."

If the break in a quotation comes at the end of a sentence in the middle of a quotation, use four periods—one for the end of the sentence and three for the ellipsis.

The ellipsis may also be used to indicate a regularly continuing series.

> The frequency will increase geometrically. The first instance may find only two cells. But it will go on infinitely: 2, 4, 8, 16, 32 . . . .

Don't use the ellipsis as a stylistic device. Don't use it in place of commas, dashes, parentheses, colons, or any other mark. The use of the ellipsis in place of other marks is cute at best, and your writing should never be cute.

QUOTATION MARKS

1. Use quotation marks for all direct quotations from any other source, written or oral, unless the quoted passage is three lines or more. These longer quotations are indicated by indenting within the normal margins and by single spacing in typescript and/or by smaller print on printed pages. When this form is used, quotation marks would be redundant and are not used.

> He said, "We will continue to market the older blades as well."

> William J. Gallagher, in his book *Report Writing for Management* (Addison-Wesley, 1969), says of unnecessary intensives:

>> Some words denote the absolute. For example *dead* does not admit of degrees of comparison. So too, a *superb* performance can be

neither *more superb* nor *less superb,* and an *impossible* task, neither *more* nor *less impossible.* Some words that can be compared gain little or nothing from the addition of qualifiers such as *quite* and *rather.*

If your long quotation is more than one paragraph, double space between the paragraphs and continue the quotation indented on both sides and single spaced.

Some publishers use single (') rather than double ('') quotation marks. This is quite acceptable, but I have not often seen this used in typescript. If you're given to pioneering, you may want to try it on your report readers.

2. For quotations within quotations use single quotation marks for the inner quotation. For a quotation within a quotation within a quotation, revert to the double quotation marks. If you start with a single quotation mark instead of the double mark, then the procedure is the same: keep alternating.

A quotation would be marked:

"............................"

A quotation within a quotation:

".....'...............'......."

If both of these quotations ended at the end of the sentence:

".............................'"

A quotation within a quotation within a quotation:

".....'...........".............." ...'....."

or

"............'...........".............."'"

When things get to that last stage, or heaven forfend, go beyond it, it's long since past time to recast the sentence. *The Guiness Book of World Records* fails to disclose the all-time high of quotations within quotations, but it was no doubt achieved by someone in the fifth grade. Keep your copy clear, clean, and unconfusing.

3. It was once common practice to put slang, jargon, and other non-standard forms in quotation marks to show that the writer was genteel and normally did not use such common locutions. Today, that practice seems snotty and as Victorian as calling a woman's leg a "limb."

If you find a word inappropriate or offensive, don't use it. If you do use it, don't apologize for it with quotation marks.

4. Use quotation marks to enclose titles of shorter or component writings such as articles, pamphlets, booklets, poems, essays, short stories,

reports, letters, minutes, schedules, or specifications. Longer works or complete works are identified, as we shall see, by italics.

5. To use quotation marks correctly with other forms of punctuation, keep a few simple rules in mind.

a. Periods and commas always go inside the closing quotation mark:

The rule says, "Time cards must be signed before Friday."
"I'll pay for the changes," were his exact words.
When you process an invoice, stamp it "Paid."

b. Semicolons always go outside the closing quotation mark:

In his letter he said, "I'll pay for the changes"; therefore, we billed him.

c. A question mark goes:

1. Inside the closing quotation mark when it applies to the quoted material only:

Mr. Jensen asked, "Why have you done it?"

2. Outside the closing quotation mark when it applies only to the whole sentence and not to the quoted material:

Did he say, "I'm going to be out of town"?

3. Inside the closing quotation mark when it applies to both the whole sentence and the material being quoted:

Did she ask, "Who is in charge here?"

d. When a quotation ends before the ending of a sentence and is followed by a dialogue tag, such as *he asked* or *Mr. Freeman said,* end the quotation with a comma instead of a period and close the quotation:

"I'm leaving for Cleveland," he announced.

If the quoted material ends with a question mark or an exclamation point, end the quotation with that mark, close the quotation and use no comma to introduce the dialogue tag:

"Were there any calls for me?" he asked.

e. Introduce a short (less than three lines) quotation with a comma outside the opening quotation mark:

He said, "Have the parts come in yet?"

f. Introduce a long quotation (three lines or more) with a colon:

Random noise is a problem because it is random. One source puts it this way:

> Random noise is characterized, necessarily, by a lack of organization. Precisely because it is random, its periodicity and amplitude are hard to predict. . . . system parameters must be adjusted to minimize its effects.

ITALICS

Italics take the form of underscoring in typescript or handwriting.

1. Use italics to indicate the titles of longer or complete writings such as books, periodicals, catalogs, long reports, and long narrative poems. Some authorities hold that these titles may be enclosed in quotation marks instead of italics in letters only, but a more consistent use suggests that they be put in italics for any form of writing.

2. Use italics for names of ships, airplanes, automobiles, works of art, and musical compositions.

3. Use italics for foreign words and phrases that have not become part of the English language. If possible, avoid foreign words and phrases and instead substitute their English equivalents. Italicize abbreviations for foreign words and phrases (*ibid., loc. cit., et al.*)

4. You may use italics for emphasis, but don't overdo it. When you emphasize much, you emphasize nothing.

5. Italicize a word when it is used for itself and not for its meaning:

Empathy signifies a feeling with, rather than a feeling for.
Enclosed herewith please find is not only cumbersome and archaic; it is, if analyzed, redundant and ridiculous.

APOSTROPHE

1. Use the apostrophe with an s to indicate possession or attribution:

the boy's hat	the customer's needs
the journey's end	Mr. Miller's office
a day's work	a month's quota

2. For nouns that form their plurals by adding s, indicate possession with an apostrophe alone:

the boys' hats (several boys, several hats)
the Directors' meeting room

But for nouns that form their plurals irregularly, use 's for the plural possessive:

The men's coats (several men, several coats)
the mice's tails

3. Use 's for the plurals of letters and numbers:

Aardvark begins with two a's.
There are four 7's in the serial number.
He raised with a full house: three 10's and two 4's.

4. Use an apostrophe to indicate omitted letters in contractions:

isn't   you're   haven't   don't

In this same spirit, the apostrophe replaces numbers missing from dates in colloquial and informal usage:

the blizzard of '04   the class of '56   *The Summer of '42*

HYPHEN

Use a hyphen to:
   1. Divide a word at the end of a line. Avoid this whenever possible. When you do divide, do so at syllable breaks. Don't hyphenate names.
   2. Separate prefixes from root words when the prefix ends with the vowel with which the root word begins:

pre-election   anti-investigation

3. Separate prefixes from proper nouns and adjectives:

anti-Administration   anti-Semitic   ex-President
pro-American   pre-World War II

4. Separate *ex-* used to mean *former:*

ex-wife   ex-champion

5. Separate prefixes when confusion with another word might result:

re-sign   resign

6. Separate the prefix *self* from the root word:

self-starter   *self-adjusting*   *self-incrimination*

7. For two-word numbers from *twenty-one* through *ninety-nine* and for fractions (*three-fourths, nine-sixteenths,* etc.).
8. For a group of words that modifies a noun following:

They had a *back-of-the-bus* prejudice.
It was a *stop-gap* measure.
an *I-don't-give-a-damn* gesture
a *twentieth-century* man

This principle of hyphenation is not followed strictly. Use your own judgment. Look at both ways of doing it, with and without hyphens; then decide for yourself which is clearer and more emphatic for your purposes.

9. For certain titles and relationships: *Attorney-General, Vice-President, mother-in-law, step-brother,* etc. All these forms are increasingly seen without hyphens, particularly in business use.

The rules and principles that govern the humble hyphen are many, varied, and often contradictory. Of those presented above, rules 1 through 7 are fairly universal and consistent. Rules 8 and 9 are more optional, and I haven't bothered to mention the others for they are, if anything, more optional than 8 and 9. Don't get tense about hyphens. No one has been indicted for misuse of a hyphen since 1937.

SUMMARY OF PUNCTUATION: A QUICK REFERENCE

The uses given here are the chief uses of the various punctuation marks. For detailed discussion and examples, see the appropriate sections in this chapter.

Period.
End punctuation for a declarative or imperative sentence, for an indirect question, or for a question that is really a request. The period is also used after an abbreviation.

Question mark.
End punctuation for a direct question. Also used to express doubt or uncertainty.

Exclamation point.
End punctuation to signal strong feeling or excitement.

Comma.
Separates independent clauses connected by a conjunction. Separates items in a series. Encloses appositives. Separates a series of adjectives. Sets off names in direct address. Used after introductory clauses, phrases, or words. Sets off nonrestrictive modifiers. Sets off interrupting or parenthetical elements. Sets off tag questions. Sets off transitional words and phrases.

Semicolon.
Separates independent clauses not joined by a coordinating conjunction. Separates elements in a series when the elements contain commas.

Colon.
Introduces a list or schedule. Introduces a long quotation. Follows the salutation of a business letter.

Dash.
Indicates an abrupt change or break in thought. Emphasizes parenthetical elements.

Parentheses.
Set off amplifying, explanatory, or classifying words from the rest of the sentence.

Brackets.
Set off editorial comment in a direct quotation.

Ellipsis.
Indicates an incomplete quotation.

Quotation marks.
Indicate direct quotations. Indicate titles of shorter or component works.

Italics.
Indicate titles of longer or complete works. Indicate foreign words or phrases. Used for emphasis.

Apostrophe.
Forms possessives. Used for plurals of numbers and letters. Indicates omitted letters in contractions.

Hyphen.
Divides words. Separates prefixes from root words.

11

Foundations of Effective Oral Presentation

Many people feel inadequate when asked to express themselves in an oral presentation. They think of oratory, elocution, and public speaking and feel that these skills are beyond them. They really have nothing to fear, for their audiences do not expect the stylized polish of oratory, the precision of elocution, or the trained eloquence of public speaking. A presentation is nothing more than a useful sharing of useful ideas expressed in the spoken word. If effective oral presentation comes close to any other form of expression, that form is conversation.

You are asked to share a subject that you know well with an audience that can use your ideas. If you take time to prepare, you'll know your audience and you'll have organized your ideas—and you'll be quite capable of giving your audience a useful experience in listening to you. No one is going to ask you to speak on a subject you're unfamiliar with. You won't be asked to entertain a group. Far from it, you'll simply be asked to share your professional competence with an audience that can benefit from that competence.

You began to prepare your presentation when you first began to gain experience with your subject. Your job in giving a presentation is to relate your experience to your audience's needs; this chapter will give you ample guidance to do that.

As I noted in the chapters on writing, perfection is a goal productive only of frustration. That applies to oral presentation too. No one has ever given a perfect presentation. No one, no matter how well qualified or experienced, ever will. Experienced speakers realize this and don't set out to do a perfect job. They set out to do a good job, a job adequate to the occasion. They know that they can achieve this goal. Having been, themselves, members of an audience, they realize that no audience expects perfection. They confine their expectations of their own performance to what the audience expects of them: sound ideas presented by a knowledgeable speaker in a useful and reasonably concise form. They direct their preparation and presentation toward this goal. It's a reasonable goal for an experienced speaker; it's a reasonable goal for an inexperienced speaker; it's a reasonable goal for you, no matter what your experience. Seek perfection and you'll never be satisfied. Aim for a good job, take adequate time for preparation, and you can satisfy yourself and your audience.

You'll be able to do a good job if you prepare. Preparation is important because it gets you ready to take best advantage of the opportunity you have to share your ideas. Preparation is also important because it shows you respect your audience, which is likely to respond in turn with respect for you. You've attended presentations at which the speakers have been obviously unprepared. How did you feel about them? Did you feel that they were showing that they didn't have much respect for you and for your time? You've attended presentations at which the speaker was obviously prepared. How did you feel about those speakers? Weren't you better disposed to hearing them out? You don't show preparation by waving a sheaf of notes. You show preparation and respect for your audience by giving an organized presentation focused on the needs and interests of your audience.

A good presentation is always audience-centered. Some speakers talk about their subjects; their whole presentation is focused on aspects of the subject. Some speakers talk about what they want to say, focusing the whole presentation on themselves, their needs, and their points of view. Good speakers bring together the subject, themselves, and their audiences. They talk about those aspects of the subject in which they are competent, those aspects of the subject that will help them to achieve their goals with their audiences. But they talk about those aspects of their subject that are of interest to their audiences—those aspects that will meet their audiences' needs, solve their problems, or in some way benefit them.

As you prepare, keep yourself, your subject, and your audience in mind. Talk about something you know. Prepare your presentation. And you'll do a good job.

ANALYZE YOUR AUDIENCE

Audience analysis is a vital part of preparation for any presentation. If you have spoken on a topic many times, your preparation for a repeat performance of that topic will, in many respects, be simplified. You should still analyze the audience, however, as though it were the first time you had spoken. For though the subject may not have changed, the audience has. Each audience you face is unique. Some may be similar, but none are identical. You may take advantage of your experience with other audiences, but don't make the mistake of superimposing the profile of a familiar audience on a new group. Even if you have spoken to an audience before on another topic, you can't assume an identical reaction to your new presentation. The topic has changed, and the time has changed; it well may be that the texture of the audience has changed.

You should try to learn as much as possible about your audience. As you speak to your audience, you're going to ask them to build ideas with you. You'll be seeking agreement and understanding. You may be asking the audience to make a decision. To do this, the members will need sufficient information to gain the understanding for making a reasonable decision. If the subject area is familiar to them, they may already have much of this information. If the subject is new, they will need a good deal of background.

You want the audience to agree with you, to know what you know. To do this, they will have to follow much the same path you did when you formed your conclusions. Make a list of the points that you must cover, the things which the audience must understand before you can expect them to arrive at the destination you have chosen for them. Check this list for the points that you may reasonably expect this audience to know. The difference between what they know and what they need to know is what you must cover.

The members may, in some instances, harbor incorrect concepts that will require correction before agreement and mutual understanding can take place. To help you counteract these misconceptions in your presentation, you should make another list with the heading "What the Audience Thinks It Knows."

What does the audience know about you? Before they are likely to accept what you say, they will have to look upon you as someone knowledgeable. In many cases, this foundation can be laid by the person who introduces you to the group. You, of course, will have to provide the information before he or she can give it to the group. It's a good idea to prepare a brief summary of your experience and qualifications so that the person who introduces you will have something on which to base the introduction. Doing this also helps to insure that your introducer will tell the audience the things about you that they should know. If you give this information orally to the chairman at the time of the meeting, he or she will probably scratch a few notes on a scrap of paper. These notes may then be translated into an incorrect and insufficient introduction. You must then remedy those insufficiencies or leave your audience in ignorance of things they should know—things which may be important if they are to accept what you say as sound. This resume shouldn't be long. It need not trace your development from birth, but it should present those items that will enable the audience to see you as knowledgeable in the area of your presentation.

There are many things that you should know about your audience so that you can direct your remarks to them and to the uses they are likely to have for the information and ideas that you will share with them in your presentation. Perhaps the group you'll speak to is one familiar to you, in which case you'll already have the information you need. But you may not know the group you'll be making your presentation to. Contact someone in the group, the person who arranged for your presentation, and get the answers to at least these basic questions:

1. How many will be in the audience?
2. What is the purpose of the meeting?
3. Why did the group choose this subject?
4. Why were you asked to speak?
5. What does the group know about you?
6. What experience has the group had with the topic?
7. What other speakers has the group heard on this topic?
8. Who are the members of the group?
    - How are they likely to use information about your subject?
    - What are their backgrounds? What do they have in common?
    - What is the age range of the audience?
9. How is the group likely to feel about the subject? About you? Why?
10. Are you the only speaker or are there others? Who are they?
11. How is the program arranged?
12. What are the facilities like?
13. What advance publicity will be given the meeting? What will it lead the group to expect?
14. Will your remarks be recorded or published?

The answers to these questions will give you a head start on preparation of an audience-centered presentation.

KNOW YOUR SUBJECT

As noted in the first section, you probably already have the substantial part of this preparation done. Your own experience has given you a fund to draw on. Much of the subject preparation will consist of editing your experience, of selecting the items likely to be of greatest interest and value to your audience. It may, however, be necessary to reinforce your knowledge with research to back up or verify certain areas of interest. You want your presentation to be accurate; so take the necessary time to recheck facts and figures if you are unsure of their accuracy. The validity of your entire presentation will be suspect if you err in a point of fact.

Your selection of material for the presentation will be guided by your purpose and your analysis of the audience. (A) Where are they now? (B) Where do you want them to be at the end of your presentation? That part of your subject that lies between (A) and (B) is what you must cover. What do you want them to know or do? What do they now know or do? What can you give them that will make it likely that they will go from (A) to (B)?

You must give them enough background so that they may reasonably be expected to agree with you. Many audiences have been left wanting to agree with a speaker but unable to do so because of confusing or inadequate information. To prepare your subject, first list the points which the audience must know in order to understand your presentation. Subtract from this the things which they do know. Give them the remainder in your presentation. If the remainder is too large to be covered in the time you have, you'll have to limit your subject to a smaller scope, one in which the remainder can be covered in a meaningful presentation.

If you expect to speak on a subject often, you can do a great deal of the research in advance if you do it on a continuing basis. If, in your everyday reading and listening, you come across a point which relates to your potential topic, note it down. Don't rely on memory to preserve it. You can work out a simple filing system to store these notes and to help you draw upon them when it comes time to prepare a presentation. It's also helpful to build a bibliography in the same way so that your research can begin without an exhaustive search of the literature.

The key word in preparation is "adequate." Overpreparation is a bore; insufficient preparation is dangerous. Take inventory of what the audience knows and what they need to know. Take inventory of what you need and compare it with what your experience has provided you. Fill in the holes.

KNOW YOURSELF

Are you ready for your presentation? What are your biases? What is your attitude toward your audience and toward this opportunity to communicate?

So far we have discussed the audience's biases, but what of your own? No one would suggest that you eliminate your prejudices. It's impossible to eliminate all prejudices, and what you do with them is your own business in the first place. If you are unaware of your biases, however, they can destroy your effectiveness. Take an inventory of your prejudices and pet peeves with regard to the subject. Are they going to color your presentation an overly optimistic sky blue or, perhaps, an unconvincing, hostile green? How do you feel about the audience? Is your attitude toward them likely to lead you to adopt a subservient or a patronizing tone?

Will you be able to relate to your audience and your subject in a reasonably friendly and objective way? Regardless of your biases, it is possible to do so, if you are aware of them. For then you can deal with them. But, if you are unaware of your attitudes, they will work unseen and unnoticed by you, but in a way quite obvious to your audience.

Knowing yourself means knowing your strengths. Your presentation will be most effective if *you* are part of it. It should reflect your ideas and your experience. As you think about the subject and the audience, ask yourself what there is in your background and experience that you can capitalize on. What experience have you had with the subject, with the audience, with the uses to which the audience is likely to put the information of your presentation? Draw on your unique experience to give your audience the best of your strengths. In most cases, you won't be the only one from your organization who could present your subject. One of your colleagues might be able to do it. Either of you could do it well—but you wouldn't do it the same way. Your way will be better for you, if you will draw from yourself the strengths of your experience and use those to shape, in part, the presentation.

ORGANIZE YOUR IDEAS

Many speakers collect material for their presentations, but not all organize that material. They often present it at random and assume the audience will be able to figure out the meaning. The audience is seldom able to do so to the speaker's satisfaction. It's the speaker's job to provide the audience with the material and with a logic through which it can be meaningfully understood.

Look at this collection of letters:

aaaaaacccdddeeeeeefggiilmmnnnnnnooppprrrssttttttuu

This alphabetical inventory contains all the letters necessary for a sentence, but there's no logic to it, no organization.

This pattern goes one step further:

understanding promotes acceptance meaningful a pattern and

This grouping adds the organization of words and is more significant than the string of letters, but it still doesn't mean much.

Clear, effective communication is most likely to come from these words organized in the logic of a sentence:

A meaningful pattern promotes understanding and acceptance.

A presentation is much like this example. Just having the facts isn't enough. We must put them in a logical order for the audience. The logic must be apparent and useful to the audience. It is not enough that the presentation seems clear and reasonable to the speaker. The audience is in unfamiliar territory; they need not only the information but also a scheme of organization that will enable them to relate the various points into a meaningful whole.

To plan an effectively organized presentation, put yourself in the audience's place. Ask yourself the questions that they would ask when confronted with the topic. Answer their questions in the order in which they would ask them.

These five questions could be the basis of an effective organization:

1.   What are the subject and the main idea?
2.   Why present this subject at this time?
3.   What does the subject have to do with me?
4.   What does the speaker want of me?
5.   What will I get out of the presentation?

With these questions, you can develop a presentation that will clearly tell the audience what you are talking about. From there you can build their interest and attention by telling them why you have chosen this subject. Once you have done this, you can move quite naturally, into the relationship of the subject to the audience or their needs. If you are successful in bringing the audience this far with you, you can next tell them what you want of them. And by relating your wants to their needs or goals, you may move them to action.

Several patterns of organization are commonly used; but all, to be effective, should respond to the audience. Cause-effect and effect-cause patterns are commonly used. When you speak of cause, the audience naturally wonders what the effects of the cause are. They expect that you will tell them; and if you don't, they may not be able to follow the rest of your presentation because of their not understanding the point, or because their attention may be diverted to speculate on the gap obvious to them. Of course, effective speakers stimulate their audiences intellectually, but doing so doesn't mean that they leave them wondering about meaning because of the gaps in the organization of the presentations. Don't raise questions in the audience's mind without answering those questions.

Many materials require a sequential development for greatest effectiveness. In other words, the points made by the speaker build on each other; they interrelate. "A" must precede "B," for before "B" can be fully understood or accepted, "A" must first be established, understood, and accepted. Organization of a subject requiring this kind of sequential development can be likened to a theorem in geometry or the proof of a scientific principle in a laboratory.

Illustration and example help to develop almost any topic. They make your presentation clear by portraying the principles in operation. A presentation on labor relations would be enhanced by case examples illustrating your points. Your topic would move from the sterile, impersonal, abstract realm of principle, policy, and procedure to a living example in which the audience could see the principles, policies, and procedures in operation. The elements of your exposition would come alive in the actions and reactions of people with which the audience can identify. Your presentation would have the concreteness of reality.

The example chosen to illustrate a point should be specific and typical of the general point being made. Illustration uses an individual example to represent and to clarify the principles common to a class. If, in discussing our space program, you wish to make the point that great care is given to ensure quality and reliability, you might trace the manufacture and preparation of a particular piece of hardware from its design to its launch. You might make the same point, or a related point, by telling of the experience of an astronaut from selection, through training, launch, and orbit to successful return. Neither example would prove your point, but either would give it concrete illustration. For most audiences, the second example would probably prove more interesting, because individuals are more interested in people than in things. To a technical audience, particularly to a group of reliability engineers, the first example might be more interesting, but not necessarily so. We often assume that an example related to the field of a specialized audience will be the most effective. Though this can be so, an example drawn from another field can, in many cases, make the point more effectively because the illustration opens new areas of thought through analogy and suggests something that might not be thought of within the traditional thought patterns of the specialized field. The "Big Bang Theory" of the universe, by giving the analogy of an explosion, suggests new dimensions which might not be brought out as effectively through the use of strictly astronomical terms.

The chief danger in the use of illustration or example is that an interesting and skillfully related anecdote may assume primary importance, while the principle which it is supposed to illustrate is lost. The specific illustration should be of little ultimate importance. The important thing should be the general concept that it illustrates.

Be careful not to charm your audiences with interesting illustrations that are not representative or typical of the general point. If the connection between the illustration and the general topic is not immediately clear, link the two in an explicit statement like, "I tell you of this incident because it illustrates how. . . ." If the audience is likely to wonder at the connection, you might explain it by saying something like, "Perhaps you're wondering what this story has to do with our subject. Well, when I first heard this story, it seemed to me that it showed how. . . ."

If you are in doubt that the audience will see the point, make an explicit transition. It seldom does harm to point out the connection, but failure to do so can damage the coherence and total effectiveness of your presentation.

Anecdotes, examples, and illustrations, like jokes, should never be used for their own sakes. Examples used in this fashion are damaging to the unity of your presentation, and though your audience will possibly enjoy them, they will serve to distract people and thus to detract from the overall effectiveness of the presentation.

SCRIPT, NOTES, OR MEMORY?

Should you write out the text of your presentation and then read it *verbatim*? Should you memorize the text? Or should you speak from notes? Let's look at these methods of presentation:

1. Read the speech.
Doing this is not effective. The audience cannot help but feel they are being read to. They cannot help but wonder why you didn't run off copies for each of them to read. It's difficult to maintain contact with the audience while reading, and most speeches that are written are read as though they were written. They don't sound like speech. In a written speech, word choice, style, structure, and tone are usually characteristic of the more formal written medium, and while the piece might be effective if read by the audience, it doesn't sound nearly as effective when they have it read to them.

2. Memorize the speech.
A memorized speech presents many of the same difficulties as one that is read. Speeches are memorized from scripts. These scripts incorporate the same pitfalls whether they are memorized or read. Memorization also has its own unique traps.

Memorization takes time. Unless you are quite skilled in acting, a memorized speech sounds as though it is being read. Contact with the audience is usually mechanical; your attention is focused on producing the lines. Then, too, it's difficult to depart from the text of a memorized speech or to alter it to respond to the audience.

Still another difficulty is posed by the enormity of the language. The total vocabulary of the English language is growing daily; even now it is in excess of a million words. The speaker who gives a presentation from memory occasionally gets stuck for the next word or phrase and draws a blank. In this predicament, there is only one word out of the million that can get the speaker and the presentation back on the track, and the search for that word can be embarrassing. The only alternative is to improvise, and doing this is extremely difficult if preparation has been for a memorized speech, especially as the memory lapse and the unsuccessful hunt for the key word have probably left this speaker quite rattled.

Memorization offers few advantages. The method is part of our legacy from orators, who considered memorization part of their art. The disadvantages of memorized speaking combine to make it the least desirable method of presentation.

3. Deliver the speech from notes.

Using notes allows you to bring the fruits of your preparation to the lectern. You can be sure that the organization you have worked to achieve will be before you to guide you. You have the security of knowing that you will not inadvertently leave out a key point. You have the disciplining influence of the notes to keep you on the track and to give you an indication of pace and timing; you can see how much you have covered and how far you have to go.

The form of notes will vary from speaker to speaker. Some use only key words to remind them of the order in which they will cover points. Others use more detailed notes. Any note system can do the job; the choice is a matter of personal preference. Equipment until you find the system that best suits your needs.

Notes should be clearly typed, triple-spaced in all capital letters. Nothing is more distracting to you and to your audience than a hunt through crowded notes for the next point. Hand-scrawled notes are often illegible; so the time spent in typing them is worthwhile.

Notes should be a tool, not a restriction. If while giving the presentation, you find reason to vary from your prepared organization, do so. Be responsive to your audience. Advance preparation is a fine thing, but no one can foresee everything. Remain alert to the silent messages the members of the audience are sending. Effective presentations have been given *extempore* by a speaker who sensed the mood and interest of the audience and who met that audience on ground they had chosen. Preparation is not wasted in these cases. It gives the speaker a good hold on the subject and the audience and allows effective "off-the-cuff" speaking. This type of speaking is not really extemporaneous, only the words and the approach are. The speaker prepared for the opportunity thought the concepts through, and analyzed the audience, himself or herself, and the potential purposes. The last-minute decision to change is based on new information that adds to, but does not replace, the data previously considered.

Many inexperienced speakers fear notes. They visualize standing before an audience to give a half-hour presentation with only a few words on a piece of paper. What is going to fill the gaps? How will those few words stretch to fill that enormous half hour? Well, to begin with, those aren't just a few words. They are the essence of experience fortified by adequate preparation. If you know your subject, the words will come. And if you don't know your subject, what are you doing there in the first place? The words will come; they may not be the best words, the perfect words. But they will do the job. If you were to write the speech or have it written by an expert word mechanic, the words might be better; they would still not be perfect, but they might be better. But there's more to a speech than words; there's the rapport, the sense of communication between the speaker and the audience. This rapport would be lost if you read the better words to or at them. The audience doesn't expect perfect words. They are interested in you, the speaker; they want to share your ideas and experience. If you have the ideas and the experience, the substance, they will accept your words.

If you use notes as a guide, as an organizing discipline, you will find that the words will come to give expression to your ideas. You'll experience the satisfaction of contact with your audience. The *verbatim* script will not be there to act as a barrier. Effective oral presentation should be analogous to conversation. Can you imagine someone bringing a prepared text to a conversation? No, but you can imagine someone thinking of what he or she is going to say before he or she says it; that's preparation, and notes are a way of bringing preparation to the presentation.

The words will come, good words, adequate words, because words are the expression of ideas, and a competent speaker has the ideas. Again, it's the ideas that are of interest to the audience. And, again, we are called on to share experience and ideas with our audience. We are not asked to orate, to enthrall, or to entertain with fine phrases and wondrous words.

HOW TO DELIVER YOUR PRESENTATION

Your presentation begins when the audience first becomes aware of you. Before you start to speak, even before you are introduced, they will have noted your appearance, your attitude, and your interest in the audience and the rest of the program. They will have noticed your alertness or its lack. Before you speak, before they hear even one of your ideas, they will have formed some biases about you that can either help or hinder you in achieving your purpose with them.

It may, at first glance, seem unfair that your audience starts to judge you before you speak, but you communicate before you speak. You don't communicate *verbally*, but *nonverbally*; you start to generate messages when the audience becomes aware of you.

We have all observed a speaker impatiently drumming fingers, obviously annoyed that the program is 25 minutes behind schedule. With apparent pique he ignores the audience and the rest of the program. Regardless of his real attitude or intentions, the audience has interpreted the nonverbal, unintentional messages to mean that he considers them, their group, and the other speakers (if any) to be an unpleasant interruption of his day. He has, in effect, told them that they are hardly worthy of interest and that they are certainly beneath his respect. He, in short, appears to be hostile or indifferent. The audience is more than ready to respond with its own hostility and indifference.

Finally, this speaker is introduced. He glides gracefully to the lectern, scintillates a gleaming smile at the audience, and begins, "It's an honor and pleasure to be here with you this evening. . . ."

But no one believes him. His nonverbal messages have given the lie to any assurances pretending his good will toward, or respect for, his audience. He will find it difficult to gain acceptance.

Does this, then, mean that you should be in terror from the time you enter the room in which you are to speak and that you should rue each conscious or unconscious gesture or movement because you are sure to offend someone in that superperceptive, highly critical audience? No, but it does mean that you should be careful not to project your pique, which you may have every right to feel. It does mean that you should try to maintain interest in the audience and the rest of the program. It does mean that you should be as courteous as you would be in any other social situation and that you should afford your audience the same respect you would afford a hostess in whose face you would not yawn even if bored.

The meaning of all of this is simply that you should be aware that your presentation will be partially nonverbal. This awareness and your own good sense will allow you to take advantage of the silent portion of the exchange you share with your audience.

Eye contact.
If you're really going to build a climate of sharing with your audience, you're going to have to be aware of their response to you. Sometimes this response will be verbal. Sometimes they will question or comment, and

you will have to listen with skill and understanding. But more often, their response won't be verbal, and you'll have to reach out for it. How? Through eye contact.

Effective communication calls for contact. Sometimes it happens through touch, but more often it doesn't. If you are really sharing a communication experience with someone or with an audience, then you must make contact. In a presentation, that means eye contact. How does it work?

Eye contact is the simplest, most natural thing in the world. If you're talking to a group of friends, you look at them. In the same way and for the same reason, look at your audience when you're talking with them. That seems a simple enough thing, but many people are reluctant to do it. When giving a presentation, they look at their notes, their own hands, the audience's shoes, the back of the room, the floor, and literally everything in the room but the audience's eyes. This can make both the speaker and the audience uncomfortable. The audience finds it difficult to relate to someone who furtively avoids even a glance at them; and the speaker is left to wonder how the audience is reacting.

If the speaker maintains eye contact with the audience, they will feel more comfortable and better able to relate to him or her and the subject; and the speaker will see from their nonverbal behavior how things are going. It's a natural, comfortable way for audience and speaker to relate. This simple technique is one of the most important delivery techniques I know. It is not an overstatement to say that an effective presentation is nearly impossible without eye contact and that eye contact alone will do much to strengthen an ineffective presentation.

What, then, are the tricks of making and maintaining eye contact? There aren't any. It is precisely the lack of tricks that makes this technique so effective. Look at your audience as naturally and spontaneously as you would look at guests seated in your living room. You shouldn't swivel your head back and forth like a radar antenna; neither should you stare at any one member of your audience. You should simply and naturally relate to your audience through your eyes and theirs. You'll be more comfortable and so will they, because your presentation will be more natural and conversational, and everyone will be spared the ordeals of formality and oratory.

Does an audience frighten you? Do you get butterflies in the stomach when you must make a presentation? Why? You don't feel that way in conversation, do you? When you're giving a presentation, however, you're not just talking to people as you do in conversation. No, indeed, you're talking to an *audience*. And an *audience* is a frightful thing. It's a soulless, shapeless beast with countless eyes. It has no identity, and so you can't relate to it.

That's not true. An audience doesn't really exist. The term "audience" is only a simple collective for a group of people seated together—

they are still just people, and eye contact will demonstrate that to you. Look around the room. What do you see? People. None of them is individually threatening. And there is no reason why they should be threatening in the collective. If you feel uncomfortable, don't let it trouble you. Many people do feel that way—and it doesn't affect the quality of their presentations. Nervous speakers can be very effective. Experience eventually lessens the nervous feelings, but until this happens, realize that the nervousness doesn't mean the presentation won't be effective. Keep in contact with the audience. That, in itself, is the most relaxing thing you can do.

Readiness.

That feeling of butterflies in the stomach is most often misinterpreted anyway. It's usually not a response to terror; it's usually a sign of readiness. When you get up to speak, and even before you do, your body gets ready for the opportunity. Extra blood goes to the brain to make you mentally alert. It's the same phenomenon that athletes call being "up for a game." The physical feelings associated with this readiness are like those we experience when we are anxious, so we often misinterpret readiness as fear or nervousness and can actually talk ourselves into a case of stage fright.

You have no reason to be afraid. You've prepared well for this opportunity. You are not looking for perfection, so you can tolerate a minor mistake or a slip. Your audience will understand; they're not looking for perfection either.

When you step to the lectern to begin your presentation, pause a moment before you begin. Take a look at the audience. Let them have a look at you. Relax physically. Don't let your neck and shoulder muscles tighten. Take a breath. Get into a comfortable position with your weight evenly balanced. Don't lean on the lectern; that throws you off balance. Begin your presentation and take command of it. You are the speaker; while you are talking, you are in charge. Share your ideas easily, sincerely, and naturally. Be yourself. Don't adopt a platform personality other than your own. It won't ring true.

Gesture and movement.

There are no specifications for gesture and movement. Once more, the only rule is to be yourself. Be natural and comfortable. If you normally gesture in conversation, do so in your presentation. Otherwise, don't force gestures or movement in your presentation. A forced, unnatural gesture is inappropriate and often ludicrous.

Avoid extremes. Don't pace like a caged beast; that's distracting and likely to make your audience uncomfortable. Don't stand motionless either. Move a little. If the conditions in the room allow it, you can move about a little; but make sure that your walking doesn't put you in a position where you keep your back or your side to your audience. If walking is impossible or if you're not comfortable moving around, you can achieve some movement by varying the angle at which you face the audience.

Have a friend or colleague observe your mannerisms during a presentation to determine if you have any distracting habits. If you do, you can overcome them by careful attention. Nervous habits are very distracting to an audience and can seriously affect the effectiveness of your presentation.

If you don't know what to do with your hands, find some comfortable position for them. Rest them on the lectern, if you'd like, but don't lean on the lectern and don't fiddle with your notes. It's a good idea to keep things out of your hands. Most of us fiddle with whatever we're holding; and though we aren't aware of it, our audience certainly is. Don't play with your notes. When you've finished with a piece of chalk, a pointer, a felt-tip marker, or any other "prop," put it down.

Any questions?

Should you have a question period? That's largely a matter of your judgment. If you have a limited time for your presentation, and that is usually the case, you will have to decide whether that time would be better spent in actual presentation or whether you can allow time for questions and comments. If you have unlimited time, it's probably a good idea to allow questions.

You can put the question period at the end of your presentation, call for questions at logical dividing points in a longer presentation, or invite your audience to break in with a question or comment at any time during the presentation. The choice is yours, and most audiences will do as you ask. In courtesy to your audience, you should tell them in advance how you want the questions handled. If there is no time for questions, it is a good idea to announce that and to tell the audience how they can obtain further information. Perhaps you could give them your address or telephone number and invite them to contact you later. You should at least refer your audience to an available reference source.

When you do have a question period, answer questions one at a time. If someone asks a compound question, break it down into individual questions and answer them one at a time or if that seems impractical, rephrase the question. If there is a moderator or a chairman at the meeting, he or she should do this for you; but more often, moderator or not, you will have to do it yourself. If you try to answer more than one question at a time, you may become confused.

What do you do with a heckler or a pest during the question period? This is seldom a problem at business and technical meetings, but it does happen. Unfortunately, the answer is that you can do nothing—nothing that will help you in the long run. You can put the heckler down with withering sarcasm, but consider the effect on your audience. The audience, consciously or otherwise, consider themselves to be a loosely formed group. If you embarrass one of them (even a member whom the rest don't care for), they will resent you for it. Thus your effectiveness with the group will be reduced. A moderator or chairman can handle the pest for you—but you can't.

Fortunately, most groups are self-disciplining. They won't tolerate bad behavior from one of their members. They are there to get something from a presentation, and they resent anyone's interfering with that. One or more of the group will usually handle the troublemaker for you. But if they don't and if a moderator doesn't, then the best thing you can do is tolerate the situation. You may gain personal satisfaction from smacking your heckler down verbally or otherwise (avoid the "otherwise" at all costs), but your effectiveness will suffer.

There is another situation that is sometimes a problem to people who give presentations: a member of the audience who knows more about the subject than the speaker does. This is really not a problem; in fact, it can be an opportunity. What do you do? That's easy. You use him or her to improve your presentation. These people aren't competition unless you make them competition. Deal with them politely. If you feel threatened and react defensively, you may force them to be adversaries; but otherwise they are useful resources. Try to get them to share this knowledge. You and your audience will benefit from it. But don't force them. They may not want to seem to take over the meeting. But, if you can do so courteously, draw them out.

No matter when you decide to hold your question period, do your best to make your answers responsive to the question. If you don't know the answer to a question, don't let that throw you. You never told your audience that you knew everything that there is to know about the subject. If you can accept the fact that you don't know everything, so can your audience. Just give them an honest response. Tell them that you don't know. You could go one step further by offering to find the answer and by assuring the questioner that you'll get in touch later with the answer. You could also refer the questioner to a source of reference. Common sense should tell you never to bluff your way through an answer. You will destroy any credibility you may have gained with that audience, and you are likely to permanently damage your professional reputation.

Your voice.

Actors, orators, radio announcers, and singers need special voice qualities; people who give presentations don't. They share ideas and information, and they need only enough voice to invite attention, to make those ideas heard, and articulation to make their words understandable. It would be nice if all speakers could sound like Orson Welles or Helen Hayes, but it isn't necessary. You can very likely give an adequate presentation with your voice. If you have a special problem, you need the professional attention of a speech therapist. Self-directed attempts to change voice quality often injure speech organs.

If you tend to be soft-spoken, speak up or use a microphone. If you tend to overproject, tone down your volume to a more conversational level. If you have a regional accent, it's not likely to give you any problems unless you do a great deal of speaking in other regions of the country and then only if your accent is very pronounced. You want to be yourself when you give a presentation, and your voice is part of you.

If you are concerned that your voice may be monotonous, keep this in mind: no one speaks in a monotone when he or she speaks about something in which he or she is interested and in which he or she believes. Show your enthusiasm for your subject, for your audience, and for the opportunity to share your ideas. You needn't shout, tear your clothes, or throw confetti, but you should allow your enthusiasm and your belief in your subject to show. Enthusiasm is contagious, and so are complacency, hostility, and boredom.

An effective presentation is much like conversation. When you are carrying on a conversation, your tone of voice expresses enthusiasm when you're speaking about something you believe in. Use that same quality of voice in your presentations. You needn't add anything to the conversational enthusiasm, but you shouldn't subtract anything either. Far too many people overformalize their presentations. They become stuffy, rigid, and pontifical. Don't let that happen to you; don't make a special effort to sound like a judge pronouncing a sentence. Speak naturally, comfortably, and with enthusiasm for the ideas that you want to share with an audience who can benefit from them.

TEAM PRESENTATIONS

The team presentation is a common practice in many organizations. Several people are chosen to develop and to present a unified presentation, with each speaker covering the part of the topic that he or she knows best. Because it presents several "experts," the team presentation can be a credible and effective vehicle for communication. It should not be used as a gimmick, though. Improperly used, it gives the impression of a tent show. Having many people just for the sake of having many people is seldom effective. But when there is a valid reason for bringing together a number of people (or for that matter, just two different speakers), the team presentation can be most effective.

The team presentation doesn't differ much from the individual presentation, except that it should be developed and coordinated as a whole. The first speaker should provide any necessary introduction and the last speaker any necessary conclusion. Speakers in the middle should confine themselves to developing only the body of the presentation, giving only as much introduction and conclusion as is necessary for the orderly and clear presentation of their content. It should never appear to the audience that they are hearing several independent presentations.

One member of the team should act as editor-in-chief to see that the content and organization of each talk are complementary. This team leader should make sure that there is no unnecessary overlap and that no important points are left out. Team members should meet together at least twice. The first meeting should be a planning session, in which everyone works together to develop the outline for the overall presentation. This session is most important, since each must be familiar with what the others will cover and with how they will cover it. A rehearsal is important too, much more so here than for an individual presentation. It will allow each participant to hear how colleagues finally developed their parts of the presentation, and it will show weaknesses in timing, proportion, and emphasis.

The presentation should be unified. It is most effective if each team member can prepare the way for those who will follow as well as build on what has gone before. This sense of wholeness is extremely important if one is to get the most from the team format. It should be *one* presentation, given by several people, with each contributing what each alone is best qualified to contribute.

There is another form of team presentation that doesn't appear to be a team presentation. Nevertheless, it's a very effective combination of the talents and resources of several people. In this form of presentation, one member of the team gives the entire presentation. Colleagues may assist in its development, but their role becomes apparent to the audience only during the question period. They accompany the speaker and sit on the sidelines while he or she gives the presentation. When questions are asked, the speaker will answer when able to. But when specialized questions are asked, the speaker can call upon a colleague who knows that area for a competent answer.

This approach is quite valuable when a presentation on a highly involved and technical subject is to be given. The speaker's colleagues provide depth and authenticity that one person alone could never have; and the team can present more inclusive information than any one speaker could give. Such a presentation suggests to the audience that the organization represented by the team is a source of strength, depth, and competence.

SPEECHES OF INTRODUCTION

Many people who will otherwise be called on for few speeches in their lives, may occasionally be asked to introduce another speaker at a meeting.

The introductory speech, which should be the simplest and least complicated kind of presentation, is often the most flagrantly abused opportunity for communication.

A good introduction should be brief, and it should establish a connection between the person you're introducing and the audience. Yet many introductions are so long that the audience begins to wonder if they'll ever get to hear the speaker. Having been the victim of many overlong introductions, I've often wished that every speaker could be given as brief an introduction as "Ladies and gentlemen, the President of the United States."

An introduction should be brief and simple, but it's an important part of the program. It links the speaker to the audience; it establishes credibility and thus makes it easier to relate to listeners who might otherwise wonder, "Who's speaking—and why should we listen?"

Introductory remarks should be brief and to the point. They should be related directly to the speaker and the topic and should tell the audience those aspects of the speaker's background which qualify him or her to speak on the subject. Extensive personal data about the speaker are seldom useful and are often tedious. The important data about the speaker are those that relate to experience with the subject.

Some don'ts about speeches of introduction.

1.   Don't compete. The speaker is the star; your role is subordinate. Play it that way. Avoid long, flashy introductions, and stick to the point.

2.   Don't oversell the speaker. Many introductions put the speaker in a nearly impossible position by promising more than the speaker can deliver. Avoid words like "expert." They can make audiences hostile by seeming to promise an all-knowing speaker. Avoid too any reference to the speaker's speaking ability—complimentary or otherwise. An audience that has been promised a "great speaker, one who will hold your attention and inspire you . . ." sits very critically in judgment of the speaker's style. It is hard to play to an audience of critics.

3.   Don't give away the speaker's method or message. If you've heard the speaker before, you might be tempted to give a preview as part of your introduction. Don't. You may unwittingly force the speaker to develop the topic out of order or to compromise the climax.

4.   Don't apologize for the speaker. Don't refer to the short notice that he or she was given. Don't, in fact, say anything that might suggest to the audience that they will hear anything other than a competent presentation of useful information. Sometimes a

well-intentioned introducer may try to get a speaker off the hook in advance by telling the audience something to gain their sympathy for the speaker. It seldom works, and it always gives the audience an advance warning that they're going to hear something that needed an apology. Instead of helping your speakers by apologizing, you do them in before they have had a chance to make their presentations.

If your speaker is a substitute for someone else who couldn't make it, don't give the audience the idea that they're about to hear a second-stringer. Unless advance publicity has given another speaker's name to the audience, don't mention that your speaker is a substitute. If advanced publicity forces you to refer to a substitution, stress the qualifications of your speaker to assure the audience that he or she is competent and not just a fill-in for the original speaker.

A good introductory speech is a simple thing that anyone can do well. It's important. To do it well, keep it simple; don't compete with the speaker for audience attention and approval; don't oversell the speaker; and do provide a bridge between the audience's interests and the speaker's qualifications and message.

12
Communication
Aids

Communication aids are mechanical and physical devices that help us to communicate useful ideas and information with our audiences. Note that they are called "aids." That means helpers. They are not called speaker substitutes, and they should not be used to do what speakers can do. They should not compete with speakers and their ideas. They are effective only when speakers use them to do what they cannot do alone.

One of the worst mistakes in presentation is made when the speaker, having prepared the outline for the presentation, looks it over to find places to use communication aids. They should never be used simply because they are available. You want to establish a relationship with your audience and they with you. People relate to people, not to things. You are the only thing on the speaker's platform that is alive and flexible and to which the audience can relate. Don't let communication aids come between you and your audience, and don't let them take over the force of your presentation. Don't feel that you must use communication aids in every presentation, but don't feel either that their use is forbidden. Use them for the things which they do best, the things which you are unable to do.

What are they useful for, and when should they be avoided? Let's see. As you review your presentation and the points that you want to make in it, you begin to think about the approach that you will take. You begin to think about how you will make your ideas and information clear to your audience. In most cases, talking about your ideas will make them clear. But sometimes you're going to want to explain things that can't be adequately communicated through words alone. To explain these things you'll need the help of a communication aid. When you find that words aren't adequate, you should begin to look for an appropriate device. To find one that will fill your particular need, let's look at the more common aids to see what they can do and how they can best be employed.

BOARDS AND CHARTS

1. The chalkboard.

This standard schoolroom device is one of the most versatile communication aids available to you. Most places in which you will give presentations will have a chalkboard, and little special skill is required for its use.

The chalkboard is inexpensive to use, and it can be used to illustrate points at any time during a discussion or question period. On the other hand, the chalkboard itself is difficult to prepare in advance; and it must be erased frequently, a time-consuming process.

Though the chalkboard can be used spontaneously, it is most effective after careful preparation. We've all witnessed people using a chalkboard by scribbling things at random, with one message squeezing and overlapping another. We've all seen someone run out of space at a chalkboard, and we've all seen illegible scrawls that confused more than they communicated. Your best defense against this is to use an index card to plan your board work. An index card is roughly the same proportion as most chalkboards. Don't wait until it is time to go to the board to decide what you will put on it. Plan it in advance on an index card. The card will give you an idea of how much will fit easily on a board and of where things should be written for maximum effect. It will give you a sense of fit and of proportion.

The chalkboard, like the other visual aids that we will discuss in this chapter, should communicate a concise message. Never use a sentence where a phrase will do. Never use a phrase where a word will do, and always keep things as simple as possible. A chalkboard is not for fancy art work and intricate drawings.

To make the most effective use of the chalkboard:

1   Plan in advance.
2.   Keep your messages simple and concise. They are easier to understand that way, and you will spend less time at the board. When you are writing or drawing at the board, your attention is away from your audience and theirs is away from your subject. For complicated drawings, use one of the other aids.
3.   Don't block the board; make sure your audience can see the message. Use a pointer if you have to indicate portions of the message.

4. Before you put anything on the board, make sure that every member of your audience can see the board and your message. Check the presentation room in advance.
5. Erase distractions. No message should be shown to the audience before you are ready to discuss it, and none should be left on the board to distract the audience after you have finished with it.
6. Use soft chalk. This is the kind that gets dust all over your clothes, but it is also the kind that writes most legibly. The harder, dustless variety leaves a fainter line harder to see, especially from the back of a large room.

2. The flipchart (or pad and easel).

This device combines the advantages of the chalkboard with some advantages of its own. Like the chalkboard it is inexpensive and almost universally available. Unlike the chalkboard, it can be prepared in advance and need not be erased.

It consists of a pad of paper mounted on an easel. Most easels can be folded up and taken with you to any place where you might have to make a presentation. The paper comes plain or lined, and can be obtained with a one-inch, light blue grid. Flipchart paper usually measures 34" × 28", although it can be obtained twice that size (34" × 56"). Its smaller size is the only real disadvantage of the flipchart as compared with the chalkboard. The writing instrument can be either a grease pencil or a felt-tip marker.

With the flipchart, you can prepare messages in advance. This saves time during your presentation. It also allows you to use detailed drawings and graphs which would take too much time to prepare during the presentation. If you should choose to prepare your flipchart messages in advance, leave every other page blank so that when you have finished discussing the material on a page, you can open to a blank sheet. If the sheet were not blank, you would have to turn to the next message, possibly before you were ready to discuss it. With the flipchart, as with all other visual aids, you should never leave a message in view after you have finished with it or expose the next message before you are ready to deal with it. Naturally, when you are writing messages on the flipchart during your presentation, you need not leave blank pages between messages. You must, however, turn a page over when you have finished with it.

Since you don't erase flipchart messages, you can turn back to them to summarize your presentation or to discuss a previous message. That's another advantage of the flipchart over the chalkboard.

Sometimes it is desirable to build up a series of flipchart messages. If this is the case, you can do so with a bit of masking tape. As you finish with a message, tear it off, and tape it to the wall. Others can be added.

I've seen this technique used to advantage in instructional presentations and in problem-solving and planning sessions. Ideas and suggestions can be charted and then taped in sequence to the wall for later discussion and reference.

To use a flipchart most effectively:

1. Plan in advance. This doesn't mean that you have to prepare your flipchart messages in advance, but you should have a good idea of why, when, and how you will be using the flipchart.
2. Remove a message when you have finished discussing it. You can easily do this by flipping the used page over the top of the chart or by tearing it off.
3. Check for visibility before using a flipchart. Its relatively small size rules it out for very large rooms. If you will be using colored grease pencils or markers, make sure all the colors will be visible from all parts of the room. Black and green can usually be seen most easily. If any of your audience will be sitting at a distance from the flipchart, they may have difficulty seeing red, light brown, and especially yellow.
4. Keep your messages simple and concise.
5. Don't block the flipchart from your audience's view, and don't talk to the flipchart. Face the audience when you speak. Use a pointer if you need one.
6. In using prepared sheets, keep every other page blank.

3. Charts.

"Charts" can refer to anything on a piece of cardboard. They certainly include drawings, diagrams, photos, posters, and montages. They can also include samples of products or other materials stapled or glued to a stiff sheet of cardboard.

Charts are portable, but cumbersome. They are hard to carry on an airplane, especially when the flight attendant insists they be stored beneath your seat, and they are even awkward in an automobile. They are portable, but I would think twice before taking a set of charts on the road. They are more likely to be useful for a local presentation.

Charts can be expensive. They normally require some talent to produce, and the services of photographers and commercial artists can be costly. Charts are, however, permanent and reusable, and they can present a more detailed message than is usually possible with a homemade flipchart or a chalkboard drawing.

To use charts most effectively:

1. Work with the artists at all stages of preparation. By all means take advantage of their skill in the graphic interpretation of

ideas, but don't lose control of the chart. It supports your presentation; make sure that it illustrates your message and not the artist's.

2.   Don't try to win a graphics prize with your charts. A chart with a great deal of art work and fine detail can be costly and distracting. Keep it as simple as possible. Simple line drawings are usually more effective than intricate and complex graphic triumphs. Make this clear to the artist, but remember that an artist may want to produce a work of art (for which you or your company will pay). You don't need a work of art. You need something that will help you to explain your idea and nothing more than that. You certainly don't need a distraction.

3.   Don't show your chart until you are ready to discuss it. Keep it covered, or better, keep it out of sight. And when you have finished with it, cover it or remove it.

4.   Don't block the chart, and don't talk to it. Plan in advance how you will use it.

4. Display boards.

These are boards of various types used for showing messages and objects. Two of the most common are the magnetic board and the flannelboard.

To use the magnetic board, which is made of steel, attach small magnets to the backs of cards with words or images on them, and then use them to build up a message. You can also attach the magnets to styrofoam models and cutouts to display three-dimensional objects.

The flannelboard is used in much the same way as the magnetic board. It consists of a large sheet of plywood or composition board covered with a nappy flannel. To attach cards and messages to it, glue a piece of rough sandpaper to the back of the card. The sandpaper is sufficient to hold the card to the flannel, especially if the board is inclined at a slight angle.

These boards were very popular a few years ago when their novelty made them interesting playthings for teachers and speakers. They still have some use when it is important to build up a message word by word or phrase by phrase. They are relatively inexpensive, reusable, and portable, but they do require some graphic skill to prepare.

Another type of display board uses a heavy pile fabric. Items are attached to it by a material made up of numerous little hooks which engage the loops of the pile and hold the object or message card securely fastened to the board. This fabric system is marketed under the trade name of Velcro. It can be used in the same way as the magnetic and flannel boards, but because the hook-and-pile arrangement will support great weight, it is possible to display heavy models and actual products.

Display boards aren't often useful, but it's good to know that they exist for certain very specialized uses. Again, you must plan for their use;

don't block them or talk to them; don't display them before you are ready to discuss them; and get them out of sight when you're finished.

MODELS, MOCKUPS, AND REAL THINGS

Sometimes it is useful to show things to the audience; the object itself may be its own best explanation. If your presentation is to explain a new fastening device, why not show the device to your audience? There is no better way to explain what it is and how it works. If the thing that you're explaining to the audience is large enough to be appreciated from a distance, you need only show them the thing itself. If it is small or if you feel that they would best learn from handling the object, bring enough of them to pass out. But do so only after you have finished talking. Never give toys to the audience while you're talking. You can't compete with that kind of distraction.

Sometimes, though, the real thing that you would like to show the audience is too expensive, bulky, or dangerous to be brought to the presentation. That is where models and mockups come in. These, as I'm sure you know, are often quite expensive, and constructing them usually requires special skills. They are portable and reusable, however, and these advantages may help you to cut the cost per presentation. If a model is to be used for just one presentation, its cost may be more than the budget can stand, but if you'll be using it over and over again, you can spread the cost over the number of times it will be used.

Real things, models, and mockups can add a note of reality or carefully simulated reality to your presentation. Instead of telling your audience what the thing is like, you can let them experience the actual object for themselves. For some presentations, that can make the difference between acceptance and rejection of a good idea.

Many sales presentations feature things and simulations of things. The salesperson knows that the product will sell itself if the customer can touch it and work it. The customer is then buying a real object, not just a description.

Technical people who develop things and then try to sell them to management have had the same experience. If the decision makers can fondle the product itself and see for themselves how it works and what it feels like, they are more likely to respond positively.

I bought the typewriter on which I prepared the manuscript for this book in just that way. I wanted a special kind of typewriter with certain unusual features. Most companies make them, but not many dealers stock them. The first three places that I went to showed me pictures and specifications, but they didn't have the typewriter. The fourth dealer, from whom I bought the typewriter, had a display model. He let me fiddle and play with it for ten minutes or so. It sold itself, and I bought it.

You don't have to be in sales to use that technique. Anyone who has a tangible thing to explain or an idea to sell can use a demonstration technique if product and purpose lend themselves to this technique.

To make the most effective use of models, mockups, and real things:

1. Prepare. Make sure you have enough samples if you're going to pass them around. If you're going to demonstrate, make sure the object is large enough to be seen by the entire audience. Make sure there is an adequate power source if your device needs electricity and that extension cords, adapter plugs, and other necessary materials are available.

2. Plan for effective use. Don't show the device until you are ready to discuss it, and get it out of sight when you have finished with it. Don't compete with the device for audience attention. Distribute samples at the end of your presentation. If that isn't possible, stop after you've distributed them, and collect them before you start talking again.

3. Don't fiddle with the device yourself. Sometimes speakers unconsciously take up a plaything. That's distracting to the audience.

4. Don't use a device just because it's available. If it will help your presentation, use it. If it won't help, it will hinder by distracting.

PROJECTORS

There are many types of projectors, and each has its own uses, advantages, and limitations. We'll consider them in order of their relative usefulness to the person giving a business or technical presentation. For other uses, such as instruction or sales, a different list would have to be made, and other comments might be more appropriate.

1. The overhead projector.
This is the most useful of the projectors. It's versatile, portable, relatively inexpensive to use; and it can be used in a normally lit room.

It projects 10″ × 10″ transparencies onto a screen or even onto a blank wall. The transparencies can be professionally prepared or homemade. The homemade variety can be made from a drawing, photograph, or printed copy on almost any brand of office copier. For this you need special transparency material instead of the normal paper on which the machine copies. Transparencies prepared this way usually cost less than $0.35 each. They are even cheaper if they are written or drawn with a grease pencil on a sheet of clear plastic.

Some projectors are equipped with a roll of clear acetate upon which you can write while giving your presentation. You wind the roll when you are finished with the material. Used this way, the overhead projector becomes a sort of electric chalkboard. Unlike the chalkboard, which requires the user to turn from the audience, the overhead projector allows the user to face the audience while writing.

The versatility of the overhead projector makes it useful for many presentations. It should not, however, be used for this reason alone. As with any communication aid, its use should be dictated by the need for clear communication. If the overhead projector will permit a clearer, more effective presentation, use it. But don't use it just to have a visual aid.

To use the overhead projector effectively:

1. Plan its use. Prepare slides in advance when possible. When you must write or draw while speaking, plan your messages in advance on a piece of paper cut to the same proportion as the slide. (Any square piece of paper will do, but it should be at least 5″ × 5″ for clarity.)
2. Keep your message concise.
3. Use color as you need it, but remember that the transparent colors needed for this process may not show clearly on the screen. This may cause a visibility problem for your audience in the back of the room. Black is clearest.
4. Remove each slide from the projector after use. If there is to be a long time between slides, shut the projector off. The white glare on the screen can be distracting to the audience.
5. If you use a pointer, use a small one on the slide itself. (A pencil will do if no proper pointer is available.) It will project a pointer shadow onto the screen. Don't use a pointer on the screen—it may damage the screen.
6. Check for visibility from all parts of the room. Make sure you design and project your slides for visibility. Every part of every slide should be easily seen from every point in the audience.
7. Make sure that a spare projection lamp is available. Lamps have an annoying tendency to fail at crucial moments.
8. Because the overhead projector sits next to the speaker at waist level or below, it must project upward to the screen at a considerable angle. Because the screen is normally mounted on a vertical plane, written messages can become somewhat distorted; and drawings, diagrams, and charts can be thrown completely out of proportion. For under $3.00 you can buy a corrective device called a "keystone preventer" at most audio-visual supply houses. It's a simple gadget that tilts the screen to a forward angle and reduces or eliminates the keystone-shaped distortion.
9. Use slides primarily for pictures and graphic representations of information, not for words. You can say words. The idea that

audiences benefit from reading what they're hearing is a false notion. Just the opposite is true: most often they're distracted from listening by cluttered, wordy visuals.

2. The slide projector.

This is a relatively inexpensive, easily stored, portable device, and its slides are reusable. It may require a moderately darkened room, which can break the visual contact between speaker and audience.

The slide projector is useful for including actual photographs of objects and sites in your presentation, and slides can be inexpensive if you take them yourself and have them developed at the local drugstore. How good they are depends on your photographic skill. It is often wise to employ a professional, but that requires a generous budget. Slides of charts, graphs, and written messages can also be made.

To use the slide projector most effectively:

1. Keep slides simple, and make sure they're visible.
2. Don't use the slides until you're ready for them, and remove them from the screen when you're through with them. This doesn't mean you must shut off the projector between slides. You can insert an opaque slide between slides when you need an interval without anything on the screen.
3. Talk to the audience, not to the screen.
4. Use slides for pictures and graphic displays, not for words. If you must use words—and it's seldom that anyone must—use as few as possible. Never use sentences. Use words and phrases.
5. Avoid cute slides, cartoons, and the like used for their own sakes. Yes, a cartoon can sometimes make an effective slide, but not very often. The audience should focus their attention on you and your ideas, not on the distracting comments made by a cute visual.

3. Motion pictures.

Movies generally take over for speakers rather than supplement their material, but there are some excellent selective uses for movies in presentations. Let's look first, however, at the disadvantages of movies:

1. They are expensive. To buy or to rent a commercially available movie, you will need a big budget for your presentation. To produce your own movie, you will need a wealthy uncle in the movie business. The costs of producing your own films are prohibitive to all but a very few of those who must give presentations.

2. Movies are generally inflexible. The commercial films that you can buy or rent have been produced for general audiences of all types. Producers usually make films for the widest possible audience. Your audience is specific, and your whole presentation, including the communication aids, has been especially designed to achieve a specific purpose with your specific audience.

3. A movie projector usually requires an operator. This means more expense and adds the problem of speaker-projectionist communication.

4. Movies are tempting to the lazy speaker. Instead of doing the work to prepare and deliver a specific message to the audience, the slothful may allow a film to do the job, and it seldom does a good job. An audience can relate to a person much better than to a movie.

5. Movies require a dark room and thus present the problem of a break in the relationship of speaker and audience.

O.K., then, what are films good for? They are sometimes useful for a carefully selective application in a presentation. Films let you bring the reality of an event or a process into the room where you are giving your presentation. For instance, if you want to show your audience the advantages of a certain type of earth-moving equipment and you can't take them to a site to see the machines in operation, you may be able to use movies to bring the operating equipment to the audience. If you want to demonstrate a complex process or a destructive test procedure, movies let you bring these realities to your audience. Video tape has the same advantages and is less expensive.

Movies have a strong sensory impact. Sound, motion, and color combine to make a sensory impact far greater than you can get from any static communication aid. If you need this kind of impact, movies can give it to you. Note that I say "need." Don't use movies or any other communication aids just because they might be novel or entertaining. The strong sensory impact of movies makes them prime distractors too.

To use movies most effectively:

1. Make sure that you need them.

2. Be selective. Choose the right film—and choose the right part of the film. Just because a film runs sixteen minutes doesn't mean that you have to show it from the first frame to the final credits. If you need to show just two minutes from the middle of the film, don't show any more. If you need to run that two-minute segment over again, do so. Use the film in whatever manner suits your purpose best.

3.   Plan for use and check for visibility. Have a spare lamp handy
as for all projectors.

4. The opaque projector.
This is a device for projecting small, solid objects onto a screen. It can
project photographs, maps, pieces of paper, pages of books, and small,
flat objects. The opaque projector reflects a strong light off the objects and
onto the screen through a system of mirrors and lenses. The lamp produces
a great deal of heat, which requires a somewhat noisy fan to dissipate. It
also produces a relatively low-intensity image, which requires a completely
darkened room. Because of the low intensity, the projector must be placed
quite close to the screen.

The opaque projector is lightweight and portable, though quite bulky.
Many places where you will give presentations will not have opaque projectors because their limitations outweigh their advantages for almost all
applications. It is the least versatile of the projectors, and except for highly
specialized uses, I would not recommend it as an aid to your presentation.

5. The film-strip projector.
This projects slidelike images from strips of film, and most of the time it
uses commercially produced presentation packages. If you need to use
such a package instead of a live presentation, this aid might be helpful.
Many packaged courses are commercially available on film strips combined
with phonograph records or audio-tape cassettes. For these uses, the film-
strip projector is ideal. The slide projector and the overhead projector are
better choices if you want to develop your own communication aids.

TAPES

Audio tapes (reel-to-reel or cassette) and video tapes offer some help to
persons giving presentations, but their uses are quite limited.

Audio tape can add authenticity to a presentation. Sometimes, for
instance, it can be valuable to you to have an authority on your subject
explain something in his or her own words and voice. Tape would be
useful for that purpose, though in many cases a simple quotation would
serve equally well. Still, I have found a few occasions when tape was
valuable to a presentation. Depending on the kind of presentation you
give, you may occasionally find it useful, but don't use audio or video tape
as a gimmick.

Video tape offers many of the advantages of movies and eliminates
some of the disadvantages, particularly the cost. You can inexpensively
use video tape to illustrate products and processes in operation. You can
videotape the dry run of a presentation and play it back to get an audience

view of your own efforts. Video tape is relatively inexpensive and easy to use, but don't use it as a toy or gimmick.

If you plan extensive use of video tape, get professional help in production. That will be expensive, but it will help you to be effective. Knowledgeable professionals can also acquaint you with the limitations of video tape for specific applications.

HANDOUTS

By handouts I mean any pieces of paper that you give to your audience, including notes, articles, reprints, pamphlets, books, magazines, catalogs, worksheets, diagrams, bibliographies, summaries, questionnaires, and almost anything else that can be written, typed, or printed.

Handouts are among the most useful communication aids; they are generally inexpensive, and they prevent distraction. If you announce in advance that you will be distributing supporting material, the audience will be spared the distracting task of note taking.

Handouts also allow you to broaden your presentation. If you haven't time to cover all the details of a subject, you can use your presentation to cover the most important points and can then distribute handouts to fill in the gaps.

Handouts provide reinforcement of the material in your presentation. The audience can review and refer to your main points later.

To achieve the most effective use of handouts:

1. Let the audience know in advance that you will be distributing them. Otherwise they may make their own notes on the material covered in the handouts.

2. Distribute handouts at the end of the presentation unless they are worksheets to be used during the presentation. If you distribute them too early, they are likely to be distracting.

   There is an exception to this advice. Sometimes you may want to use a handout to prepare the audience for your presentation. A handout explaining background material or other preparatory information may be distributed to the audience a few hours to a week in advance of the presentation. You can't always assume, though, that every member of the audience will have taken the time to read the advance handout. People are reluctant to do homework, so don't base the level of your presentation upon the assumption that your advance handout has been digested and understood by the audience.

3. Select handouts as carefully as any other communication aid. Don't use them just because they are available. If they don't

apply to your purpose and to your audience, they distract from your presentation. Some speakers, both inexperienced and experienced, try to achieve effectiveness by the pound. They give their audiences great quantities of material. Faced with this mound of litter-ature, the audience most frequently discards it all, the useful information along with the padding.

Properly used, handouts can add fullness to your oral presentation and can help you provide specialized detail to those members of the audience with the competence and the interest to understand it. And, like the appendixes of a written report, handouts can do this without cluttering up your main presentation.

Handouts are also useful for presenting masses of numerical, statistical, or financial data. People find it impossible to understand or to retain great masses of figures when they are presented orally. Some speakers try to remedy this problem through the use of slides or charts presenting the numbers, but the audience can't absorb all that information in one gulp. The most effective way to handle quantities of figures is through handouts. Use the spoken word, perhaps augmented by slides, graphs, or other aids, to explain the significance of your figures. Use the handout to give the figures themselves. Later, your audience can study the handouts and, armed with your comments, can interpret and absorb the vast quantity of information represented by the numbers.

An illustrated oral presentation of an equation can be effective, but for most presentations, the derivations of the equation are best dealt with in a handout.

Use handouts any time you are concerned that you might be giving your audience more than they can absorb immediately—and any time that you think they should take with them something which will later jog their memories.

STATISTICS AND NUMBERS

Figures, numbers, and statistics are often the least interesting and sometimes the least credible parts of any presentation. If you must use numbers to support your ideas, do so carefully, and use the best techniques available. For great masses of numerical data, use a handout. Large batches of quantitative data from your presentation can't be immediately absorbed by the audience. Use graphs or other visual material to represent quantities when you can. As we noted before, relationships are easier to perceive when presented graphically.

However you present your numbers, do so ethically. One of the reasons that statistical presentations are mistrusted by many people is that statistics are so often misused—sometimes in ignorance, sometimes by intention.

Statistics and their graphic representations are specialized fields with their own rules. Properly used, statistics can compress reality into a concise form. Improperly used, they deceive and distort, and they can tarnish the image and credibility of the speaker.

If you plan to make frequent use of statistics in your presentations, you'd be well advised to make a careful study of the science of statistics. If you plan to use them only occasionally, make sure that the statistics you use are correct and that they are used in a way which reflects reality. Never use them to deceive. It is not ethical, and you are not likely to get away with it in front of any competent audience. Once you're caught in an attempt to deceive, your credibility is all but destroyed. Ethics makes sense in a world where you're judged by results.

A FINAL WORD ABOUT COMMUNICATION AIDS

At the beginning of this chapter, I warned against the overuse of communication aids and urged you not to use them unless they are absolutely necessary. I want to stress that again, but I want to be sure that I don't leave you with the impression that there is something wrong with the proper use of communication aids. They are quite useful for many purposes. In my experience in both giving and observing presentations, I have found them to be most useful for:

1. Adding authenticity. Photographs, models, mockups, slides, and many other aids can help you to bring reality into your presentation. They can bolster your information with material that will help your audience to understand the things you're trying to explain. If your presentation needs a dose of reality to make it acceptable, use a communication aid if you can find one that will add without distracting.

2. Showing relationships. A flow chart can be an excellent way to show the relationships of the elements in a process. An organization chart can depict very clearly the relationships between people and their functions in an organization. A chart or a graph can illustrate the quantitative relationships of data. Any concept involving relationships among things, values, and ideas can often be more clearly expressed by using a communication aid.

Use aids whenever you *need* them. Use them wisely and selectively and you will use them well.

13
Foundations of Effective Listening

Most people have had little formal training in listening because up until quite recently little was available. Most of our communication education has centered on those skills necessary to get *our* points of view across. This overemphasis on the skills of expression may have led many of us to underemphasize the role of listening in our day-to-day communication. But listening is important because each of us needs information that cannot be had except by listening. Even if our listening skills are not what they should be, we can improve them.

If we see people writing, it's obvious that they're communicating. It's even more obvious when we see people speaking. They're communicating, no doubt about it. They're active.

Look at people listening. What are they doing? Nothing, apparently, unless they respond with a noise or a nod. Listening appears to be passive; but, in reality, it's quite an active process.

Listeners hear words. Effective listeners see the physical behavior of the speaker. They interpret those signals; they compare them. Does what the speaker says square up with the way he or she says it? Effective listeners try to see the meaning in the message; they try to relate it to their own needs. If we look very closely at effective listeners, we see that they respond to the speaker. They respond without words, but they respond nonetheless. They tell the speaker that they're following him or her and that they're willing to hear. Perhaps they say it with a smile or with a nod or maybe with their eyes.

Listening seems passive as we watch someone listen to someone else.

Yet, when someone is listening to us, we are aware of whether or not he's really listening. We know whether he's interested or bored or merely faking attention and we know all of this from the nonverbal signals that he or she sends to us, consciously or otherwise.

Good listening is active. When we listen well, we are very active intellectually. We are constantly asking questions and seeking answers. We ask the questions of ourselves, and we seek answers in the message we receive from the speaker.

We speak 125 to 150 words per minute, on the average. We can think much faster, perhaps 400, 500, or even 1200 or more words per minute. What do we do with the differential? The answer to that question is important, for it determines the effectiveness with which we listen. It can be a liability or an asset. Which it is for you depends on how you use it.

The ineffective listener allows this speech-speed/thought-speed differential to provide time for distracting excursions into other areas.

Effective listeners realize that their think speed is greater than the speaker's talk speed. They know that they can't help but remain mentally active. Instead of succumbing to the temptation of distraction, they channel their thoughts to the topic. As the speaker expresses ideas, the effective listener forms mental questions and seeks the answers to these questions:

What is the speaker saying; what does it really mean?
How does it relate to what the speaker said before?
Where is the speaker going; what's the point being made?
How is it helpful; how can I use it?
Does it make any sense?
Am I getting the whole story?
How is the speaker backing up points?
Is the speaker leaving anything out?
How does what the speaker is saying relate to what I already know?
Do I understand what the speaker is saying?
Should I ask for clarification?

These are just some questions that effective listeners might ask. The important thing is that they do ask questions and that these questions involve them actively in the communication. They're not passive observers; they're active participants working along with the speaker to develop ideas and to achieve understanding. The effective listener is a communicator, for effective communication, like electricity, must have a closed circuit. When we join the speaker in seeking understanding, we help to close the circuit.

When I say that listening should be active, I refer mainly to mental activity. Physical alertness, however, has its place in the process. If we remain physically alert, we are more likely to be mentally alert. Sit upright; don't allow yourself to become too comfortable. An overly relaxed posture is an invitation to daydream. The speaker, too, will benefit from your alertness, will see that you aren't daydreaming, and will be encouraged by your attention; you'll be more of a target and less of a distraction. Of course, you'll benefit also from the speaker's increased effectiveness.

Good listening is selfish. Courtesy should prompt us to listen. However, if it were only courtesy that motivated us, it's most unlikely that we would listen for long. Most of us, in fact all of us, are motivated by those things that will be helpful to us. And listening is helpful, even necessary. There's a lot of information in other heads, and the only way that we will ever get most of it is to listen—to listen actively, to listen selfishly for what we can get out of it.

THE CONTENT-DELIVERY EQUATION

It's easy to listen to people who express themselves well. It's hard to listen to people who express themselves poorly. Those two simple statements are the basis for the content-delivery equation, which leads us to believe that something well expressed is useful and that something poorly expressed is not.

If people express themselves poorly, we tend to assume that they have little of value to say. So we listen half heartedly, if at all. If people express themselves well, we enjoy listening, and it's such a pleasant experience that we evaluate what they say lightly, if at all. We are much more likely to accept the ideas, suggestions, and persuasions of someone with a good delivery than we are to accept those same things from someone with a poor delivery. But we don't listen for entertainment—not if we're effective listeners. We listen for ideas, for meaning.

Does the content-delivery equation affect your listening? Do you take the easy way out? Or do you listen for meaning regardless of style of delivery?

DEFENSIVE LISTENING

When we listen defensively, we don't listen at all, so perhaps we should call this defensive nonlistening. We often listen defensively when we are involved in dispute or a difference of point of view. We state a point of view; someone disagrees or offers a differing point of view. And while he or she is stating the case, we take that time to think of what we will say next. That's bad listening and bad debating strategy. We can't deal effectively with another point of view unless we know what it is. Don't listen defensively. State your case; then listen to other points of view. You'll have ample time to think of what you're going to say next while you're saying it. You can think faster than you can speak. The think-speed/talk-speed differential allows plenty of time for composing rebuttals during delivery.

SOME LISTENING TIPS

1. Listen with purpose.
We all do this, but how often do we define that purpose clearly in our own minds? As you listen, use some of that lag time in the speak-speed/thought-speed differential to make a declarative statement of purpose. Don't be satisfied with a vague, abstract, semiconscious feeling of purpose. Put your purpose in a simple, declarative sentence:

- My main purpose in listening to this guy is to find out what kind of a product manager he'll make.
- I want to learn the *real* reasons for the increased number of gripes from the shipping section.
- Before I can sell this firm, I've got to know its power structure. This woman can give me some good insights on that; I'm going to listen to her.

The last statement goes one step further. It anticipates a use for the information. We should always take that step. But, first, we've got to size up the speaker. Who is she? What has she to offer us? What can we learn from her?

Part of our statement of purpose should include a prediction of what we might do with what we get from listening. Then, as we listen, we have an outline to which we can relate the points that the speaker is making. *I'm going to listen to this person because . . . , and this is what I'm going to do with that information.*

A statement like that will help keep you on the track. As you are tempted to wander away from the subject, you can bring yourself back by recalling your purpose.

If all speakers were supremely skilled, we wouldn't have to worry about listening, purpose, and attention. The effective speaker would, right at the beginning, tell us what we could get from the speech and why it was so valuable we couldn't afford to miss it. He or she would go on to give us a beautifully organized, unified, coherent, emphatic, and clear exposition of ideas and their relationships to our needs. Wouldn't that be lovely? Every lecture, meeting, interview, and conversation would be a joy, and our listening would reach undreamed heights of effectiveness.

Sure, people should all speak that way, but they don't and they aren't likely to get much better than they are now. You can't make people much better at giving you ideas, but you can make yourself a better getter of the ideas that you are exposed to every day.

2. Listen for meaning.

Don't listen for words alone. As we noted earlier, listening involves more than hearing. Sight is also involved, and effective listening is a matter of integrating all the information we receive.

Effective listeners listen with their eyes as well as with their ears. They look for meaning wherever it may be found. They listen for what is not said as well as for what is said. They listen for tone, gesture, and implication and relate the verbal and the nonverbal clues of the sender of the message.

Effective listeners are aware that much of the meaning they attach to a message may come from within themselves, from their own biases, experiences, and needs. They try to sort out the sender's meaning from their own. Good listeners sort, sift, scan, relate, integrate, synthesize, and compare.

An honest attempt to understand someone else will help us to find meaning. It should also earn us new respect from those to whom we extend the courtesy of trying to understand them. Respect for a person or for a point of view tends to be mutual, and it's quite difficult to withhold respect from people or their points of view when it's obvious that they're trying to extend that respect to us and to the views we hold. The converse is also true. It's quite difficult to respect others when it's obvious that they hold no respect for us or for what we believe. If true understanding is ever to be achieved, someone has to take the first step. Effective listeners who are concerned with getting meaning will take that first step, even if only in the purely selfish desire to perceive meaning.

3. Eliminate distractions.

All of us are easily distracted whether we are speaking, listening, writing, or reading. Distractions are everywhere to be found, and it's probably impossible to eliminate all of them from any environment. But many times, distractions that could be eliminated persist because no one takes the time to eliminate them.

The physical setting is the source of many distractions: noise, activity, drafts, too much or too little heat. When you've some serious listening to do, try to schedule it in a place and at a time when you can be reasonably free from distraction. If you do a great deal of your listening in your office, look it over; check it out for possible distractions and eliminate as many of them as possible. Note the times of the day when uncontrollable distractions occur, and try to avoid appointments at those times.

You can eliminate many distractions by holding calls and visitors when you have someone in your office. Now, this seems almost too basic to mention. Everyone knows that we should do this. So why mention it? How many people do you know who fail to do it? What about you? It's impolite to subject a caller to a constant series of interruptions. It makes it hard for your guest to develop ideas if you both are constantly being thrown off the track by interruptions.

We ourselves can distract speakers. And, if they're distracted, they are less effective and we get less from them. There are the obvious distractions to be avoided: fingers drumming on the table, pencil tapping, change rattling, clock watching, or any other visible manifestations of impatience or disinterest. They tell the speaker that the listener isn't an active listener.

How to cure it? Be an active listener.

4. Don't jump in too soon.
Let the speaker finish before you begin to speak. Most face-to-face communication situations require that we play many roles; we are alternately a speaker and a listener. We often become so engrossed in the point of view that we are trying to get across that we find it difficult to listen. There is an atmosphere of tenseness, of anxiety, or of combat that brings all our energies to bear on the difficult problem of getting our ideas across to others. In these cases, we cease to listen and, instead, concentrate on what we have to say. We are impatient; we can hardly wait for the other person to finish before we jump in with our next point. There are no formal rules of order at most meetings, discussions, interviews, or conversations; who can get the floor is who can get the first word in and then keep words coming fast enough to prevent someone else from interrupting. In meetings or conversations like this, we hardly dare to take a breath. We fight not only for our point of view but also for time to express it.

We are impatient. We center our interest on what concerns us. We jump in too soon. We jump to conclusions by deciding what others are going to say and what they mean, and we respond to that. They don't like being cut off, so they don't listen to us. Rather, they look for a chance to cut in. When you've got the floor in a meeting like that, you hardly pause to breathe. One phrase is repeated over and over again, "Now, wait a minute." But nobody waits a microsecond, much less a minute.

Get into the habit of pausing a second or two after someone else has spoken. This applies to two-person conversations as well as to multiperson meetings. Let people finish. Give them a second for an afterthought or an addition or a clarification. Let them correct their own mistakes.

The goal of communication is understanding. Listening, effective listening, may be defined as the quest for meaning and understanding.

14

Foundations of Effective Interviewing

For those who feel that a discussion of interviewing should be preceded by a definition of the process under consideration, I would offer the following as a working definition of the interview. *It is a situation in which people, usually two people, meet to exchange information.* An interview is not a conversation, an opportunity to "nice" someone, nor an in-depth probing of the interviewee's unconscious. It is not couchless analysis, bloodless exploratory neurosurgery, or psychofluoroscopy.

An interview is an exchange, two-way communication. An interview is purposeful. Interviewers have purpose. They have information to give, and they expect to receive information. That the interviewer should have purpose is obvious. Not as obvious are the purposes of the interviewee. Interviewers are aware of their own purposes but are often unaware that the interviewees have purposes other than satisfying the interviewer. An interview will be successful only if both parties are able to achieve their goals.

What makes a successful interviewer? There is no one personality type, no sure-fire technique that guarantees good interviews. People with many different personalities employ many different techniques and do so successfully.

An effective interviewer should have the ability to relate to the interviewee and to share the interview experience. Both interviewer and interviewee have something to give, and each has the expectation of gaining. The ability to share the interview doesn't require any special sort of personality. Indeed, the interviewer would be ill-advised to put up a false front, to create a special image for interviews. The most effective technique is the absence of visible technique. Naturalness is easy to accept; falseness is always suspect, and few of us have the acting skill required to project and maintain a personality that is not our own. Interviewees are perceptive people. They can spot an assumed personality, and they will distrust it. Be yourself; think of your own reaction to someone who is trying to impress you with a false personality. The people whom you will interview react to falseness in the same way.

Interviewers should be objective; they should know their own prejudices, positive and negative. It's impossible for any human being to be completely objective, but we can, if we know ourselves, keep our judgments and our responses more nearly free of our biases and prejudices.

SOME INTERVIEWING TIPS

Prepare for the interview.

Successful interviewers know that preparation is required for good interviews. They begin by making a checklist of their purposes and of the information that they hope to elicit. If you do no other preparation, at least formulate a purpose in your mind. What do you want to give? What do you want to get? Who is the interviewee? What does he or she want to give? What does he or she expect to get?

Look at records or files before the interview. Don't take time from the interview for this homework. Stopping the progress of an interview to dig out a file or record and then taking the time to analyze it is a distraction. If it's a recruiting interview, you should analyze applications, resumes, test data, and the like before you meet the candidate. Such an analysis will allow you to direct your interview to the amplification or clarification of information already available. It will keep you from going over the same ground twice.

A candidate is given a poor impression of you and your organization when the interview begins with paper shuffling. There are several ways to begin an interview; the poorest is probably, "Well, now, let's see what we have here" (shuffle, shuffle, shuffle).

The same holds true for other interviews. The interview is no place to review appraisal forms or personnel records unless they are part of the subject being discussed, and the interviewer and interviewee review them together. Certainly, you should not give the impression that this is the first time that you have seen these documents.

Provide a proper setting for the interview.

The setting for the interview should afford as much privacy as possible. The setting should avoid placing physical barriers, such as desks and tables, between the interviewer and the interviewee. Such barriers heighten the dominant status of the interviewer and may increase the tension felt by the interviewee. The scene of one person behind a desk and another in front of it is reminiscent of an interview in the principal's office; unless your experience differs markedly from mine, you will recall that as a not-too-pleasant experience.

The setting for the interview should be free of tension-producing items. Unfamiliar items produce tension; explain forms to the interviewee and why physical equipment, particularly dictating machines and other sound-recording devices, are in the room. The same is true of other people in the room. If you have a colleague present, introduce him or her to the interviewee and explain the reason for his or her presence. Don't allow the interviewees to assume that they are also being double-teamed or clandestinely evaluated. No one likes to feel outnumbered.

Keep tension at a minimum. You want to understand the interviewee's normal reactions. Tension adds another significant variable and makes accurate evaluation difficult.

Avoid writing during the interview.
Avoid writing because:

1.   It is distracting to both parties.
2.   The pauses for writing fractionate the interview.
3.   The notes taken during the interview are usually incomprehensible when read after any period of time has elapsed.
4.   The notes are made upon the basis of your impressions at that time in the interview; they don't allow you to evaluate the whole of what is said, only what has been said to that point.
5.   Notes tend to emphasize the dominant status of the note-taker.
6.   Notes tend to heighten the tension.

It's usually best to make summarized notes after the interviewee has left. If you have scheduled several interviews in a row, allow time between them, at least ten or fifteen minutes, to summarize the previous interview in your mind and in your notes and to take a few minutes to review your preparation for the next interview. Summarizing at the end of an interview allows you to consider the interview as a whole. You are able to edit out the unimportant data and focus your summary on the most significant elements in the entire interview. You deal with dominant impressions rather than with instant reactions. Notes made in this way can be more carefully drawn and are more likely to be understandable when used for later reference. The interviewee is spared the trauma of wondering what has been written, and the interviewer is free to listen during the interview.

Don't worry that you will forget something important by the end of the interview. If it's important, you'll have no difficulty recalling it for your summary.

Occasionally it is desirable to note a key word or fact during the interview. If this is so, then don't try to do it as you listen. Pause, let interviewees know that you consider their comments important, and let them know what you are doing by saying something like, "That seems important. I'd like to make sure that I remember it correctly. Let me make a note of it." Other than pausing to make occasional notes of names or other factual data, devote your entire attention to the interviewee. You'll both get more out of the interview.

Let the interviewee talk.
Transcripts indicate that many interviewers fill the majority of the interview with what they have to say. The interviewee's participation is limited to brief responses to direct questions. This kind of interview may tell the interviewee a great deal about the interviewer, but it doesn't give the interviewer much of a chance to learn. Other transcripts indicate a preponderance of talk by the interviewee. The interviewer provides topics and questions to stimulate response and the interviewer devotes most of the time to learning. Interviewing is really formalized listening. Of course, if part of your purpose is to give information, take the time to do so clearly and concretely, but allow the interviewee time to respond to the information. Allow the interviewee to seek clarification, to test for understanding.

Open-ended questions usually produce helpful responses. These are questions that require a detailed response from the interviewee. Questions that can be answered "yes" or "no" normally result in an interview in which the interviewer does most of the talking. A question like "Do you feel that you could do this job?" usually elicits a one-syllable response (usually "yes"). Putting that same question in open-ended form ("Which of your abilities and interests do you feel would be most helpful in this job?") requires the interviewee to open up a bit.

In the rest of this chapter, we'll look at some specific interview situations, but as a general rule we can safely say that an interview is a shared conversation with a purpose. It will be most effective if you plan for it and try to be yourself while allowing the interviewee to be natural too.

Allow interviewees to choose their own words.
If they're having difficulty finding the right words, be patient and let them find the words. You want to learn about them, not about yourself. Many interviewers who assist interviewees in finding the words are amazed to find how many people are just like themselves.

Avoid coaching the desired response. The interviewee will be grateful for the hint, and, in most instances, will be happy to supply the "right" answer. "We feel that it's important for our employees to be interested in their jobs. We're not much for clock watching. Now, how do you feel about putting in a little extra time, if it's necessary to get the job done?" What sort of a response do you expect this will elicit from a candidate who wants the job?

Don't play games.

Gimmicky interviews seldom produce valid information, but they often drive away people exposed to them. Fortunately, few resort to the gimmick interview, the pet question, or the set-up situation.

An interview should be conducted naturally and in a dignified, businesslike way. Few skilled interviewers resort to cheap tricks and shoddy gimmicks. They may indeed have favorite questions, questions which have proved successful in eliciting helpful responses, but they don't have pet answers.

THE SELECTION INTERVIEW

Effective selection interviewing begins with a consideration of purpose. Let's look at the usual purposes for selection interviewing and your likelihood of achieving them.

To determine which of a group of candidates are most likely to make suitable employees.

Note "most likely." No process of selection is foolproof. As a sole selection device, the interview is unreliable, but combined with other information it can be helpful in raising the probabilities of successful selection.

To motivate suitable candidates to accept the job offer.

Depending on the skill of the interviewer and, of course, on the quality of the offer and the organization making it, the interview can be most helpful in achieving this purpose.

To give candidates not accepted a positive view of the organization and the industry as a whole.

Few organizations and industries can afford to alienate candidates. You may need them in the future—you'll probably need at least one of their friends or relatives.

The interview as a selection device.

In discussing interviewing with managers, supervisors, employment specialists, and recruiters, I've asked them if they ever formed judgments or made tentative decisions to hire or not to hire a candidate solely on the basis of documents (resumes, application forms, test results, and so forth) about the candidate, before they had a chance to interview the candidate. Almost all responded that they did make these predictive judgments.

I further asked these people about the correlation of their before- and after-interview judgments. The overwhelming majority reported that their preinterview judgments to hire or not to hire were unchanged after the interview in over 90 percent of the cases they handled.

Is this bad? I think not. It indicates that a detailed summary of experience is a reliable tool and that the interview most often supports this summary. It could also indicate that the interview yields very little additional information. In addition, it could indicate that people are stubborn and that once having made up their minds, they are unwilling to change. Do you often find that your preinterview impressions are supported in your postinterview judgments? Or to put it another way, how much are you learning in your interviews?

In many cases, the interview is a cultural institution. Why do you interview candidates? Perhaps, because you're expected to. Perhaps, because everyone else does.

Has the interview, then, a contribution to make to the selection process? It certainly does. It gives candidates a chance to learn about the company and the job. It gives them a chance to interview the recruiter. (Just as recruiters make generalizations about a school from contact with a few students and one or two faculty members, so do candidates generalize about your company and industry from their limited contact with you.) The interview gives you a chance to get information not available on the resume or application.

Is public contact or contact with other employees an important part of the job for which the candidate is being considered? If so, you have an excellent opportunity to learn about grooming, poise, tact, verbal fluency, enthusiasm, forcefulness, and ability to organize ideas. You can learn about voice, manner, cooperativeness, ability to establish and maintain contact, and potential skill in relating to others. From the candidate's record of experiences and activities, you can infer many of these things; the interview gives you a chance to validate your inferences.

The interview can also be useful for gathering further information about critical points in the experience documents or for resolving apparent inconsistencies or contradictions. You can use the interview for all of these things and more if you plan by analyzing the resume or application and by cataloging the skills and abilities required for the job.

Of course you'll make predictive assessments about the candidate.

You couldn't avoid doing so. Fine, make those predictions, and use the interview to test them. After you review the candidate's resume, make a brief checklist of the points that you want to cover, the things you want to learn.

Analyze the candidates. Who are they? What are they likely to want from the interview? Be prepared to provide those things that they want to learn. If an interview is planned for, it can become an important element in the selection process; but to be most effective it must be integrated with other sources of information.

The value of the interview as a selection device is most often over-rated. This probably stems from our concept of ourselves as a keen judge of human nature. This self-concept doesn't square with the facts; for, in reality, you can learn very little about a person in the hour or less normally scheduled for an interview. You seldom see the candidates in their native habitats. They're on their best behavior. They know their weak points, and, consciously or otherwise, will try to keep you from seeing them.

But, if the interview is properly conducted and given its proper weight in the overall hiring judgment, it can be an effective recruiting tool.

Other sources of information.

Among the sources of data available to managers who must recruit and select are the following:

1. Applications or resumes.
2. Letters of recommendation and references.
3. Comments of previous employers or supervisors.
4. Test results.
5. School and college transcripts.
6. Security, credit, and background investigations.
7. Publications of candidates.
8. Professional societies.
9. Comments of other interviewers.
10. Personnel files and peer ratings for candidates who are already employed by the organization.

Let's look at these sources and draw some conclusions about their helpfulness.

Applications or resumes.
The candidate prepares these documents, or has them prepared, to sell you. They are one-sided. Yet, they are perhaps the most valuable source of information you have about the candidate. They indicate a pattern

or lack of pattern from which you can predict future performance. This pattern is not a certain predictor, anymore than a track record is a sure predictor of the winner of the fourth race. But it's something to go on.

Does the pattern of experience indicate growth? Is the growth likely to continue? Does the candidate show signs of having reached his or her potential? How does he or she work under pressure? Has the candidate shown indications of creativity? All these questions must be asked, and the answers must be compared with the requirements of the job you're trying to fill. If you were to buy a piece of equipment, you would first draw up specifications and compare the available equipment with those specifications. You should do the same for a job. Before you can make an intelligent selection, you must know what you are selecting for. All of this seems obvious, and all managers think that they can choose the right person. But do they? Or do they look for the best person that they can find, when perhaps they don't need the best? What answers do managers want to the questions above? For almost all jobs, many managers would say that they wanted a person who had shown signs of growth and the promise of continued growth, a person who has not reached his or her potential, a person who works well under pressure, and who has demonstrated creativity. Yet, do all jobs call for this? Aren't there many jobs that call for a person who has demonstrated competence, but not necessarily creativity? Aren't there many jobs which offer little growth potential and cry out for a person whose potential, already achieved, matches the requirements of the job?

Resume reading calls for arithmetic. Are all periods of time accounted for? If not, why? How long has the candidate spent on each job? Don't be fooled by some of the folk myths that seem to surround time-on-the-job. The myths tell us that a person who changes jobs often is probably unreliable, a "drifter." The myth also states that someone who has stayed on a job for a long time is in a rut. Generalizations like these are invalid. They seem to suggest that a person should change jobs every three to five years just to keep the record clean. This doesn't make sense. Of course time on the job is significant. But the meaning is different in each case. The fact that someone has changed jobs often is not significant; the reason may be. And what has been the quality of the jobs held? What has been gained from them? What is the pattern of experience taken as a whole? The fact that he or she has held one job for a long period of time does not, in itself, signify stagnation. What were the personal and professional reasons behind the stability?

Study the resume or application for these patterns. Check out the patterns in the interview or by reference checks. If you have questions, raise those questions in the interview. Get the candidate's interpretation of the facts. Then you decide what makes sense.

Letters of recommendation and references.

Letters can be of some help if they are specific. If they are merely abstract testimonials to character, friendliness, and integrity, then they are of less value.

If the candidates supplied the names of the references, then the letters are less likely to be helpful. They would not have given you the name of anyone likely to malign them. If you ask the candidates to supply the names of previous employers, faculty advisors, major department chairpersons and the like, the information received may be of greater value. If the reference is a specific statement describing what the candidate has done, it may tell you quite a good deal about ability.

Comments of previous employers or supervisors.

Some people will respond more candidly to a telephone call than to a letter. Fear of suits for defamation of character often keeps people from expressing negative opinions in writing. If the person on the other end of the phone line doesn't know who you are, he or she may be unwilling to tell you much, for this person has no way of knowing if you are who you represent yourself to be. You can often overcome this reluctance by asking him or her to verify rather than to supply information. Instead of asking when Stephen Marelli worked for the company and what his salary was, you might get better results if you asked, "Stephen Marelli has applied to us for a job as a project engineer. He tells me that he worked for you from the fall of 1964 to the spring of 1967." Most supervisors would probably verify that. "Steve tells me that his salary with you was $9500 a year. Is that about right?" Your stating the salary indicates that you aren't just fishing for information and that you are probably what you represent yourself to be. If you are able to establish your credentials and establish rapport with the supervisor, he or she may even volunteer information that will help you.

If you find it difficult to get this kind of information, you could ask your personnel office to obtain it. If the former employer is in the same area, your personnel manager probably has a working relationship with the personnel manager from the candidate's previous job.

Test results.

This is a difficult area to comment on. There are many different tests, some valid sometimes and many not valid at all. None is always valid. The most nearly valid tests are probably those that measure skill directly, that is, performance tests. If you want to hire a typist, a typing skill test will probably give you a good idea of his or her ability. As the level of jobs goes up, skill tests become impractical. The skills required to be a company president, an engineer, a department head, or an office manager are not amenable to testing.

The ability to do simple jobs can be more easily evaluated than can the ability to perform more complex ones. In simple jobs, the variables that control success are more easily isolated, and a testing analogy can be more easily constructed. In all cases, tests and their construction, evaluation, validation, and interpretation should be left to highly qualified experts. This is no field for amateurs, whether in line management or on the personnel staff.

Tests are most helpful when used as screening devices rather than as selection devices. If, for example, you were confronted with 100 applications for 3 or 4 openings, you would find it impossible to give each of the 100 applicants a thorough consideration. A test battery might help you to screen the group down to a manageable size of 10 or 20. You should, however, realize that some good applicants will be screened out and some poor applicants will pass the screening tests. Final selection should be based on considerations other than, or in addition to, test results.

By all means, use tests under expert guidance, but don't harbor unrealistic expectations of what they can do. On the other hand, if you don't use tests, it's still quite possible to make sound decisions based on the other data available to you.

Many laws and regulations govern the use of tests. In general, their purpose is to assure that people will not be the victims of unfair or irrelevant tests. As these laws and regulations are constantly changing and being reinterpreted by courts and regulatory agencies, you'd do well to check with your personnel and legal staffs for guidance.

School and college transcripts.

These are of most value when the candidate is a recent graduate and you have nothing else to go on. For people who have been out of school for some time, the record of experience will probably be of greater value. The transcript deals with academic skills which have only an indirect relationship to on-the-job skills. Of course the transcript can be valuable in assessing a candidate's academic preparation for the technical aspects of the job.

Security, credit, and background investigations.

The value of investigations is determined by the nature of the investigation and the nature of the job. Acquaint yourself with the method of the investigation so you can interpret the results of the investigation in terms of the way in which the data was collected.

Publications of candidates.

These can give you an insight into the candidate's viewpoint on professional topics.

Professional societies.

These groups can be useful in acquainting you with the candidate's peers, who may be able to give you some idea of his or her reputation in the professional community.

Comments of other interviewers.

The candidate will, if hired, deal with many people. If others in your company have interviewed the candidate, get their impressions. Interviewers should, however, form their own impressions and record them independently. After each has done so, they should meet to discuss the candidate. But if this discussion takes place before the interviewers have formed their impressions of the candidate, then a dominant personality or a status authority at the meeting may force or influence compliance with his or her viewpoint, and the advantages of having several points of view will be lost. A pooling of independent judgments and impressions should result in a broader profile of the candidate.

Personnel files and peer ratings.

These materials can give added information on a current employee. These data are generally not available on people outside the company.

Conducting the selection interview.

Recognize the candidate as a person, rather than as *Candidate #73.* Do this by frequent, natural use of the candidate's name. Some interviewers use the candidate's first name, feeling that this technique promotes warmth and informality and reduces tension. This is an individual decision, but I feel quite strongly that the use of the candidate's first name should be avoided. It seems patronizing. It is the form of address used by an elder to a younger, by a senior to a junior, and by many teachers to their pupils. It heightens the dominant status of the interviewer who says, in effect, "Now, kid, what can I do for you." Few of us would call a candidate "kid." More would use the first name. The candidate, however, is not there as a student, but as a professional seeking employment. The use of Mr., Mrs., Miss, or Ms. recognizes the professionalism of the candidate and puts the interview at its proper tone. If the interviewer's manner is otherwise cordial and receptive, this form of address will certainly not overformalize the situation.

It's interview time, and the candidate is here. How do you begin? Of course, you want to keep tension low. How about a little small talk? You're wasting time. The value of small talk is overrated. A tense candidate is likely to get more so as you postpone the agenda of the interview. You both know why you're there. This small talk isn't fooling anyone.

If the candidate wishes to begin, allow it. You're there to learn. You can't do that while you're talking.

While it is quite true that you, as an interviewer, should prepare in advance for the session, it is unwise to overstructure the interview by using a series of canned questions with predictable answers. This practice increases the likelihood that you'll hear the expected answer, regardless of what the candidate says. It will also tempt you to focus your attention on your "script."

Summarize from time to time. It gives both you and the candidate a chance to check on mutual understanding. Don't allow the interview to decelerate into a random social interchange. Many a good interview has been ruined by giving the candidate a poor last impression. Allow candidates to summarize, if they wish. For almost all interviews, the final point should refer to follow-up and possibly to a source of further information.

You can be a capable interviewer. To do so most effectively, be yourself. Set your own goals for each interview within an overall philosophy of purpose. Realize the limitations of the interview as a selection technique. Take maximum advantage of the other sources of information available to you, and integrate the interview into this system of sources.

When you interview, listen; allow candidates to be themselves. Give them the information they need to make the judgments they will have to make if a job offer is made. Just as you are interviewing them, so are they interviewing you, your company, and your industry.

FORBIDDEN QUESTIONS

Lawsuits and complaints to federal and state commissions with jurisdiction over discrimination have made many people afraid to interview. They fear that they'll ask a forbidden question and thus invite litigation and sanction. To some extent the fear is justified. It could happen. But, if you use your head and if you confine your questions to matters that are genuinely job related, you're not likely to get into trouble.

For guidance on current laws and regulations and for help in conducting legally correct interviews, consult the specialists in your organization. If you do much employment interviewing, they've probably already contacted you. If not, get in touch with them.

THE APPRAISAL INTERVIEW

In this section we'll look at the manager's role in preparing for and conducting the formal appraisal interview. Perhaps I should say the *ritual* of appraisal interviewing, for it often seems to have a ceremonial quality.

Both the interviewer and the interviewee approach the ceremony with misgiving and apprehension, and each wonders how it will come out.

Employees are concerned because it's their performance that is going to be discussed. They're on the spot. Managers often dread the annual or semiannual ritual because it forces them to give specific, concrete consideration to employee performance. Sure, we appraise people every day. Every time we make a work assignment we appraise the skill of the employee who gets the job. But that sort of appraisal can be done casually; a manager can operate on the basis of feelings about the work force. We don't have to give objective justification to our feelings, and we don't have to discuss them with the people concerned. The appraisal interview must sometimes deal with individual shortcomings, and that's never pleasant. Managers, like other people, find it discomforting to have to discuss another's shortcomings.

Many managers resent the fact that the organization expects them to appraise their employees. They don't feel that they should be placed in the role of judges. They feel that they have no business sitting in judgment on other people; they know that they themselves need to improve their own job performance. These managers are quite correct in assuming that they have no business judging other people. But, as managers, they have an obligation to judge performance. As managers, production and performance are their concern. An appraisal interview is not the place to discuss people. It is the place to discuss their performance and what can be done to maintain effective performance or to correct inadequate performance. Performance, not personality, is the basis of an effective appraisal system and of a productive appraisal interview.

People react defensively and emotionally to personal criticism, and an interview based on discussion of personality is likely to produce only hostility, defensiveness, resentment, and an argument. A supervisor cannot change the personality of a subordinate, nor can the subordinate. But both can work together to develop or to continue acceptable performance.

Systematic appraisal interviews let employees know how the boss thinks they are doing and what they can do to improve their performance. The manager in an organization with an appraisal system is forced to break away from prejudices and preconceived notions. Each of us has a tendency to type people and then to see them and their performance in terms of that typing. Managers don't give very close supervision to "good" workers. They assume that the employees so typed are producing well. They tend to underrate the performance of employees typed as "poor" workers or as "shirkers." A periodic, objective appraisal that focuses on performance, actual performance, forces the manager to reconsider these typings. Appraisal and a discussion of performance pinpoint training needs and other developmental needs of individual employees.

An appraisal interview has two goals: improved job performance and better relations and improved communication between managers and subordinates. If the appraisals are based on sound, objective, performance-based criteria, and if the interviews which follow the appraisals are well planned and well conducted, both of these goals should be met.

Preparing for the appraisal interview.

Preparation for the appraisal interview is a continuing process, for an effective interview can be conducted only in a climate of mutual trust and respect. Mutual trust and respect can come only from satisfying day-to-day relations. When the appraisal interview is the sole communication between a subordinate and a manager, it's bound to be fraught with tension. If the interview is another element in a manager's day-to-day contact, it will be easier for both parties to the interview. It will have less of a connotation of a trial, less of a feeling of "give an accounting of thy stewardship," with its implication "for thou canst be steward no longer."

Complete your appraisal before the interview. You aren't meeting to decide what the appraisal should be; that's too likely to result in argument and haggling. As you appraise, keep your own biases in mind. Focus on performance. Remember that you're appraising performance over a period of time. Don't allow a recent experience to color your judgment of overall performance during the period of the appraisal. Be specific in your standards; you'll have to discuss them in the interview. Look for specific, concrete behavior; you may have to refer to it during the interview.

Give the employee advance notice of the interview. A day or two should give ample opportunity to prepare for the interview.

Ensure privacy for the interview. Think of the implications of timing. If you schedule an interview to begin a half hour before the end of the work day, you are implicitly telling the employee that this is going to be a 30 minute interview. The interview should take as long as necessary. On the other hand, it shouldn't be stretched to fit a preconceived time block. Allow plenty of time. The employee has a contribution to make in the interview. You can estimate the time that it will take you to say what you have to say, but you can't accurately estimate how long the employee will take or how long it will take to permit you both to interact on the subjects raised. An employee looks upon the interview as important. It may be one of several for the manager, but it's the only one for the employee. Employees don't want to feel short-changed. They want this to be as important to you as it is to them. Rushing the interview connotes impatience and suggests that the manager feels that the employees' views aren't worth wasting time on.

Conducting the appraisal interview.

There are several ways an interview can be conducted. The manager can state the employee's shortcomings and then order improvement. This was the procedure at Scrooge and Marley.

The manager can speak understandingly of the employee's short-comings and then motivate with a Pat O'Brien locker-room half-time pep talk. There won't be a dry eye in the department on appraisal interview day. There won't be much improvement in performance either.

The manager can tell the employee how to improve. This is fine if the employee agrees with the manager's assessment of the situation and is willing and able to follow the manager's guidelines. The trouble with this method and the others that we have described is that they are not interviews; they are lectures, sermons if you will. They revolve entirely around the manager; the employee is relegated to the role of audience. An effective interview, on the other hand, is an interaction between the manager and the employee.

To begin an appraisal interview, explain the purpose of the interview to the employee if the employee's not familiar with the system. Explain what happens to the appraisal sheet. Tell what the appraisal is used for and by whom. Don't weasel. Don't blame the procedure on "policy."

Summarize your appraisal. You can bring out specific points as the appraisal develops. Don't skirt weaknesses, but don't fail to emphasize areas of strength. The appraisal interview isn't a chewing-out session. Indicate areas of improvement as you see them.

Encourage employees to participate. Listen. How do they see their performance? What do they think of the criteria by which performance has been judged? What do they see as areas needing improvement? What do they propose to do to improve or to maintain good performance?

Summarize from time to time. Restate what you understood the employee to have said. This shows you have been listening and allows you to check on the accuracy with which you have comprehended meaning.

Keep calm. If the employee becomes angry or emotional, don't reply defensively. Try to understand the anger and its cause, but don't become angry yourself. Don't try to gloss over emotional response. It's real and it's part of the situation. Discuss it. Listen. Let the employee blow off steam. You can't solve the underlying problem by pretending that the employee's emotional response never happened. Human beings are creatures of emotion. It's part of all of us. None of us likes to hear about our shortcomings; none of us likes to be told that we need to improve, though, intellectually, we all realize that we do. When we are in a situation like this, we tend to react emotionally. Angry response is, however, less likely if the manager concentrates on performance rather than on attitude. Most of us can take criticism of what we do, but we reject someone else's com-menting on what we are.

Encourage employees to propose their own methods of development. Behavior will be more productive if they set their own goals. But encourage long-range goals with short-range steps. Progress to a long-range goal is hard to measure, but if milestones have been set up along the way, we can progress as we move from milestone to milestone.

Relate the values of improvement to goals, but avoid threat. An employee may be told, "If your performance in this area doesn't improve, there's very little chance of your getting that promotion that you want." Or he could be told, "When you are able to improve your performance in this area, you'll be a better candidate for the promotion that you want."

When you discuss performance improvement with an employee, try to do so in specific terms. Phrases such as *better work, higher quality, more cooperation, better relations with customers, lower costs, considerable improvement*, and the like are abstract. How will the employee and the manager know when these goals have been achieved? What goal should the employee shoot for? What will please the boss?

If goals are tied to specific performance, they will be clearer and more likely to motivate improvement in performance. If we speak of *reduction in scrap of 15 percent over the next six months, cut rejects by 10 percent, reduce customer complaints to no more than two a week*, or some other concrete indication of improvement in the specific job, we are setting goals that can be achieved, and both the subordinate and the manager will know when those goals have been achieved.

At the end of the interview, summarize. Restate your appraisal. Restate the major points of the interview—the employee's and yours. Restate areas of agreement and solutions, plans, and goals. Indicate agreed on follow-up and be specific in what form follow-up will come.

After the interview, make notes on these points. They'll be helpful when you follow up. You may even find it to be a good idea to send the employee a memorandum outlining the criteria and goals upon which you have agreed. This should prevent future confusion, if the memo is specifically worded.

Appraisal interviews don't have to be an ordeal. They can be an opportunity for sincere, meaningful communication on matters of great concern to both the manager and the managed.

THE EXIT INTERVIEW

Exit interviews should be conducted with all employees who leave, not just with those who leave because they appear dissatisfied. The purpose of the exit interview isn't to find out what's wrong. What, then, is its purpose? There are several.

The exit interview can give you an unthreatened view of the department. The departing employee, secure in a new job, may not be afraid to speak frankly.

The exit interview can give you a picture of the job from the point of view of the incumbent. You're probably going to have to get a replacement for the job. It would be well to know what the person who has held the job thinks of it and its duties.

The exit interview can produce suggestions for the improvement of procedures and relationships within the department, and it can give you a look at yourself through someone else's eyes. This view is no more objective than your own self-concept, but it may suggest a different viewpoint.

The exit interview is a form of employee attitude survey. It may help you to take steps that will correct a situation causing turnover.

Of course, there are reasons why employees may not be frank in comments to you. You'll have to listen very carefully to what they say, how they say it, and for what they don't say. Then you'll have to integrate all of this information with what you know about the employee and the situation. But don't let your past experience determine the meaning that you attach to the exit interview. Listen with an open mind; evaluate later. You may learn something new if you listen well.

Employees may be reluctant to be honest in their comments because they feel that what they say will affect their references. No one wants to leave a disgruntled manager behind. Your attitude and manner of conducting the interview, as well as your reputation for fairness, will have a great deal to do with the frankness with which employees speak during the exit interview. The values in an exit interview are all one-sided. You can learn from it, but employees may be reluctant to be open and honest because they see nothing in it for them. They may be willing to do you a favor, but they'll have to believe that you really value what they say. If so, they may find the opportunity to express themselves satisfying. If the whole thing seems like a ritual, employees will respond in ritualistic fashion. They'll say what they think they're expected to say. An employee leaving a job because it's too much for him or her may be reluctant to admit this and may exaggerate the difficulties of the job or blame the problems on poor personal relations. It's much easier for someone to blame external causes than it is to fault one's own lack of ability. The employee who restructures reality in this fashion may be unaware of what he or she is doing. Because this person can't admit shortcomings, he or she may attack people, policies, or procedures as the cause of the departure and failures on the job.

In general, however, people are willing to cooperate in giving their views. Don't make the mistake of thinking that every criticism comes from an inept employee who is taking out his or her frustration on the system. Much of what is offered in criticism may be quite real.

Preparing for the exit interview.

Don't wait until the last minute for the exit interview. If possible, schedule it soon after the employee has submitted a resignation. You may find the information you get from the interview to be helpful in hiring a replacement.

Of course, arrange for privacy during the interview. And make sure that you let the employee know that remarks will be treated in confidence.

Take time to review the employee's history, if this isn't already well known to you. The employee's comments will be related to his or her experience, and it would be embarrassing for you to admit that you don't know the employee well enough to understand what he or she says.

Conducting the exit interview.

You want to get a complete picture of the employees and their reasons for leaving. You should know what their jobs have been—as they have seen them. The job as outlined in the job description and the job as actually performed may be quite different. As you recruit a replacement, you are concerned with filling the job as it was actually performed, not the job that was written up on the job description. If the actual job performance does not match the job description, then you will have to consider rewriting the job description or reassigning the tasks to someone else, unless you feel that the tasks should not have been performed at all. In that case, it might be well to find out how and why the incumbent was performing those tasks.

You'll want to know why the employee is leaving and what his or her future plans are.

You should listen for the employee's attitudes toward the organization, the job and its functions, the department, fellow workers, supervisors, and you.

Keep the interview as informal as possible. In fact, avoid calling it an interview. Don't grill the employee. Don't question too intently. And, above all else, *listen.*

You can steer the discussion to the point by asking what the employee thinks you should look for in a replacement. Answers to this question can be most revealing. You might also wish to ask the employee where you might look for a replacement. He or she may suggest a likely candidate.

The answer to "When did you start to think of making a change?" can be very revealing. If the time given in the answer corresponds to some specific experience or event, you may be able to pick up a fruitful thread for further discussion or exploration.

If the employee criticizes you, the department, the organization, or people in it, don't be defensive. Listen. You can evaluate later.

The *reason for leaving* stated in a resignation or in a separation form is, of course, not always the real one. Even if it is the real one, it doesn't always tell the whole story. It may be true that Ruth is leaving for "professional advancement" or for a "more responsible job and higher pay." But what started her looking? The answer to that may be most helpful to the manager who wants to improve a department. Exit interviewing can sometimes provide the answer to that question and to others.

The employee who is leaving your department or organization has a lot to tell you. Are you willing to listen?

15
Coaching and Counseling

Managers communicate with their employees in many ways. Some of the messages are related to getting tasks completed; some to problems; and some, perhaps most, to the maintenance of the normal functioning of the organization. Managers are coordinators and controllers responsible for the maintenance and proper use of the material and financial resources of their areas of management. But managers (whether they're called executives, managers, supervisors, or working leaders) have another key responsibility: the maintenance of human resources, the people who report to them. In discharging this responsibility to their organizations and to their subordinates, managers provide a service to both their organizations and employees. This service is much like that of a counselor. Certainly, managers are not just a counselor to the people who report to them—that is but one of their many functions—and managers who understand and are able to function in this role of counselor, or coach if you prefer that term, will best discharge their obligations to their organization and to their subordinates. This chapter deals with that role and with the philosophy and techniques that will help a manager to function most effectively in it.

Rather than attempt a definition of counseling, let's look at some of the purposes of this process, keeping in mind that we are limiting our consideration to the kinds of counseling that managers might engage in with their employees. We are not talking about clinical counseling, school guidance counseling, or personal adjustment counseling. We are not talking of the activities of psychiatrists, psychologists, social workers, clergy, educators, marriage counselors, or probation officers. Each of these practitioners has a legitimate area of concern. So, too, does the manager or supervisor.

The purposes of an individual counseling relationship will be determined by the goals of the counselor and the client,* but the following would seem to encompass most situations:

1. To help clients make the most of their potential.
2. To help clients adjust to change.
3. To help the clients assess their strengths and limitations and to translate these into reasonable goals.
4. To provide a setting in which clients can blow off steam or resolve misunderstandings.
5. To meet the clients' basic needs for security, adequacy, and response.
6. To provide a setting in which clients can recognize and face their personal problems, whether work-related or not.

The client is the focal point of the description of the purpose of the counseling. This is as it should be. Counseling, to be effective, must be centered about the client's needs. The counselor functions to promote the client's development. There are, of course, other purposes for two-person face-to-face communication, but these other purposes describe an interview.

In an interview, primary purposes may be ascribed to either the interviewer or the interviewee, or to both. The interview is primarily a device for sharing information. The interests of the interviewer and of the interviewee are equal. One is no more important than the other. This is the primary difference between the interview and the counseling situation. In the interview, each person has the right to pursue goals; it is a communication device. The counseling session, on the other hand, is not primarily a communication device. It is a situation which uses communication to aid the client's development. Counseling is education. It aims at the enrichment of the client as formal and traditional education aims at the enrichment of the student. Counseling is a helping relationship. The counselor is the helper; the client is the helped. We'll look more at the quality of this relationship as we explore it in greater detail, but to begin this exploration, let's examine each of the purposes previously mentioned.

*Throughout this chapter we will use the term *client* to refer to the person being counseled. This is the term commonly used in the literature of counseling, and it avoids the repetition and possible confusion which may come from the term *counselee* because of its similarity to the designation *counselor*. The *counselor* is the person providing the service, whether a manager, staff specialist, or staff member with the official title of counselor.

1. Developing potential.

After reading what we have thus far said about counseling, managers might wonder why they should take time to counsel employees. If counseling is so centered about employee-clients and their needs, is it a legitimate function of the manager? Should managers take company time to counsel employees or should they instead send them to some other person or agency more properly concerned with helping people just because they need help?

There isn't a "yes" or "no" answer to that question. Certainly, clergy, social workers, and psychiatrists should help people in areas involving their professional competencies. But just as certainly, managers have their own charters to counsel within the scope of their competence and responsibility. We need people who have proved their potential, people who have shown, by growing, an ability to grow.

Many of these people with growth potential are right in our own departments. Many more could grow but don't know that they can grow, and nobody else knows that they can grow. Nobody ever took the time to discover that potential or to provide the employee with an opportunity to discover the existence of unrealized potential.

Isn't professional development the job of the personnel office? Shouldn't the company training staff give employees a test or something? Managers are responsible for running departments. Are they supposed to take the time to be guidance counselors?

A manager is responsible for the allocation and most efficient use of the resources of the firm; this includes the human resources. It would, I think, be safe to say that the majority of our employees have never had any counseling, have never had the opportunity to assess their potentials and be given assistance in developing a plan for personal development.

We have talked to our employees, but have we listened? We have given advice and told them of our plans for them, but have we counseled? We have devoted most of our time to the promising people, the *comers*, the ones who least needed our counsel. It's rewarding to counsel the comers. We can feel that we have helped them to grow, and as we watch their progress through the company, we can easily feel a warm glow of parental satisfaction. "That's my boy. I brought him along. When he first came to work for me, I saw something in him, and I worked with him . . ." That's fine. We all like to identify with success. And, of course, we should try to develop our most promising candidates. We gain a great deal of reinforcement from these developmental activities. The tragedy is that we spend most of our time developing those people who least need our help, the people who would probably grow without our help or anyone's, and we neglect the employees whose potential is less obvious. They are a challenge, and we're not sure that we're equal to it. The prospects of reward, of reinforcement, are not nearly as certain. It's much easier to write these employees off with the observation that they've reached their peaks, that they're happy where they are, and that they just want to be left alone.

In some cases, perhaps in many cases, this is true. In many other cases, there is a potential that is not self-actuating. It needs cultivation. And even with those who are happy where they are, that may be because even they are unaware of their potential. We need talent. We can't recruit enough of it to meet our needs. We're going to need more talent in the future. In the future a manager's success is going to be judged by ability to use and to develop people, human resources, in the most effective and creative ways.

Most counselors deal in the actuation of potential. Managers' roles as counselors are unique in that they can shape the environment in which their clients can pursue their development. Most other counselors must help their clients to adjust to their environments. Managerial counselors must do this too, in some cases, but in other cases, they can change the client's environment. They can shape and mold the environment of the client to make the actuation of potential more likely. They can create opportunities for growth. Of course, there are some things that cannot or should not be changed, things to which the client must adjust. But the supervisory relationship with the client gives the manager an advantage not enjoyed by other counselors.

This supervisory relationship imposes a drawback as well. Because managers can control the client's environment and destiny, they are in a position to make decisions for the client. Counseling should make it possible for clients to learn to make their own decisions more effectively; thus the manager who makes decisions for the client is not counseling. Obviously, managers must make many decisions involving their employees, and the purpose of this discussion of counseling is not to suggest a free-wheeling, *laissez-faire* administration in which everybody does as he or she pleases. The point is that managers have many functions. One of these functions is to counsel employees. In this role they should not make decisions for employees. We'll explain why later. For now let it suffice that managers are seen as people with many roles to play. The requirements of these roles cast them in several relationships with the people whom they manage. One of these roles is that of a counselor, and one of the purposes of counseling is to help employee-subordinate-clients make the most of their potentials for growth and achievement.

2. Adjusting to change.

Change is a fact of life in organizations. We hope most change is for the better, at least from the standpoint of organizational goals. Some change brings new advantages to individual employees; other change works to their disadvantage. But the reality of change and its *real* effect on the individual employee is often not the issue. The issue from the standpoint of human relations is the way in which the employee perceives the change. This perception, whether it mirrors or distorts reality, is in itself a reality.

Effective managers are realists. In addition to considering the objective realities with which they must deal, they also must consider the social realities. Many managers, however, are so schooled in the perception of objective reality that they too easily dismiss employee attitudes that don't conform to what they, the managers, perceive as reality.

Think back to the most recent incident when someone, your boss perhaps, imposed a change on you. Perhaps it meant moving to another state. Or maybe it was an additional assignment, a change in work procedures, or a different organizational relationship. Whether the change was great or small, you probably resisted it at first. Later, maybe a little later or maybe not until quite a while later, you probably accepted the change. Depending on the type of change, your need for security, and your previous relationship with the person who imposed the change, you may have tried to avoid the change. You may have tried to change the changer. Maybe you quit your job; that's the ultimate resistance to organizational change. If you didn't quit and if you were unable to avoid the change, you probably came to accept it and now it's part of the routine. If somebody now tried to change things back to the way they used to be, you might even resist that change because you are change-resisting. We all are.

Our initial reaction to a change is frequently emotional and negative. As time passes and we have a chance to think about the proposed change, we analyze the situation and react more rationally to it. Then, as we look at the change rationally, we decide to accept it or to fight it. Our decision, at that time, is more likely to be based on the merits of the proposed change rather than on the fact that someone is trying to change us.

Let's look at an example. Bob's boss has just told him that he is going to be assigned to a new job. The boss selected Bob for this assignment because he saw a good deal of potential in Bob. The new job will give Bob valuable experience and will prepare him for future promotions.

Bob accepted the promotion, but since he started the new job, his performance has suffered. He has exhibited poor morale. What is the boss going to do? Will he dismiss Bob's reaction as that of an ingrate? Many managers would. Or will he realize that Bob may not see the change as he does? Bob may feel unsure of himself in this new environment. He may want a chance to talk it over with the person who will judge his performance in this new job. Bob may be unwilling to initiate this conversation. He may feel that to do so would be to show weakness to the boss. But he may welcome the opportunity to talk if the boss provides that opportunity.

It may also have been a good idea for the boss to have had such a conversation with Bob before making the assignment. In fact, almost any situation involving change is probably a situation that should involve counseling. Counseling is often nothing more than creating an opportunity for talking things over. Counseling doesn't require a couch or a 50-minute hour or even a formal announcement that it is occurring.

3. Setting goals.

It is a cardinal principle of behavioral science that all human behavior is goal-directed. The goal, the objective, the motivation determines where we are going. Where we are going determines the route we take to get there.

We often say that phlegmatic employees have no goals. Not so. They have a goal: stability. Their actions are motivated by the maintenance of the *status quo*. They are strongly motivated to avoid making waves and to maintaining personal security.

Each of us is so involved with our own value systems that we find it difficult to understand the motivations of others. Our own motivations seem real and natural, and it's hard to understand why others don't share them. Counselors must understand and respect other motivations. They must first know themselves and their desires and needs. They must realize their patterns of personality are not universal and that other patterns are reasonable. They must realize they cannot impose their own values on others. They must strive for empathy.

An unreasonable goal promotes frustration, and frustration destroys relationships and productivity. When we establish a goal, we make an emotional investment in its realization. When we achieve it, our investment pays off. If we fail to achieve the goal, however, we lose the emotional capital we invested—we experience frustration. Each of us is familiar with the results of frustration in our own lives. Frustration hurts so much so that we will, if we are frustrated often enough, avoid setting goals so that we may avoid frustration.

Achievement has the opposite effect. When we achieve a goal, we feel rewarded, reinforced. The experience is pleasant and satisfying. We set other goals so that we may achieve the satisfaction that comes with attainment as well as the more tangible rewards that may be associated with the goal.

Reasonable goals help us achieve the satisfaction of attainment and avoid the frustration of failure. We do, however, tend to set goals without analyzing the reasonableness of those goals. In so doing, we increase the odds against attainment. It is often helpful to talk over our goals with another person who can help us to determine their reasonableness. We use the other person as a sounding board. Those who help us best allow us to set our own goals; they don't set them for us.

Goal setting is an individual matter, for each of us has our own strengths and limitations. Note the use of *limitations* rather than *weaknesses*.

This is a helpful way to look at these factors. We can accept limitations, but we tend to feel guilty about weaknesses; we tend to deny, even to ourselves, that we have them. Part of an effective goal-setting process is an inventory of our strengths and limitations as they relate to the proposed goal. A manager-counselor can be of great value to clients by encouraging them to make such inventories and by helping them to see the relationships between the results of those inventories and the reasonableness of the goals.

Employees who have often been frustrated may be unwilling to set goals for themselves. They can sometimes be brought out of this lethargy if they can be helped to realize that minor, short-term goals exist and can be achieved. If they are short-term goals, they may not require much staying power and, if achieved, may bring satisfaction and confidence to the client. Having achieved some of these goals and having reaped satisfaction from that achievement, the client may feel more ready to tackle larger, intermediate-range goals. These small achievements may help to break a pattern of frustration.

Managers should help clients assess their strengths and limitations. They should encourage the client to set reasonable goals. These goals should have at least some short-range applications. There's nothing wrong with long-range goals; they're fine. But it's difficult to see progress toward those goals. The goal seeker receives very little reinforcement and encouragement and thus may abandon the goal, even though it is not beyond reach. Of course, the case of the legendary office boy who rises to become president of the firm alters all that we have said about becoming discouraged in trying to achieve a long-term goal.

If we should be counseling a clerk who has her eye on Mahogany Row, we might be better advised to encourage her to set some intermediate goals. The presidency is likely to be a long time coming. If this young woman were to shoot for leading clerk in one year and office manager within five years, she might achieve these goals. She could at least see them within her range. Achieving the clerk position could reinforce her, give her the feelings that come with success. We should not discourage ambition, but we should encourage it by urging our clients to set steps along the way as intermediate goals so that the time between achievements will not be so long as to discourage that ambition.

Part of the process is to analyze strengths and limitations, not always in a spirit of passive acceptance. The strengths are there to capitalize on. The limitations may suggest a plan for self-development, which, after all, is merely another term for pushing back the boundaries of personal limitation. The manager-counselor is often in a position to help the client overcome many limitations by providing training, either in formal classroom courses or through work assignments; additional counseling; or assignment to special projects or committees, for example.

Limitations should be viewed creatively. They should not be seen as barriers to success but rather as conditions that will influence the kind of success to which the client may reasonably aspire.

Of course, there are many employees who may have reached their potential or who want no further advancement. It might be well to remember that people and their motivational patterns change. While we might have been quite right to put Anne in the low-potential category five years ago or even last year, she may have changed. Periodic counseling will help us to spot these changes, if we approach them with an open mind. Too often managers look upon these sessions as part of an administrative ritual. Seeing it in this light, they don't listen.

Counseling of this sort may be connected with a formal company or agency appraisal plan, or it may be conducted independently. The climate in your organization and in your own department will have to guide your decisions about re-evaluating potential.

4. Providing a setting in which clients can blow off steam or resolve misunderstandings.

Emotional pressure, the sort of pressure built up by anger or confusion, requires a safety valve. A person will have an emotional outburst without an appropriate device to release and reduce pressure. Much of this emotional pressure results from misunderstanding and from lack of opportunity to communicate.

Many managers are reluctant to allow such opportunities for communication. They feel threatened by them. They find it difficult or unpleasant to allow their employees to ventilate their feelings. They feel that their authority status should insulate them from the need to be responsive to the employees' feelings; people shouldn't question their assignments and orders; they should do what the boss tells them to do. Very few managers would express it this way; it's no longer fashionable to be authoritarian. Almost all managers would pay lip service to what they would consider a *human relations* approach, yet many fail to manifest this approach in action. A few lack the necessary skill, but the vast majority are afraid to expose themselves to their subordinates on a one-to-one basis. They are afraid to come out from behind their desks.

Managers who take this head-in-the-sand approach and avoid open communication gain nothing. Employees will express themselves. If they can't do so in conversation, they will do so in their production records or through absenteeism, the grapevine, job hunting, or any one of several other outlets that exist in any organization. None of us will tolerate this build-up of pressure within ourselves; we will ventilate our feelings; and in most cases, the least costly ventilation to manager, organization, and employee is open communication.

If you fail to communicate, people who feel that they have a right to a message from you will put words in your mouth. They'll respond to those words, and thus you'll be party to a dialogue of which you may have been completely unaware. By the time this dialogue is processed through the grapevine, you'll be amazed to hear the direct quotations ascribed to you. Don't communicate by omission and don't allow yourself to be deluded by the false assumption that you can avoid communication.

For situations which involve the build-up of pressure in employees or the clarification of confusion which plagues them, counseling offers a solution. Counseling in these situations also acts to reassure your subordinates of your recognition of them as persons. This leads us to the fifth purpose.

5. Meeting needs for security, adequacy, and response.

Did you ever feel that you were working in a vacuum, at least where the boss was concerned? How did you like that feeling? Most of us have felt this way at one time or another. The boss was not inhuman, probably just busy. Most managers are busy people. We are so busy that we find ourselves managing solely by exception; when something goes wrong, we take action to correct it. The management of things or processes can often be best handled by dealing with exceptions, by reserving our time and energy for those matters that scream for our attention. We let things go by themselves if they are going well. We haven't the time for constant checking, and experience has taught us that this constant checking is not a very productive way to spend our time.

In managing things and processes, many managers have found they can most effectively allot their time to getting things organized. Once things are organized and the work seems to be moving smoothly, they turn to other projects and return to the original project only when things foul up. Well, there are several opinions on the philosophy of management by exception. But we are concerned with the management of people. Management by exception in this sphere is not a very good idea.

I don't mean that managers should constantly look over the shoulders of their employees. No, doing this would raise havoc with the morale in any organization. What I'm getting at is the frequent complaint of many employees: "I wish that I knew how he thinks I'm doing. When something fouls up, I hear from him soon enough. And if we do an exceptional job, we get a pat on the back. But I mean in the day-to-day operation. How am I doing? What does he think of me, and of the job I'm doing? Does he even know I'm here most of the time?"

When managers are told that their employees feel this way, they often respond:

> Well what the heck do they expect? Sure I chew them out when things are fouled up, but I don't think I'm unreasonable. And, I make sure that I tell them when they've done an outstanding job. But what am I supposed

to do, go out there every day and tell them all what fine people they are? In the first place, I haven't the time, and in the second place, I'm no house mother. This is a place of business, not a clinic for emotionally immature whiners. They know when they're doing a good job; they know they'll damn well hear from me if they're not. And besides, we have an appraisal interview once a year. And besides, what would I say anyway?

We don't complain about reprimands or correction when we have fouled up. We may not like criticism, but, unless it's unduly harsh or overly public, we expect it and accept it. And, it's well that the manager reserves special comment or praise for special performance. But the vast majority of us don't foul things up very often, and we don't do a really exceptional job very often, but we do like to hear from the boss in the intervals between great successes and failures. We want to know how we are doing. No, it's more than that. We *need* to know how we are doing; we are insecure in a vacuum.

People have varying degrees of personal security. Many of us are quite confident of our ability. Others are less secure. But none of us is completely secure. Each of us needs assurance of our adequacy from time to time, some more often, others less often. Many of us are quite skillful in presenting a front of confidence and self-assurance. We are so skilled at it that we fool almost everyone, and in so doing we convince them that we don't need reassurance. And we don't get it. And we are uncomfortable without it.

We all have needs for security. We all need to know that we are adequate. We all need feedback from our boss; we all need the opportunity to give feedback to the boss. These needs cannot be satisfied in group meetings. Group meetings can do part of the job, but they must be complemented by one-to-one, face-to-face communication opportunities. And that is managerial counseling and coaching.

6. Dealing with personal problems.

Of all of the areas of counseling that we shall discuss, the personal problems of employees is the most controversial and the one about which we can say the least with any degree of confidence. The first questions that come to any discussion like this are: Should the manager be concerned with the personal problems of employees? Should the manager be concerned with employees' personal problems that have no relation to the employee's job or work performance?

Let's duck this question. Its answer is a matter of personal philosophy. Beyond that we can say sometimes yes and sometimes no. The question is, I think, philosophical, for the fact remains that regardless of whether the manager should or should not be concerned with the strictly personal problems of employees, employees will continue to have personal problems and they will continue to bring those problems to their managers. Every manager has had this happen, and I would dare say that every manager has, at one time or another, brought a personal problem to the boss.

We can divide personal problems into those related to work and those not work related. In the work-related area are those personal problems that, though they may be centered outside the work place, nonetheless have an effect on the work performance of the employee. The manager is interested in the solution of these work-related problems, though he or she may not have any hand in their solution. The manager sometimes becomes involved in personal problems because an employee is performing poorly. When the manager discusses the work performance with the employee, the personal problem comes to light.

Some people are compulsive busybodies. They love to hear of the personal problems of others; they're just plain nosy. Being nosy is a poor quality in a manager, in anybody, but particularly in a manager.

Other managers shun the personal problems of employees. When an employee introduces a personal problem into the discussion of work performance, they terminate the interview quickly with a hasty, almost embarrassed, "Well, try to work it out. I'll try to talk to you later. Right now I have to go to a meeting."

Many managers are reluctant to become involved with personal problems because they are unwilling to accept the responsibility that comes with giving advice in these personal areas. They should be. But that should not keep them from listening. One of the worst things that any counselor, particularly a manager-counselor, can do is to give advice on personal matters. But we can listen.

Do people come to us for advice? Generally not. They come to us because they want someone to listen while they try to unravel their own problem. Most of us, in fact, resent advice on personal matters.

When people have a problem, work-related or not, in most cases they also have the answer. It's somewhere inside them, but they have to dig for it. And talking is one of the ways in which they dig.

Has anyone ever come to you with a personal problem, wondering what to do? Do you recall what happened if you simply listened? The person talked about the problem, maybe decided that the real problem was something different, wondered what could be done, listed a few alternatives, considered each briefly, and then chose one as a solution. "Yeah, that's what I ought to do," the employee said. "And thanks for your help. The whole thing seems a lot clearer now. Thanks."

And you wondered what the employee was thanking you for other than for your time, because you know that you didn't offer a thing. You did, though. You offered a listener. And the employee should have been grateful, for listeners are hard to find.

For nonprofessional counselors, that's the best way to deal with personal problems: listen. You might do some good, and you'll never do any harm. When you go much beyond simply listening, you are running the risk of doing harm.

People instinctively defend themselves; they protect themselves from harm. Very often we fail to recognize a personal problem on the conscious level because we are afraid to face it. We are not yet ready to deal with it, thus we keep it hidden. A skillful prober, an astute questioner, may be able to bring this problem to the surface. But if we are not ready to deal with the problem, we shall not be in a better state for having recognized it, but we may be in a worse state. Our natural defense mechanisms kept us from having to face this problem, but if someone successfully infiltrated our defense mechanisms, we might be unable to avoid facing something we were not ready to face. The results could be quite serious.

Probing of this type, if it should be done at all, should be left to skilled clinicians. Managers, teachers, and the like who engage in this sort of probing often do immeasurable harm in spite of what may be the best of intentions. It can take surprisingly little skill to penetrate the defense mechanisms of another. It takes a great deal of skill to know how to help that person deal with the results.

But if we simply listen, clients will protect themselves. They will share only those thoughts and feelings with which they are ready to deal. They will retain their integrity while taking advantage of our function as a sounding board, as a listener.

The manager is best advised to confine intervention into the lives of employees to those matters related to the job and to leave the introduction of personal elements to the employee. Of course, it is quite true that the employee's personal life and performance on the job may be related. Financial problems, health problems, difficulties with spouses or children, excessive drinking, and the like may be reflected in poor quality of work, absenteeism, inability to get along with other workers or customers, general irritability, and the tiredness that may come from moonlighting undertaken to solve financial difficulties.

These are difficult situations. The manager must try to bring the employee to an acceptable level of performance but must also avoid being a busybody; status as a manager gives no right to invade the private life of the employee. In many cases, the manager will be aware that the personal problem exists and that it is contributing to the employee's poor performance. Should the manager raise the issue? What can the manager do?

Part of the answer must be found in the manager's relationship with the employee. Is the manager a personal friend as well as boss? If so, he or she may be able to deal more directly with the personal issues—as a friend, not as the boss, and this presents an interesting tightrope for the manager-friend to walk.

Whether friend or not, a manager can't go too far wrong by concentrating on work performance in discussions with an employee. The employee may not like being reminded of shortcomings in this area but will recognize it as a legitimate area of the manager's concern. The employee may choose to raise the personal problem in this discussion. The manager-counselor will then be in a dual role. As a manager, he or she may have to prescribe standards of conduct and performance on the job; but, as a counselor, will have to avoid doing the same for the personal aspects of the situation. Here the manager cannot prescribe and, in most cases, should not even suggest or advise. All the manager should do is listen.

THE TECHNIQUES OF COUNSELING

Counseling is basically a helping relationship centered about the needs of the client. This view of the process is obvious in therapeutic counseling, but it also characterizes managerial counseling. Counseling may achieve company goals, but to be effective it must be conducted to benefit the client.

The several schools of counseling vary in the ways in which they prescribe the active roles of client and counselor. On the one hand, the nondirective school places the counselor in a passive, catalyst role. The directive school, in contrast, assigns the major active role to the counselor. The eclectic view has the counselor vary role in accordance with the situation and the needs of the client.

Several processes occur in counseling. The situation must be analyzed. The causes must be diagnosed. Alternatives must be considered, and a course of action must be chosen. In all cases, the choice of a course of action must be left up to the client. The counselor's active role in the other areas should vary inversely with the client's ability to do these things alone. This relationship of the client's active role and the counselor's active role can be seen in Figure 15–1. The height of this rectangle represents the functions to be performed in the counseling situation. The counselor never occupies the full vertical axis. As the role of the client increases, as the client is better able to solve problems, the role of the counselor lessens. Ultimately, it should disappear as the client becomes able to assume a totally active role. Certainly not all counseling starts with the client in the dependent position represented by the extreme left of the rectangle, and the purpose of the illustration is not to suggest that. Rather, the graph is presented to emphasize the interaction of the active roles of the client and the counselor.

Even when the counselor is playing an active role, it should be a teaching role. The goal of counseling is not the solution of the client's problem. The goal is to teach the client how to solve problems.

If the goal were merely to solve the problem, then the counselor's

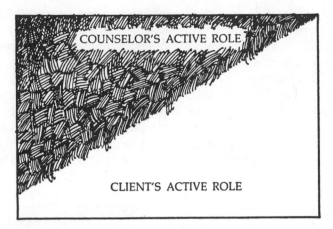

COUNSELOR'S ACTIVE ROLE

CLIENT'S ACTIVE ROLE

Figure 15–1

function would be to listen to the problem and then to suggest the solution. The counselor, if skillful enough, would take care of the problem. But what would happen when another problem arose? The client would be back to the counselor looking for another solution. The solution to the first problem would not have assisted development at all. The client would become increasingly dependent on the manager-counselor. Many managers and many counselors foster this type of counseling relationship. Some do so because they are under the mistaken impression that they are helping people by solving their problems for them; these counselors are sincerely motivated to help the client. Others do so because they like to have people dependent on them. This kind of counseling gives them a great degree of control over people, feeds the managerial ego, and creates a feeling of self-importance. It raises hell with the clients, for it is not in the nature of a healthy adult to be dependent upon a manager. Dependency is the easy way out, but it really does nothing to promote personal security.

The counselor's contribution should be to teach and help the client toward self-development and independence. Managers who feel that they must create dependencies need to examine their own motives very closely.

In a given situation, the counselor's active role may include analysis of the problem, diagnosis of its causes, and suggestion and consideration of alternatives and their consequences. To be of maximum benefit to the client, the counselor should teach. As the counselor analyzes, the client should be learning to analyze; as the counselor diagnoses causes, the client should be learning to diagnose causes; as the counselor helps the client to develop alternatives, the client should be learning to develop alternatives; the counselor should then help the client to consider the consequences. In all cases, the decision as to which alternative will be chosen should be left to the client.

One question frequently raised by managers with whom I have discussed this view of counseling is: "Suppose that an employee makes the wrong decision—and that I know at the time that it's the wrong decision, I certainly can't allow that decision, can I?"

Yes, you can. If the decision would harm the organization, you may, as a manager, have to prevent it. But if the decision is chiefly concerned with the employee you can allow what you feel would be a wrong decision. You can suggest the consequences of this decision, but if the client persists in it, it is, after all, this employee's decision, and he or she must accept the responsibility, the rewards, and the consequences of that decision. To make a decision for the employee is to deny him or her responsibility for adulthood. Of course, the employee may not allow you to make decisions— but, on the other hand, may ask you to or at least be quite relieved when you urge or recommend a choice. When you do this, it becomes your decision. You bear the consequences of it and the responsibility for it.

For how many lives can anyone be responsible? Most of us have trouble taking care of our own. We can help others, but we can't take over for them. Many managers have tried to avoid counseling and coaching employees just because of this; they feel that they are assuming too much responsibility. This will not be so if they simply counsel. It will be so if they advise or direct in matters of development, but not so if they help others to learn to solve their own problems and to make their own decisions.

Nonverbal communication in counseling.

Much of our attention has been focused on verbal communication, since we first learned to communicate and to understand the messages of others. But we have all become aware of the part which nonverbal communications, messages without words, play in the dynamic system through which human beings exchange ideas and feelings. The counselor must sharpen skills in interpreting nonverbal messages. We must be aware not only of what is said but of how it is said. We must be aware of what is not said. We must look to the whole communication, verbal and nonverbal, to find a pattern of meaning.

Nonverbal communication is, of course, a two-way street. Clients can perceive the nonverbal behavior of counselors and will add meaning to it. Thus, in addition to developing a sensitivity to the nonverbal behavior of others, counselors must be careful to control their own behavior, particularly when it might seem to connote impatience, value judgment, hostility, disinterest, approval, or threat.

The most effective counseling is, in many cases, listening, and the most effective listening is nonevaluative. Effective listeners neither agree nor disagree with people. They say, verbally and nonverbally, "I'm trying to understand you and what you say. I'm listening. I'm still with you."

When counselors express agreement or approval, they build dependency. When they express disagreement or disapproval, they stimulate defensiveness or hostility. When counselors indicate understanding and acceptance, they establish the base for meaningful communication.

When people are face to face, there is potential meaning to every act and lack of action. Many inexperienced counselors have difficulty dealing with the nonverbal aspects of counseling. The most bothersome nonverbal phenomenon is silence. Silence, pause, is a natural part of any conversation. In casual conversation, we accept pauses without attaching any special significance to them. But when we must communicate in any formal setting, from public speaking and conferences to interviewing and counseling, we fear silence. We feel that we must fill in the gap with a comment, a question, or a restatement. We suffer silence poorly; it makes us uncomfortable. In reality, pauses are natural. We pause when we have said all that we want to say. We pause when we feel that we have said more than we want to say, when we feel that we may have shown too much of ourselves and we want a moment to reflect on it and on the listener's reaction to what we have said. We pause to organize our thoughts and feelings. We pause to invite a reaction. We pause to try to force the listener to take the burden of the conversation, and we pause because we are unable to find the words to express what we want to say.

Allowing a pause to occur naturally provides both client and counselor with an opportunity to recapitulate what has gone before. Clients pause to think, to reflect on what they have said, to organize their thoughts and feelings, and to search for the words to express themselves. Some counselors will, in a situation like this, try to fill in the gap by supplying the words for clients. Clients may allow counselors to do this. It takes the burden away from them. But the words that counselors supply may not be the right words. The words supplied by counselors may reflect their own feelings and judgments, and the counselors' evaluations have no part in the processes by which clients express themselves. The sense of urgency which the counselors emit as they fill in pauses often charges the atmosphere and makes it difficult for either counselor or client to relax. And a tense counselor is of little value. Effective counselors must remain as calm as possible.

Nonverbal behavior is an essential part of counseling. Counselors must be aware of the client's nonverbal messages but must control their own. It is difficult for us to verbalize, to put into words, many of our feelings. Verbalization is basically an expression of the intellect and our conscious thoughts. The emotions we communicate nonverbally.

It's quite easy to confuse nonverbal messages. People have few ways of showing emotion. We laugh, cry, blush, perspire, twitch, stammer, and become visibly excited in a very few ways. When happy, very happy, we dance around in a physical outpouring of joy; when angry, very angry, we are "hopping mad." When very happy, we may cry; yet our tears may also flow when we are sad. When happy, we laugh, yet laughter may signal depression.

The total meaning of a statement must come from an integration of the verbal and nonverbal behavior of the client, and the counselor's search for meaning must take into account all information. The counselor should listen with an understanding ear. In this regard, as in all others concerning counseling and indeed concerning all communication, a desire to understand, to accept, and to be of help is of greater value than any technique, if we confine our counseling to those areas where an understanding manager can help.

A manager has an obligation to keep in confidence anything which an employee offers in confidence. Managers may act to keep from hearing in confidence those things which cannot be kept in confidence, but if they do not do so and an employee-client says something in the expectation that it will be kept in confidence, then managers must protect the employee's privacy. People are in turn managers and subordinates, but they are primarily people. And a person has a sense of responsibility to others.

An effective counselor is acceptive and reasonably permissive. In dealing with employees in a counseling situation, the effective counselor plays down the status differential that separates manager and subordinate. Counseling is above all else a chance to talk things over, a chance to say what's on your mind. If one must watch each word and surround oneself with defenses, one cannot express oneself. A client must be free to let off steam or to express gripes.

Effective manager-counselors must be personally secure, or at least be able to see beyond their own insecurities, for it is doubtful that anyone is ever totally secure. To counsel effectively, one first must have achieved self-respect and self-understanding. We should know our own needs, our own attitudes, and our own biases. We should know our own frustrations. We should avoid confusing our own personalities with those of the clients. If we do not know ourselves, there is great likelihood that we shall see ourselves in our clients and that we shall project our own goals, needs, desires, and even our guilts onto the client. And if our clients come to see themselves in our reflection of them, they will leave us more confused than when they came.

Many manager-counselors, particularly those with dominant personalities, have tried, and some have appeared to succeed, to shape the client to their own image and likeness. Others have done so without consciously trying. These men and women have counseled to conformity and in so doing have produced employee-clients who, on the surface, appear to be much like themselves, but who, within themselves, feel the pressures that have forced them into molds into which they cannot comfortably fit. Each human being is unique, though he or she may be like others in many ways. Each unique personality has its own goals, needs, desires, frustrations, and patterns of motivation. Thoreau summed this up quite eloquently: "If a man does not keep pace with his companions, perhaps it is because he hears a different drummer. Let him step to the music which he hears, however measured or far away."

The counselor should be neither a drummer nor a music critic. Counselors should, however, know the tunes which make them march. They cannot help others nor respect or accept them until they have accepted themselves. Counselors must realize that they are emotionally involved with the clients they counsel; they must be aware of their own humanity. And, just as they must avoid projecting their own personalities on clients, so must they avoid identifying with clients and their problems. Counselors must control their involvement. The problems must remain the client's problems. When counselors come to think of it as "our problem," then they limit their usefulness.

Counselors must understand their own motivations in the counseling process. Do we counsel to help the client or do we do so because it makes us feel parental? With whose needs are we primarily concerned? Counselors must ask themselves this question often, and must answer truthfully. When counselors' own needs are the primary concern, then clients become foils, and counselors are in danger of deliberately structuring dependency relationships.

Counselors must avoid being busybodies, insinuating themselves into the problems and personalities of others, compulsively involving themselves in other people's lives for the satisfaction of their own needs. Effective counseling must revolve around the needs of clients and must promote their development. Any other counseling is fraud.

Certainly, counselors will experience satisfaction from their activities. This is good, for unless our activities receive some positive reinforcement, we are not likely to continue them. The question is one of determining the primary beneficiary of the counseling; to whose development does it contribute?

Some counseling tips.

1. Listen.
We have repeatedly stressed the importance of listening. It's impossible to overstress the importance of listening in face-to-face communication. Good counseling is often nothing more than good listening.

2. Don't play psychiatrist.
Most managers would probably hesitate to perform surgery on their employees, but many have tried to indulge in the sort of bloodless neurosurgery that is best described as pop-psych. Pop-psych is a good deal

more dangerous than unlicensed surgery. Employees can see when you are coming with a knife and can defend themselves, but pop-psych is subliminal and clients may well be unaware of what is going on.

If you always wanted to be a doctor, or if your mother always wanted you to be a doctor, then quit your job and go to medical school, but don't try to satisfy this yearning by taking up psychiatry as a hobby.

Avoid interpreting the client's motivations. Avoid symbolic interpretation of all kinds, or at least avoid expressing these interpretations to the client.

Don't lead clients. Let them express themselves in their own ways. When we lead the expressions of another, we most often find that we are projecting our own problems, weaknesses, guilts, and motivations.

3. Don't be a busybody.

Avoid crude interference in the lives of others. The fact that you manage a person does not give you any rights to invade privacy. Be available, but don't be unnecessarily intrusive. If an employee's performance compels you to speak to him or her, concentrate on performance.

4. Know yourself.

Polonious' oft-quoted advice to his son, "To thine own self be true . . . Thou canst not then be false to any man," has a place here. It's quite easy to confuse our own motivations with those of our clients. Before we counsel another, it would be well that we know ourselves, our motivations, our goals, our desires, our frustrations, our guilts, our fears, our biases and prejudices, and our needs. We may not be able to resolve all these facets of our personality, but if we are consciously aware of them, we are less likely to impose our own personalities on those of the client. We are less likely to try to live our lives over again through those whom we counsel.

5. Be reliable.

Make sure that the information you pass on to the client is valid. Don't guess; know. If necessary, verify before you communicate. Be personally reliable. Respect confidences, and once you have undertaken to counsel an employee, see it through to the end. Allow the client to terminate the counseling.

It's easy to become impatient. Often counselors feel that they can see the solution to the problem when the client cannot. The counselor becomes impatient and tends to push the client aside. The client begins to seem dull and the problem interminable. This situation calls for empathy, for an understanding of the client's view. Curtness has no place here.

6. *If counseling bothers you, don't counsel.*

If you find other people's problems utterly boring and find the process of counseling distasteful, you probably cannot avoid communicating this to your employees. This limits your effectiveness as a counselor.

If you tend to identify with or to become overly involved with the problems of other people, then you should, for your own sake as well as theirs, avoid counseling, for to be of help to your client, you must remain outside the problem. Once you lose your objectivity, your value as a counselor decreases markedly if not entirely.

But, if you can retain your objectivity and control your identification, if you can listen in a spirit of helpful empathy, and if you can maintain an interest in the development of your subordinates, then you can experience the satisfaction of helping in the development of other people through meaningful face-to-face communication.

COUNSELING AS A TEAM ENDEAVOR

Often, an employee's most readily available source of counsel is the manager, but often it is necessary to go beyond the department for specialized counseling. Some organizations have a formal employee counseling structure; in others it is less formal. Normally, specialized help should be available, either in-house or by referral, in several areas: occupational specialists, educational specialists, personnel specialists, clinical specialists.

Occupational and personnel counselors can usually be found in most personnel offices. Organizations too small to employ people full time in these capacities usually have consultants in these areas.

Educational specialists can usually be found in the training department. If the company has no training department or if more specialized information is desired, then local schools and colleges that have part-time programs for adults will provide counseling for students and prospective students. In addition, most universities have a testing and counseling center which can provide detailed educational and career counseling.

Clinical specialists in psychiatry are normally not on the payroll of most organizations. Referral to these specialists can be obtained from the medical department or medical consultant, local hospitals or community mental health organizations, or the state or local medical association.

Effective managerial counselors know their limitations and abilities. They do not rush each client off to a specialist, nor do they refrain from referral when it is called for. Referrals should not be made casually. When one refers a client to a specialized source of counsel, one retains responsibility; one must be sure that the resource to which the client is referred is skilled and reliable. The effective counselor will take the time to check out referral resources before suggesting them to clients. Take the time to investigate the available resources; get to know them and their capabilities. Find out the kinds of problems with which they can be of greatest help.

Effective counseling can be greatly facilitated if the managerial counselor, the most common first source of help, knows the available referral resources and makes intelligent use of them.

A FINAL NOTE

Effective managerial counseling can be the most important resource an organization has to develop its employees. A manager who is willing to listen, a manager who can achieve empathy and recognize the reality and validity of other points of view will be better able to manage the human resources of the organization.

Counseling need not be seen as *head shrinking or hand holding*. Counseling is not coddling; it is not an indication of softness. Effective counseling is strong and vital when conducted by managers who are able to respect themselves and their employees.

Counseling has been traditionally seen as an interaction between a skilled, objective, uninvolved, emotionally detached outsider and a client. The manager may be none of these things. Preparation for management may not have included the development of skill in counseling. The managers' objectivity may be obscured by involvement with the client in other manager-subordinate relationships. And then there is the problem of status differential and the authority relationship of the manager-counselor to the subordinate-client. This relationship may impede free and open communication. Yet, we know that meaningful two-way communication is necessary for the effective coordination of organizational activity. Certainly, some problems must be handled outside the manager-subordinate relationship, but it does not necessarily hold true that because managers are part of the problems, they must be ruled out as counselors. They may, indeed, be the most effective counselors if they are willing to listen non-defensively and if they are secure enough to do so.

The outsider who counsels is concerned with helping clients to adjust to their situations, to solve problems, or to achieve goals within the context of an existing situation. The outside counselor can seldom do anything to affect the environment within which the client must function. Outside counselors seldom have to change themselves.

The manager-counselor, while trying to help the client adjust to the environment of an existing situation, may also have the power to change the environment in which the client may function. Through work assignments and other managerial prerogatives the manager may create opportunities for development or mitigate the pressures under which the client functions. Manager-counselors may gain new insights into their own impact on their subordinates, they may find it desirable to change their own attitudes or behaviors.

Managerial counseling can be most rewarding in terms of human satisfaction and increased managerial effectiveness. The effective manager is an effective communicator, and counseling offers opportunities for sincere, real communication.

16
Meetings and Conferences

Many people resent the time they spend in meetings because so many of them are poorly planned and conducted. They waste valuable time. Take many Monday Morning Meetings, for instance. Why are they held? Because it's Monday morning, and we always have a meeting on Monday morning. A meeting needs a better purpose than its periodic recurrence on the calendar. A meeting needs a purpose, and all of the people at the meeting need to know that purpose. If they don't, then they can't contribute effectively and intelligently to that purpose, and they are going to feel they are wasting their time.

All participants should have an advance copy of the agenda so they come to the meeting prepared to contribute. All too often, meetings have to be recessed while someone goes to get information that could have been brought had he or she known what was going to be discussed. It's the leader's job to see that this advance word goes out, but if the leader fails to do so, then an effective meeting participant should ask what's going to be discussed and suggest that everyone else get the same information.

People should be invited to meetings because of their potential to contribute to the meeting's purpose. Unfortunately, many people are invited according to status or even custom. A potential participant who is invited to a meeting on one of these bases should suggest that he or she be left out of that meeting and others like it. That could amount to organizational *hara-kiri* in some groups, but it would produce better meetings in organizations mature enough to hold effective meetings.

Noncontributors at a meeting are not neutral; they are a negative force leading to inertia in the dynamics of the meeting. To have an effective meeting, it's important that the leader and each participant take a creative initiative from the setting of purpose to the sending of the minutes.

An insecure leader might feel threatened by an "upstart" participant who offered suggestions. And if the conference leader is obviously insecure, it might be best to avoid becoming involved in any of these ways. But a good suggestion tactfully made to a capable and reasonably secure conference leader can greatly improve the meetings you attend. Thus, you and your colleagues will be able to make better use of your meeting time.

Conferences are useful for several things:

1. Getting the word out.
2. Resolving interpersonal or interdepartmental grievances or problems.
3. Bringing together different viewpoints and experiences to solve problems.
4. Defining problems.
5. Providing a setting for internal communication.
6. Stimulating the creative flow of ideas. Conferences are not useful for making decisions.

Useful or not, conferences are often called to:

1. Assemble a captive audience.
2. Communicate the power structure.
3. Spread the blame in case something goes wrong.
4. Give the participants their social kicks.

Conferences are useful for getting the word out to many people at the same time, but they are also more expensive than written messages, which can serve the same purpose. (Consider the sum of the hourly salaries of the people who are attending the meeting multiplied by the number of hours the meeting takes.) But meetings offer advantages that written messages can't give: two-way communication and persuasion.

People at meetings can ask questions, and if the topic to be discussed is new or involves change, two-way communication allows an opportunity to clear up misunderstandings. Oral communication is more persuasive than written. In fact, face-to-face communication in a small group is even more persuasive than oral communication in a larger meeting.

So, to spread the word should you decide on a meeting, a memorandum, or a conversation? That depends on your purpose, your subject, and group feeling about the situation. If it's a simple message that doesn't involve any need for two-way communication or if cost is a major factor, send out the word in writing. If two-way communication or persuasion are important, call a meeting. If persuasion is of extreme importance and cost is no object, then choose the small group sessions. Of course, it's possible to combine these methods. First, you could send written background information and explanations to a group of people. The next step might involve a meeting with a brief presentation, but with the rest of the time devoted to two-way interchange for questions, clarification, or discussion of objections. The third phase could be a series of individual meetings. Writing up the information would reduce the meeting time, and the combination of the written material and the meeting would pave the way for persuasive and individualized face-to-face sessions.

This technique is frequently used to sell a product or an idea, and it can be quite successful. Land development companies have developed this technique into a ritual. First, they use direct-mail solicitations, giving some attractive details and inviting the prospect to a free dinner. At the dinner meeting, the prospects are given the chief pitch, which sometimes includes an offer of a free weekend at the property site. The third phase is the persuasive face-to-face closer.

Don't assume that this scheme is suited only to land deals, however. If you have to persuade or inform a large group, a two- or three-step approach involving written material and group or individual meetings can be effective.

Not all meetings, of course, are held to spread information. More are held to bring people together for discussing or defining problems. Most organizations consist of a few generalists and many specialists. Many organizational problems require the assembly of different experiences and different viewpoints, and bringing these together means a meeting. Meetings discuss problem areas and attempt to define problems that can be solved. One person alone might attempt to solve the problems but would be limited by specialization and incomplete knowledge. If a meeting is to be effective, then, it must be conducted so that each participant who has something to contribute can do so.

Group thinking can be an important vehicle for the defining and solving of organizational problems. But so can individual thinking. A well-planned meeting will allow opportunity for both to occur and for the benefits of both to be brought to bear on the problem. Solving organizational problems is best done in three stages:

1. Briefing.
2. Individual thinking.
3. Group meeting.

The problem-solving or problem-defining process should start with a briefing of all of the participants. It can take the form of an oral presentation at a meeting or a written report on the background of the situation. The briefing should include as much information as can be provided to help the participants understand the problem they will be asked to deal with.

Following this briefing, enough time should be allowed for each participant to let ideas incubate a while and for each to develop ideas without distractions or interference.

LEADING A MEETING

Leadership is more than *charisma*, more than the force of personality. A good conference leader, like a good orchestra conductor, does most of the work beforehand. A good conference leader does much of the work after the meeting as well. I've stressed the importance of preparation, and that's certainly something a good conference leader will attend to. Preparation for most meetings will involve the following:

1. Define the purpose for the meeting.
2. Select the participants.
3. Prepare an agenda.
4. Decide whether or not a briefing is necessary, and prepare one if it is.
5. Notify the participants.
6. Prepare the facilities.

Two steps remain after the preparation:

7. Conduct the meeting.
8. Follow up the ideas that are generated and the action that's assigned.

Let's examine these steps individually.

Define the purpose for the meeting.
A meeting should be a purposeful gathering. As leader of the conference, you should determine what that purpose is and ask yourself if a meeting will help you to achieve that purpose. If the purpose is to disseminate information, can it be done by distributing simpler, less expensive written material?

If the purpose is to define or to solve a problem, what specifically is the problem? Is its scope narrow enough to permit creative action by a group?

Choose a purpose the group is likely to deal with effectively. Of course, if you pick a subject that is too broad, the group may change the purpose of the meeting after it starts. If that seems a good idea, don't fight it. Your purpose isn't sacred, and if the group finds a more productive way to spend its time, let it happen. For example, suppose your original purpose for the meeting was to discuss ways to make the company more profitable. Sometime during the meeting someone says, "This seems awfully broad. Why don't we focus on just one way to increase profits today—say we discuss ways to make best use of subcontractors?" You could then ask the group if that purpose suits them. If it does, there is no reason not to follow the suggestion.

We sometimes make a fetish of the democratic process, however, by assuming that any good conference leader will accept every suggestion from the group and that a totalitarian would reject something that came from the group. That isn't so. It is true that you shouldn't silence anybody with your gavel; that's the fastest way to stifle all participation. But in the previous situation, you could, if it seemed wise, reject the suggestion to limit the agenda. You might do so with comments like these:

> I see what you mean, Dale; these are pretty broad areas we're getting into, and we could work more productively if we tackled something as narrow as the subcontractor issue. But since this is our first meeting, perhaps we should spend some time just listing the areas in which profitability could be improved. It looks as if we're going to have more to talk about than can be handled today.

> Suppose we try this. Let's list as many problem areas as we can right now. We'll arrange to meet later on the specific issues. If we have time before lunch today, Dale, maybe we can start talking about the subs. If not, why don't you arrange a meeting for first thing next week with all of the people who are concerned with the subs? I'll plan to be there too.

Putting your rejection that way tells the group that you're going to stick to your agenda but that you recognize the worth of the suggestion and are willing to deal with it. No one should feel turned off. And maybe many people who came to the meeting to talk about their own ideas rather than about subcontractors will stay interested.

There's nothing wrong with changing the purpose or the agenda of a meeting while the meeting's in progress; but if people came prepared to deal with the original purpose, they may resent the change unless it is obvious that it is a change for the better.

Select the participants.

Once your purpose is set in your mind or on your scratch pad, you can start to select the participants. Who in the organization (or out of it, if necessary) is most likely to contribute to the purpose of the meeting? How are the participants likely to work together? You'll want them to function as a cohesive group, so it's important to select people who can work together.

Prepare an agenda.

A meeting should not be a rigidly organized discussion directed by the chair constantly gaveling participants out of order. However, there should be some planned direction to keep the discussion from wandering off on one tangent and another. Participants should have some idea in advance of what the meeting will cover so that they can prepare to contribute. As we noted before, the agenda can be changed at the meeting if there is good reason to do so, but since the meeting should begin with a stated purpose, it helps the participants to know in advance what the purpose is and how it will be pursued.

Put the agenda in writing and send a copy to each participant well before the meeting.

Decide whether a briefing is necessary.

Sometimes the participants will be familiar with the subject. Their daily work or common experience may have already brought them in contact with it. At other times they may not have sufficient background information to enable them to prepare for the meeting. If the latter is true of the group for your meeting, plan for a briefing. It can take the form of a written briefing to accompany the agenda; it can be an oral presentation given at the opening of the meeting; or it can consist of individual briefings for just those participants who require the information.

As you decide whom to brief and what to brief them on, remember that the quality of participation will depend in part on the quality of preparation. And briefing, where necessary, allows the participants to prepare for the meeting.

Notify the participants.

The agenda can do this, or you can do it personally. If it is necessary to solicit participation, let each prospective participant know what the purpose of the meeting is, what can be accomplished, and why you have chosen him or her.

Let your participants know when the meeting will begin and end and give them a realistic estimate of how much of their time the meeting, its preparation, and its follow-up will take. Once you've done this, stick to the schedule. Begin your meeting on time. People don't like to hang around. End it on time. Your participants have planned other parts of their day around your meeting; don't force them to reschedule other things because your meeting runs late. You won't have trouble getting people to come to your meetings if you earn a reputation for starting and ending on time.

Your notification should also include a list of participants so that all participants will know who is attending. A meeting should have as few surprises as possible.

Conduct the meeting.

Your meeting is being held to give the participants a chance to contribute their combined talents and ideas to the subject under discussion. Your job as conference leader is to make this possible—more than that, to make it happen.

When you are giving a presentation, your role is paramount. *You* must share *your* ideas with the audience. *You* provide most of the content of the meeting at which you give a presentation. But your role at a conference meeting is another matter. For a successful conference, you should provide as little of the content as possible. As conference leader, you have an opportunity to dominate and to influence the thinking and the expression of the participants. Don't do it.

If you want a successful conference, allow the group members to make the maximum contribution. Make sure that each member has the opportunity for expression. It's never a good idea to force someone to contribute, however. Doing this embarrasses the person and makes everyone else uncomfortable.

You should avoid dominating the meeting yourself, however, and you should try to prevent anyone else from doing so. But remember that a successful meeting isn't one in which everyone says the same number of words. Some people will say more and speak more often than others. That's fine. In fact, one person might make most of the verbal contribution. That's fine too. What isn't acceptable is the situation in which one or more participants are not given a chance to speak. You don't want to run a meeting by Robert's Rules in most cases. That's far too formal, and you want to encourage free discussion. There is no need for all remarks to be addressed to you or for you to give formal recognition before someone can take the floor. Still, you should interrupt any monologues, perhaps by inquiring if anyone else has any thoughts to contribute.

While you don't want to interrupt the free flow of ideas, you should make sure participants have the chance to finish what they want to say. Many people will handle interruptions themselves, but if your participants should have difficulty expressing themselves, you should cut the interrupter off to allow the speaker to finish.

It's also your job to keep the meeting on the track. If the group wanders off the subject into an unproductive area, gently bring them back by reminding them of the subject under discussion. If another subject seems to interest them and if that subject is worthy of pursuit, you can tell the group that it will be discussed later.

It is usually unwise to give your own viewpoint too early in the meeting. It is not a good idea for you to introduce the subject and then immediately offer your own suggestions. This preconditions the participants' responses to the topic. You, of course, are a participant as well as a leader, and you have every right to offer your thoughts. But wait until the others have had a chance to express their ideas before you do so. Avoid judging the contributions of the other participants. If someone suggests an idea, reserve your own comment on it; instead ask the group to comment on the suggestion. Don't set yourself up as judge or supreme authority. That's bound to inhibit participation.

A very important job for you as leader (and for every participant as well) is listening. Stay alert and listen actively. If the real issue is being hidden by the words being spoken, state the real issue. If there's disagreement, let it happen. A meeting doesn't have to be an exercise in harmony, and debating the issues can be an excellent way to explore them. But try to listen well enough to identify the issues. Listen to identify points of agreement, too, and bring them to the attention of the group. Identify the real areas of disagreement and try to keep the discussion productively focused on them.

Listen actively and listen for meaning. If no one else is listening actively, a common occurrence, you can help to make the meeting more productive by sharing with the group the results of your listening. Follow up ideas and actions. Your first task following the meeting is to prepare and distribute the minutes. If a secretary has taken notes at the meeting, ask for a rough draft of the minutes. Look the minutes over before they are prepared in final form. Have all action items been included? Have all points of view been represented and summarized fairly? When you are sure that the minutes honestly represent what went on at the meeting, send them out to the participants.

Many people are reluctant to go to meetings because they feel a sense of incompleteness when the meeting is over. They've discussed a topic; they've made suggestions; they've become interested; they've given their time, their ideas, and their interest. And they never hear another word about what happened to the ideas, the subject, and the momentum that were generated. They feel as though their time had been wasted. As conference leader, it's your job to see that this doesn't happen. Follow up with the participants. Let them know the results of the meeting.

If there's to be another meeting in the near future, you can begin it by telling the participants what has occurred since the last meeting and by giving them a status report on items still in progress.

But what if there's no second meeting? Not all situations call for a second conference. In that case, it's your responsibility to get the word out to your participants. Let them know what happened. Let them know the results of their contributions and of their interest. Do it by mail, by phone, or face to face, but do it. Following-up is an important part of your job as conference leader, and it's a good way to insure that you'll have willing participants if you ever want to conduct another meeting.

PARTICIPATING IN A MEETING

Like the conference leader, the participants have duties before, during, and after the meeting. Their duties before the meeting are to prepare themselves to participate productively.

The first step is self-selection. People are invited to meetings for a number of reasons, not all of them valid. The first question to ask yourself is whether or not you can contribute to the meeting. If you feel you can't, you ought to suggest that to the person who invites you. If there's a good reason for participating (or if your boss tells you to participate), then by all means go.

Day in and day out, people go to meetings and then complain about their being a waste of time. To whom do they complain? Usually to their coworkers at lunch or back in the office. If they would register their complaints with the people in charge of the meetings, things might change. Perhaps the leader of the meeting invited the reluctant participant in fear that feelings would be hurt if he or she were left out.

If you're going to a meeting, get ready for it. Look over the agenda and think about the contributions you might make. Prepare any material that you might need to take with you. Many meetings are held up because a participant announces, "I think I have some information on that in my office. Wait a few minutes and I'll get it." Of course, there are times when you can't anticipate a need, but there are more times when you can. Do so whenever possible.

Prepare for a meeting. If you think that you'll be presenting data at a meeting, make sure they're in their best form. Don't present an assumption or an opinion when you could make it a fact by taking the time to verify data before the meeting.

If you have some data that you think may be useful and interesting to the other participants, take copies along. If your review of the agenda suggests other items that should be included on the agenda, suggest them to the conference leader. They may have been intentionally excluded or overlooked—and might be welcome.

If you agree to attend a meeting, note it on your calendar, and be sure to keep that time free. If your participation is important, the meeting cannot proceed as well without you.

You have three duties at the meeting: to think, to speak, and to listen. Most meetings have enough speaking. Unsuccessful ones have a pronounced lack of thinking and listening.

There are no rules for the amount of vocal participation that you should allow yourself. You can't be said to "talk too much" as long as you are contributing every time you speak and as long as your speaking doesn't deny others the opportunity to express themselves. Keep your comments as relevant and as concise as possible, consistent with clarity and effectiveness.

Obviously, if you have nothing to contribute, you should be quiet; don't talk just to hear yourself. And don't feel that you should talk so that others will know you're there. If you don't feel that you have anything to say, keep quiet. You can still think and listen. And if your thinking and listening suggest something that you can contribute, do so. If not, keep thinking and listening.

But if you have something to contribute, talk. And if you have a lot to contribute, talk a lot. Just make sure that you allow others with something to contribute the opportunity to do so.

You have two follow-up duties:

1. If you have accepted responsibility for any action items, take action promptly.
2. You went to the meeting to share ideas. Your thinking doesn't stop when the meeting ends. If an idea occurs to you after the meeting has been adjourned—the next day, perhaps, or even a week later—tell somebody about it. Tell the conference leader or another participant who may be following up on your idea.

One final note on your participation. Some people are reluctant to suggest ideas at meetings. They are afraid that in the dynamic atmosphere of the meeting, the Important People may forget whose idea it was. They prefer to buttonhole the Most Important Person after the meeting and to make their suggestion then, when they can be assured full credit. That's a most unproductive strategy, for if the idea were raised at the meeting, it might have been combined with other ideas to produce an even better idea. Or it might, when exposed to other viewpoints and experiences, have been refined and improved. Don't worry about credit. If you are competent and if you contribute your share to the meetings that you attend, you'll be rewarded. There's no limit to what can be done as long as it doesn't matter who gets the credit.

17
Foundations of Professional Reading

When you read, read actively. Like listening, reading appears to be a passive form of communication. But like effective listening, effective reading is active. To read effectively, think along *with* the writer. Read with purpose; read for what you can get out of the reading; read for useful ideas and information.

How do you feel when you've finished reading something from your in basket, satisfied or relieved? If you feel just relieved, then you probably aren't getting what you should from your reading. Do you read with purpose? Do you know what the writing is about? Do you have an idea of what you might do with the information you may get? Do you know why you read a particular piece? Or do you read because you're afraid not to?

Good readers have many reading styles. They read purposefully and questioningly. They have different questions for different purposes. Some things they read quickly; others, slowly. But before they read, they determine purpose. Only then do they select their reading tools. And with that purpose in mind, they apply those tools to get the most from their reading—their active, purposeful reading.

You should know what you are reading and what probable use you may have for the ideas or information. Note the word *probable*. It's there to include purposes other than immediate purposes. Sure, you may not have a specific immediate use for the information, but it should relate to an area in which you have specific professional interest. Effective readers don't feel that they have a license to read everything that *might possibly someday* be helpful. *Might* and *possibly* and *someday* are the words of the ineffective reader with the bulging briefcase who is afraid not to read everything. So, be honest with yourself. Have you a probable use for what you read? This question can help you to become a better reader. Don't duck it. Ask it and answer it truthfully.

PREREADING

Prereading, or previewing as it is sometimes called, simply means looking over the material before reading. If you saw the preview of a movie, you would learn who had made the film and who the stars were. You would know whether it was a musical, western, mystery, satire, farce, comedy, documentary, or drama. You would know whether it dealt with contemporary or historical subjects. You would know whether or not you would bring your children to see it. You might decide whether it was worth seeing or not. And, if it was, whether you should make a trip into the city now to see it or whether you will wait until it comes to a local theater or to television. You would know many things about the picture from the preview.

There is an important difference between the movie preview and your prereading. The preview was made by someone who wants to persuade you to see the film. It accentuates the positive and eliminates the negative. *You* control your own prereading. You don't have the things that you preview selected for you.

A prereading of business documents helps you to manage your reading because it helps you to answer several questions. It gives you an idea of the general content and organization, a conceptual framework, and an advance sampling of layout and style. It prepares you to work with the writer in developing ideas. Prereading gives you an indication of the parts that should be skimmed or skipped and of those that should command greatest attention. Prereading helps you to delegate some of your reading.

Prereading allows you to divide the pile on your desk into five smaller piles.

The first pile contains documents that should be discarded. Your preview has indicated that these pieces are not likely to be helpful to you or your subordinates, superiors, or associates now or in the future.

The second category includes those pieces that should be read by someone else more directly concerned with the subject or by someone with a more appropriate background.

In the third category are those pieces that should be filed away for later reading. All that you need to know now is:

1. That the document exists.
2. The general subject with which it deals.
3. Whether it deals with new matter or cancels or changes old matter.
4. Where it is filed.

A cursory prereading is all you need to get this information. A more detailed reading at this time would not be productive, since you will have to read the document in the future when you need to use it. Yet, many managers waste time in reading everything completely when they receive it. They are afraid not to read every word. It's this fear that bulges briefcases.

The fourth category contains pieces which must be read for general information now. Read them with the same speed and attitude with which you read a newspaper. Don't try to memorize each detail.

The fifth category contains those pieces that must be read in detail now. This category calls for careful, detailed, analytical reading. The pieces in this fifth category are the most time-consuming. But, this pile should be the smallest. Because you have managed your other reading, you should have more time for this fifth pile.

Prereading techniques vary with the types of reading materials. Since your own pile of reading is unique, you'll want to develop your own style, but the following techniques will help you to develop your own system of prereading.

Prereading books.

1. Examine the title.

The title tells what the book is about. But a moment's reflection may give the author's viewpoint.

2. Note the author's name and other data accompanying the name.

This information may be on the title page, in the foreword, or on the dust jacket. Learn the author's qualifications on the subject. If the author's affiliations are listed, see if they give any clue to a possible bias about the subject.

3. Look for the publisher's name.

Sometimes you can get an idea of the value of a book from the publisher's reputation in the subject field. Have you ever read anything else in this field by this publisher? How was it? What do you know of this publisher's work in the subject field?

4. Note the date of publication.

Books used to carry the year of publication on the title page. They seldom do now. The copyright date on the copyright page will tell you how timely the material is. Your own knowledge of the subject field must tell you how important freshness is.

5. Read the introduction or preface.

Most of us skip this preliminary material in our haste to get to the meat of the book. This is a mistake. These sections can give you a great deal of information. Authors may tell you why they have written the book or what their hypotheses are. They may give an indication of method. They may tell you how they intended their books to differ from others in the field. Authors may express their biases, which you should know to judge their opinions.

6. Look over the table of contents.

The contents page is more than a where-to-find-it guide. It's an outline. Here, the author has set forth an orderly breakdown of topics and the order of coverage that gives you an advance view of subject development, logic, and the scope of the book. The more detailed the table of contents, the more valuable it is. Even a simple listing of chapter titles can help, however. If the table of contents lists only chapter titles, you can learn more by thumbing through the book quickly, glancing at headings and subheadings. These are easy to spot, as they are generally set in distinctive type.

7. Now, thumb through the book quickly.

Get a quick idea of the physical arrangement of the book. You may want to stop for a quick look at graphics or other visual aids. A picture or graph may, indeed, tell more than a thousand words and give you a big boost in your attempt to gain an understanding of the book through prereading.

8. Read the summaries or abstracts.

If your book has these features, they can give you an understanding of the book surpassed only by actual reading. If summaries or abstracts aren't part of your book but questions at the ends of the chapters are included, these may often be as enlightening as summaries.

If you have decided to put the book into one of the first three categories (discard, delegate, or save for later reading), then your work is done. Just put it aside, file it, or put it in the interoffice mail. If you have marked the book for a general or detailed reading, then you have a familiarity with it and a conceptual framework that will make your reading more productive.

Prereading reports.

1. Examine the title.
2. Note the author's name, company, and department.
3. Check the date.
4. Note for whom it was prepared.
5. Look for the stated purpose or reason for the report.
6. Examine the table of contents.
7. Read the summary or abstract.
8. Read the introduction or background statement. If it's a research report, examine the research methods if they are summarized here. They are an important key to determining the validity of the data and indicate the competence of the writer or researcher.
9. Thumb through to note headings and subheadings.
10. Look over graphic exhibits.
11. Read the conclusions and recommendations.
12. Put the report in one of the five categories and go on from there.

Prereading letters.

Reading and prereading short letters is sometimes the same thing. You have probably developed your own quick system for sifting through a pile of correspondence and categorizing it. You probably note the following:

1. Letterhead.
2. Date.
3. Name and title of writer.
4. The main idea. If the letter has been written by a regular correspondent, you can probably predict style and quickly get to the heart of the letter. A glance at most letters can usually tell you what they're about, as the essentials are generally found in the middle. The beginning usually consists of introductory remarks, a rehash of correspondence, and some polite or institutionalized formularies. The message is in the middle, and the end returns to formularies and assurances of good will and interest.

Prereading articles in periodicals.

1. Examine the title.
2. Check the author's name and any biographical notes.
3. Determine the type and purpose of the periodical.
4. Look for the date of publication and for the date of submission, if given.

5. Read the abstract.
6. Read the introductory statements.
7. Note headings and subheadings.
8. Scan any graphic exhibits.
9. Examine conclusions and the summary.
10. Put the article into one of the five categories, and go on from there.

HOW TO READ STATISTICS, FIGURES, AND GRAPHS

Approach numbers and graphs with four questions—and keep those four questions in mind as you read them:

1. Is the information valid?
2. Is it all valid?
3. What meaning does it suggest and is that meaning valid?
4. Is the information useful?

Most of us can recognize untruth and will immediately dismiss it. But the half truth contains just enough truth to escape this fate and gets into the mind where the falsehood can work its deception. To avoid this, consider the whole statement.

Half truths are often found in implied statements. In this case everything that is said is true, but the implication is misleading (For instance: "When Smith took over as manager, sales were less than one million a year. Now, as he completes his first year, sales exceed two million.")

While the figures may be quite correct, there is no reason to accept the implication that Dave Smith was responsible for the additional sales. Though he may well have been, it is also quite possible that the sales were achieved despite his incompetence. Stating two facts together in this way implies a relationship, but before you accept this relationship, look for more information.

Are comparisons tied to something solid? Beware of the open-ended comparison. "O'Malley's bread is fresher." Fresher than what?

Are the figures factual? Are the data on which they are based reliable? When and how and by whom were they gathered and processed? Who paid for the study?

Statistics can be helpful, but statistics never give the full picture. Indeed, that's why we use them. They are useful in reducing great masses of data to usable units. Statisticians, to put it another way, are editors. They edit reality. If they're good at their trade, they can be helpful, if we understand them properly. If they're dishonest, we must be very careful, for theirs is an intricate science, one in which it's quite easy to become lost.

The following examines some of the more common statistical dead-falls to help you know what to look for when you read figures.

1. The great American average.

It seems almost irreverent to say anything about the average. Democratic folklore has imbued it with a sort of holiness. But, nonetheless, it is well to offer a few cautions about this word "average." What would you say is the average income of the group depicted in Table 17-1? Have you finished your calculations? You may count your answer correct if you responded either $8,000, or $13,000, or $14,700, or "none of the above." The mode (that which occurs most often) is $8,000. The median (as many earn more as earn less) is $13,000. And the mean (the arithmetical average) is $14,700. It would also be possible to say that you can't tell the average from the table, as the frequencies represent the income of a sample rather than that of a whole group.

Table 17–1

Figure 1	
Annual income*	Number in sample earning that amount
$30,000	12
25,000	14
20,000	8
15,000	16
14,000	7
13,000	4
12,000	3
11,000	2
10,000	9
9,000	13
8,000	18
7,000	14

Is it proper to refer to mode, to median, and to mean as "average"? It certainly is. They are three different types of average, and each is validly used in its own proper circumstance.

In what statisticians call a "normal frequency distribution curve" (the bell-shaped curve), mean, median, and mode coincide. In other distributions, such as the one we have just seen, they do not coincide. Some writers take advantage of this; they calculate all three and then report the one most favorable to their point of view as the "average." When you see something described as an average, be careful.

The data in Table 17–1 might cause the careful reader to ask several other questions:

- How was the sample chosen?
- Why is the middle so light and the upper and lower limits so heavy?
- Why are amounts up to $15,000 presented in intervals of $1000 and amounts over that in intervals of $5000?
- Has there been some rounding of figures, or did everyone have an income in even thousands?
- Were incomes below $8000 and over $30,000 arbitrarily excluded?
- Why is that asterisk at the title of the first column?
- How were the figures obtained?
- If the information was obtained by questionnaire, were the questions worded so that respondents would tend to inflate their incomes? Or deflate them?
- Who gathered the figures and why?
- And anyhow, so what? What's the point?

The uses of "average" can also be seen in the answer to this question. What was the average income in the United States in 1964? We could respond in several ways by citing the 1966 edition of the *World Almanac* as our authority. We could note on p.382 that the *median* income of employed male civilian full-time workers was $6302 that year. If we don't care for that figure, we can cite p.753 as we blithely report that the *per capita* personal income in the United States was $2566 for that same year. The average reader would, I assure you, think of either figure as the "average income in the United States." We could, of course, eschew the average, and looking elsewhere in that estimable publication, dazzle our reader with the figure $494,996,000,000.00 (the total personal income in the U.S. in '64). If we were feeling particularly churlish, we would simply make a casual reference to that year's Gross National Product, $628,699,000,000.00. We could then feel free to attach any significance we chose to that figure, secure in the knowledge that only a few economists have any idea at all of what the Gross National Product really is.

I certainly don't.

Do you? Yet how many times have you read some reference to it without batting an eye? Beware the unknown, particularly if it's expressed in figures. Don't take statistical terms for granted or at face value.

2. The simple sample.

Sampling is a statistical technique that attempts to describe the behavior or condition of a class through study of only certain members of that class. Sampling can be a valid and an accurate technique. The political polls attempt to predict how the entire electorate will vote. They survey only a minute percentage of the electorate to do this. Very often they are correct. But, then too, there was the case of Harry Truman.

Market research, quality control, industrial engineering—all these sciences and more make use of sampling techniques; so you're quite likely to come across data that are the result of sampling as you move through the reports on your desk. As with most things, common sense provides the best guide. You certainly wouldn't place much faith in a national political sample which attempted to predict the behavior of U.S. voters after limiting their study to male Republican osteopaths over 67 living west of the Rockies. Certainly, you'll want to know the group studied and how it was chosen. It should be a representative group.

You'll also want to keep in mind that even valid data from unimpeachable sampling yield only probabilities of what will happen to a large group, usually over a relatively long period of time. A sampling may accurately predict that the voters of Massachusetts will cast 67.4 percent of their ballots for a given candidate, but it should not be taken to mean that Clara Jones will vote in any given way—or even that she will vote.

A biased and less-than-scrupulous writer can manipulate a sample to reflect a point of view. If the sampling is to be done through personal interviews or a written questionnaire, the questions can be worded to suggest a response favorable to the sample taker. Indeed, even an honest sampler can often unwittingly cause respondents to favor certain responses. People, when responding about their own behavior, tend to give the answer that reflects what they think they should be doing rather than what they really do. Thus, reality to the contrary, a survey would probably show that almost all Americans bathe and brush their teeth daily, attend church more or less regularly, read wholesome literature and eschew anything prurient, and always say grace before meals.

Another example of rigged sampling can be seen in Table 17–2. This table represents the results of my coin flipping this afternoon. It shows 27 heads to 23 tails. That's only a little off the 50–50 ratio we would expect. It certainly isn't a significant deviation from the laws of chance. We know that if I were to continue flipping for, say, a thousand trials, I'd come out pretty close to 500 heads and 500 tails.

Table 17–2   Results of 50 successive flips of a 1968 U.S. quarter.

1 H	6 H	11 H	16 T	21 H	26 T	31 H	36 H	41 T	46 T
2 T	7 H	12 H	17 H	22 T	27 T	32 H	37 T	42 H	47 H
3 H	8 H	13 H	18 H	23 H	28 H	33 H	38 H	43 T	48 T
4 H	9 T	14 H	19 H	24 T	29 H	34 T	39 T	44 H	49 H
5 T	10 T	15 H	20 T	25 H	30 T	35 T	40 T	45 T	50 T

(H–heads, T–tails)

Suppose I failed to report the whole sequence to you—suppose that I wanted to prove through these figures that I was endowed with mysterious powers to control the tumbling of coins in the air. I could give you just the data yielded by flips 11 to 20 and state that, "In a series of trials, I demonstrated the ability to flip heads 80 percent of the time."

Anyone using sampling can do the same. The person can choose a favorable sequence within a larger neutral or unfavorable sequence. In addition to this type of editing I could further bolster my claim by having it certified by "independent observers."

By the way, did you notice the title for the table? Wasn't it scientifically precise? That's a nice touch, making the whole thing a little more believable.

Sampling is a valid technique if properly employed. But don't assume that all samples are valid, even though they may be couched in impressive scientific jargon. If it doesn't make sense, don't believe it. And don't accept figures as such. Ask who gathered them, where, how, and why.

Graphs give the writer another way to present data, and they give us our third trap.

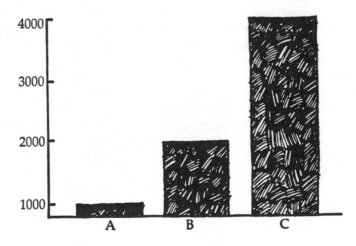

Figure 17–1

3. The flexible graph.
Graphs are marvelous things. They are among the writer's best friends. They enable us to tell in a page what would take chapters of text to explain. They depict relationships better than words could ever hope to do.

Take your own organization, for instance. How many words would it take to describe the relationships of the people in your group? Yet an organization chart could do it in just a page. Graphs bear out the ancient maxim that a picture is worth a thousand words. But graphs, because they are so simple and because they are able to present so much information in such a small space, can deceive. The effective reader would do well to guard against two of the more common types of deceptive graphs by (1) looking for the bottom line and (2) noting the vertical axis. Figure 17–1 illustrates the need for observing the first of these durations.

As the vertical axis clearly shows, bar A represents 1000, bar B twice that amount, and bar C 4000. Yet the height of bar B is not twice that of bar A; it is five times the height of A. Bar C is not four times the height of A; it is 13 times as high.

The graph does not lie. The correct figures are given at the vertical axis, but the overall impression is gained, not from the numerals at the axis, but from the observation of the relative heights of the bars. The casual observer would get the impression that the quantity represented by bar C was 13 times as great as that represented by bar A, and this is not so. The false impression is created by having the bottom line represent a quantity greater than zero. In the case of Figure 17–1, the bottom line represents 750.

If these same figures were to be represented on a graph that started at zero, then the impression would be quite different (see Figure 17–2).

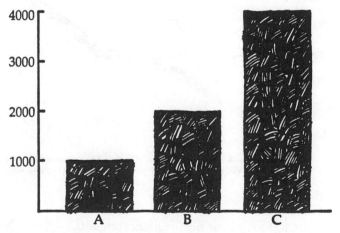

Figure 17–2

A similar effect can be achieved by varying the height of the vertical axis. Figures 17–3 and 17–4 represent the same data. Their vertical scales give the correct figures, but the overall visual impression is something else again. The writer can maximize or minimize at will by varying the vertical axis. When you read graphs, go beyond the immediate visual impression. Check the figures on the axes. If the bottom line doesn't represent zero, wonder why and judge for yourself the effect this has on the overall impression you receive from the piece.

When you read a graph, then, don't just look at it. Study it. Note the figures. Look for what's there. Look, too, for what isn't there and wonder why. Ask yourself if the graphic presentation represents the figures fairly. If not, begin to be suspicious of the whole presentation.

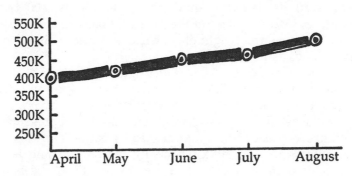

Figure 17–3

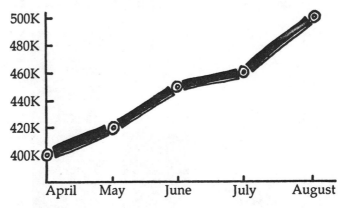

Figure 17–4

Be suspicious, too, of our next statistical deadfall—that which Vance Packard has so aptly called:

4. The hidden persuaders.

There's nothing wrong with persuasion. Each of us is persuaded daily to something. But we might be surprised if we ever stopped to think what in us was being persuaded.

Cigarette advertising, perhaps the prime example, convinces many of us that we should buy a product labeled hazardous to our health. How does the advertising persuasion overcome the warning? Many different appeals can be seen: sex, youth, status, social needs. One ad proclaims that its cigarette is lower in tar and nicotine and cites "official government figures" to prove it, thus suggesting that the government has somehow endorsed this cigarette as safe. This, of course, isn't so.

I'm not suggesting that you stop being persuaded by advertising or by reports, proposals, or letters. I am suggesting that as you are being persuaded, you pause a moment and reflect on which aspect of your personality the appeal is working. Getting into the habit of reflecting that way may help you to make sounder decisions.

Expertness in understanding statistics and graphs is hard to come by. Most of us will never achieve it. Thus, we must rely on common sense. Ask the significance of the data. Ask who compiled it and how and why. And never forget to ask, "Does it make sense?"

There are many more questions that can be applied to a particular piece of writing, but the four above should be included in any list. Their use is not confined to evaluation of the written word alone. They may and should be used to evaluate the spoken word too.

MANAGE YOUR READING

The management of your reading has two aspects: (1) the development of personal reading skills and (2) the use of management control and personal influence to create the best possible climate for your own reading and that of your associates. In this section, we'll look at the second aspect, some techniques that can ease the reading burden and, in some cases, improve the climate of written communication in your organization.

1. Delegate.
We looked at part of this technique when we discussed prereading. In the second category, we said we would refer material to a superior, colleague, or subordinate who would be able to get more from it than we could. But delegation doesn't stop there.

Delegation includes having your staff do some of your reading for you. They can prepare abstracts or digests for you or they can brief you on the points most important to you. Of course, they will have to know you and your job well enough to be able to do this. You will have to give them periodic guides as to what you want. You will have to establish two-way communication. Before you can start to rely on your people, you will have to train them in this concept.

You may feel that only a top-executive reading load justifies such help and that only a top executive would have such a staff. You can adapt the concept to your own level. You may ask your secretary to look at the correspondence and underline the operative parts. You may even delegate the authority to reply to some letters without your having to see them.

Whatever your job may be, and however you may employ the technique of delegation of reading it will take you a while to have confidence in your subordinates; it will take them a while to learn what you want. Thus, two-way communication will be important at the beginning. If you can apply this technique successfully, you will find *your* confidence and *their* skill increasing and you will probably broaden your use of the technique. You'll find that it saves you a great deal of time and that it can be a very useful way of keeping subordinates posted, thus enabling them to do a more effective job.

2. Control.

Control the volume of paper that comes to you. If you are a "Copy to" addressee on much routine correspondence and you find most of it going in the *discard* category, let the originator know you have no need for the copies.

Take a look at the periodic reports and correspondence that come to you. Are they necessary? Could any be eliminated or shortened? Many times you'll find that a periodic report is no longer of value to you, but it persists in being sent to you because no one ever stopped it. Pieces of paper are costly. They are costly to prepare, transmit, read, and file.

Is every piece of paper which comes to you worth that cost? If not, shouldn't you do something about it?

What about the *form* of periodic correspondence? Does the message say the same thing each time, except for a figure or two? If so, wouldn't a standard form be cheaper? And, with a standard form, the important, changeable figures would stand out.

3. Communicate and train.

Many managers and executives complain about the quality of written matter that comes to them, but they do nothing to correct the situation. They send things back with general criticisms scrawled on them in an angry hand and raise hell in general. Subordinates know that the boss is un-happy, and they scurry in random experimentation to find what will keep the old grouch quiet. Like rats in a maze who excitedly probe their environment in random movements to get to the food pellets, the writers can only try and try again. Like the rats who eventually learn through trial-and-error experimentation, the writers too eventually settle on a solution. Learning takes place. The learning has been crude, expensive, and perhaps has damaged morale and the communication networks of the organization.

Specific response can get you the writing you want and can train writers to provide it in a far easier and less traumatic fashion. Both positive and negative response are necessary to accomplish this.

Did you like a particular piece of writing? Was it helpful to you? If so, don't simply award the source of the piece a "well done." Analyze it for a moment. Ask yourself why you liked it. When you know this, make it known. Include the "well done," but amplify it and make it meaningful and helpful by telling why you felt it was so. A comment like the following would be complimentary and helpful too. "Good report. The illustration of the machine failure in packaging tied the whole thing together. It gave us a good picture of the overall problem."

This type of response is meaningful; the originator of the report has been given a pat on the back, which is always pleasant, but has also been given an opportunity to learn.

Writers can learn from negative comments, too, if they are constructive and specific. Comments like "too general," "not what we want," and others serve to reprove and don't allow for learning except as an element of a trial-and-error pattern. The following comment indicates lack of satisfaction and yet allows learning to take place.

> This isn't what we want. Before we can make a decision, we'll have to know not only what happened, but *why*. The *why* should be included in your report. Give us specifics on several cases and see if you can find any common factors. Even if you can't, it will be helpful to know the incidents are not part of an overall pattern. Please condense your introductory remarks; the people who will receive this report have a working knowledge of the background.

A comment like this has much more meaning than most of the tail-chewing epigrams that come boldly scrawled to writers.

The people who prepare reports are often chosen to do so because of their competence in the subject matter. Do your technical specialists spend much time writing? If so, do they deserve some formal training in writing skills? Or, do they need some editorial help? The answers to these questions must be determined at the local level, but they should be asked from time to time, for all of this is part of managing your reading.

Providing specific comments to writers can do a great deal to help them, but judged even on selfish, personal grounds, doing this is of great value to you as a reader. The result is better raw material to which you can apply your reading skills.

Managing your reading simply means applying what you know about the process of effective reading to the improvement of your personal reading skills and to the improvement of the climate of written communication in your organization.

Part TWO
THE GUIDE

This guide contains, in alphabetical arrangement, entries on grammar, usage, pronunciation, spelling, and diction chosen for their usefulness to business and technical writers and speakers. Each entry deals with problems most often associated with it. The entries are cross-referenced to one another and to applicable sections in Part I of this book.

The guide may be used in two ways:

- As a reference source to be consulted when you have a problem in expression;
- As developmental reading. Read one or two pages a day until you have completed the Guide. It will acquaint you with facts to help you in speaking and writing, and it will make you aware of the kinds of help that you can find here.

No matter how you choose to use it, take a moment to look through the Guide. Read a few sample entries to get an idea of how information is presented.

The entries have been prepared to give immediately useful guidance to business and technical people. They do not present in-depth academic or scholarly information or points of view.

A

a The normal pronunciation of this article is the short sound of the *u* in d*u*ck, and *uh* sound. When speaking formally in a presentation and especially when reading aloud, many people give the word the long *a* sound of the *a* in f*a*te. To keep your speech natural and conversational, use the shorter *a*.

a-   As a prefix, *a-* means *not*. It's used in words like *amoral, atypical, asexual,* and *aplastic.* It's usually pronounced as a long *a* (the *a* in f*a*te), though the short *a* (the *a* of *a*pple) is common for *amoral*.

a/an   Use *a* before a word beginning with a consonant sound. Use *an* before a word beginning with a vowel. If a word begins with *h*, use *a* if the *h* is sounded, as in *a house, a horse, a hotel.* Use *an* if the *h* is silent and the word begins with a vowel sound, as in *an hour, an honor.* In British usage, probably because of British pronunciation, *an* is used before many words beginning with *h*. Normal American usage prefers *a* unless the word clearly begins with a vowel sound.

abbreviations   Use abbreviations when it's important to save space or when the frequent repetition of a term would be tiresome. Abbreviations are acceptable, particularly in technical writing where they represent standard terms. But don't coin abbreviations for most uses.

Use standard abbreviations. If you must coin your own, explain it in parentheses immediately following its first use. Coining abbreviations is an acceptable economy if you will use a term many times, but don't do so for a term that you will use infrequently.

Abbreviations for most titles are acceptable when the title is used with the full name, such as *Prof. Louis H. Mall, Rev. David Flood,* but spell out the title when using the last name only, as in *Professor Mall, Reverend Flood.*

Abbreviations for titles such as *Mr., Mrs., Ms.,* and *Dr.* are acceptably abbreviated whether used with full names or last names alone.

Many abbreviations, such as *NASA, FBI, USN,* and *IBM,* are written without periods. For a fuller discussion of this and the punctuation of abbreviations, see p. 85 in Chapter 10.

abdomen   The preferred pronunciation is with the accent on the first syllable (AB-do-men), but a second-syllable accent, though chiefly regional, is also acceptable (ab-DO-men). The adjective has one acceptable pronunciation, that with the accent on the second syllable: ab-DOM-i-nal.

ability to   A roundabout way of saying something that could be expressed more simply. "He has the *ability to* swim" would be better expressed as "He is *able to* swim" and even better expressed as "He *can* swim."

above   Use this word as an adjective or an adverb when directing your reader's attention to a part of your writing that comes before: the *paragraph above*, the *list mentioned above*, the *above paragraph*. Don't use it as a noun, as in the phrase "see the *above*." *Above* is preferable to the cumbersome *the aforementioned*.

Use *above* to direct your reader's attention to something that is, in fact, above. If you want to send the reader back more than a page, give a specific page reference to prevent a search of everything that has come before.

abstract and concrete words and phrases   Abstract words are imprecise; they can have any number of meanings. *Promptly, quickly, warmer, soon, in an efficient manner, suitable compensation,* and the like can easily mean one thing to the writer or speaker and another to the reader or listener. Avoid abstract words in favor of concrete expression. A more detailed discussion of abstract/concrete begins on p.18.

accent marks of foreign words   These should be used if the word has not become a part of the English language *(città, forêt, père),* but they should not be used for words that have become part of our language, such as *resume* and *cafe*.

accept, except   *Accept* means *to receive* (He *accepted* the award). *Except,* when used as a verb, means *to leave out* or *to exclude* (We *excepted* temporary employees from the pension plan) or *to object to* (He *excepted* against the judge's ruling). As a preposition, *except* signifies a leaving out (Everyone *except* the treasurer was present).

Be careful not to confuse these sound-alikes. Use *accept* for the positive notion of receiving something. Use *except* for the negative notions of leaving out or objecting to.

accessory   The first *c* in this word is pronounced as a *k;* the second as an *s* (AK-ses-o-ree) (ak-SES-uh-ree). Don't pronounce both *c*'s as *s*'s (ass-ses-uh-ree).

accurate/correct   These words are nearly synonymous in most uses and should not be used together (The account is *accurate and correct.*) Use one or the other, but not both.

acoustic/acoustics   The form without the final *s* is an adjective: the *acoustic properties,* the *acoustic qualities.* The form with the final *s* is a noun referring to the science of sound: *Acoustics is her field.*

acquiesce   Simplify this word. Use *accept* instead. Thus, instead of saying "He *acquiesced* to our demands," say "He *accepted* our demands."

ad/advertisement   *Ad* is generally acceptable as a short form of *advertisement* in business and technical use. It is a short form rather than an abbreviation and should not be written with a period. (We saw your *ad* in *The Wall Street Journal.*)

A.D., B.C.   *A.D. (anno domini,* in the year of the Lord) used to be written before a date (*A.D.* 68), but now it's generally written after (68 *A.D.*). *B.C.* is written after the date (44 *B.C.*) and should be used for all years which predate the Christian Era. Use *A.D.* only when there's a possibility of confusion (Nero, 37–68 *A.D.*, is reputed to have burned Rome). Other than to avoid possible confusion as to which date is meant, leave *A.D.* to historians and state legislatures.

     You may sometimes see the abbreviations *B.C.E.* and *C.E.* These stand for *Before the Common* (or *Christian*) *Era* and *Common* (or *Christian*) *Era.* They correspond to *B.C.* and *A.D.* respectively.

adapt, adopt, adept   Don't confuse these sound-alikes. To *adapt* is to change to make more suitable. To *adopt* is to take as one's own. *Adept* is an adjective meaning highly skilled.

additionally   Often and incorrectly used when *also* would provide a better sentence.

> *Poor:*   *Additionally,* we will provide field service.
> *Better:*   We will *also* provide field service.

address   As a verb (He *addressed* the meeting. She *addressed* the envelopes.), address is pronounced with the stress on the second syllable, ad-DRESS. When address is used as a noun, the stress may be on either syllable.

ad hoc   This Latin phrase means *to this.* It is used most often to refer to a temporary committee (*ad hoc* committee) formed for a specific purpose. The opposite of *ad hoc* committee is *standing* committee. Though the phrase *ad hoc* is widely used, it would be better to use the designation *temporary* or to use no designation at all and simply call the committee by its descriptive name, such as *Building Committee.*

ad hominem   This Latin phrase means *to the person* and it refers to attacks on a person rather than on his or her ideas when the ideas are the point of discussion. It's a weak argument and one usually designed to camouflage a weak point of view. One who argues *ad hominem* seems to say, "I can't counter your ideas; so I'm going to try to discredit you."

     According to an old law school maxim, "If the law is on your side and the facts are against you, argue the law. If the facts are on your side and the law is against you, argue the facts. If both the law and the facts are against you, give the opposing counsel hell." As that maxim indicates, the *ad hominem* argument is usually a last resort. It's usually ineffective with an intelligent audience, and it often turns on its users by exposing the weakness of their own cases. Avoid it.

adjectives   Adjectives are words that modify nouns and pronouns. They do so by describing (the *red* house, the *tall* man), limiting (*seven* cartons, *several* employees, *every* agency), or pointing out (*this* program, *those* books).

Adjectives may be linked in two ways to the words they modify:

1.   By placing them next to the words which they modify:

   The *red* house at the corner of the *wide* street is mine.
   Put the *complete* story in the *monthly* report.

2.   By joining them to the words they modify with the predicate (verb) of the sentence:

   I am *hungry*. (In this sentence, *hungry* tells about *I*, not about *am*. It modifies by describing the pronoun *I*; so it's an adjective.)
   She is *ready* to type the report. (Similarly, *ready* tells about *she* and is an adjective.)

Adjectives linked by verbs to the words they modify are called *predicate adjectives*. Adjectives placed next to the words they modify are called *attributive adjectives*.

For more on adjectives and their uses, see Chapter 3, "Guide 5," pp. 20–21; and Chapter 10, "Problems with Adjectives," pp. 81–83.

adjourn/recess   These words are often used interchangeably and incorrectly. To *adjourn* is to suspend until another day. To *recess* is to suspend for a period of time. It would be correct to say that a meeting *recessed* for lunch, but it would be incorrect to say that it *adjourned* for lunch. When a meeting is finished for a day but is to meet again another day, it is said to *adjourn*.

   Incorrect: We'll *adjourn* until four o'clock this afternoon.
   Correct: We'll *recess* until four o'clock this afternoon.

As *recess* can mean any suspension, it would be correct to say "We will *recess until tomorrow*," but, as the meeting is to resume on another day, "We will *adjourn until tomorrow*" is preferable.

administrate   Use *administer; administration* and *administrator* are the noun forms. *Administrate* is the unfortunate result of an attempt to turn the noun forms into a verb. There's no need for that because *administer* is the verb form.

adverbs   Adverbs modify verbs, adjectives, and other adverbs.

> The price dropped *quickly. (Quickly* modifies the verb *dropped.)*
> He wore a *dark* blue suit. (*Dark* modifies the adjective *blue.*)
> The price dropped *very* quickly. (*Very* modifies the adverb *quickly.*)

There are several types of adverbs, distinguished by the information they provide:

1. *Adverbs of manner* tell *how* something happened.

    > The price dropped *quickly.*
    > He spoke *quietly.*
    > He did it *dishonestly.*

2. *Adverbs of time* tell *when* something happened.

    > I saw him *recently.*
    > Do it *soon.*
    > I'll see you *Wednesday.* (Wednesday can, of course, be a noun, but used like this—to tell when something happens—it's an adverb.)

3. *Adverbs of place* tell *where* something happened.

    > He went *north.*   Put it *there.*
    > I'm going *home.*   It went *up.*
    > Come *in.*   You'll go *far* before you rest.

4. *Adverbs of degree* tell the *extent* of the words they modify.

    > It was *very* quiet.
    > She's *almost* ready.

Adverbs such as *very, rather, quite, extremely,* and *somewhat* are overused. They usually add little to meaning and tend to weaken rather than to strengthen the words they modify. Leave them out if they are not essential, unless leaving them out would drastically change the meaning you are trying to convey.

Conjunctive adverbs, sometimes called *transitional connectives,* modify entire sentences or clauses. There's no particular reason to think of these words as adverbs or to treat them as such. They are, or ought to be, in a class by themselves, but some grammarians list them as adverbs. Conjunctive adverbs are words like *therefore, perhaps, moreover,* and *however.*

> *Perhaps* you'll be able to go.
> *Therefore,* we have granted his request.
> We have, *however,* insisted that he come to Boston.

Conjunctive adverbs pose special punctuation problems. See *semicolon,* pp. 90–91.

advise   To *advise* is to give counsel to. It doesn't mean *tell* or *inform,* and it shouldn't be used in that sense:

> *Incorrect:*   Please *advise* us of your billing procedures.
> *Correct:*   Please *tell* us about your billing procedures.
>
> *Incorrect:*   Please *advise* us of any change in address.
> *Correct:*   Please *tell* us of any change in address.
>
> *Incorrect:*   This is to *advise* you that . . . .
> *Better:*   This is to *inform* you that . . . .
> *Best:*   *Drop the whole phrase and state the information without any lead-in.*

adviser/advisor   Take your pick; either spelling is acceptable. *Advisor* has a slight edge in preference and frequency.

affect, effect   Usually, these sound-alikes are different parts of speech. *Affect* is a verb meaning *to influence* (His example *affected* all of us), and *effect* is a noun meaning *result* or *influence* (We saw the *effect* of his work. The drug has side *effects*). In these common uses, the difference is clear. Use *affect* as a verb, *effect* as a noun.

But *effect* can be a verb as well, though with a meaning different from that of *affect.* As a verb, *effect* means to *cause* or *to bring about* (He *effected* changes in the department). Usually, *effect* is a weak verb that indicates a need for recasting the sentence:

> He *effected changes* in the collection policy.

would be better stated as:

> He *changed* the collection policy.

and

He *effected a reorganization* of the department.

Would be better written as:

He *reorganized* the department.

Afro-American   This term is usually associated with cultural aspects of black life which have their origins in African forms or traditions. It is not descriptive of race or color. One would speak of *Afro-American art*, but one would be more likely to say of a person, *"He is (a) black"* rather than *"He is (an) Afro-American."* The words *black* and *Afro-American* and their distinctions from *Negro* and *colored* are relatively new in our language and our total American culture, black and white, and they are still evolving. See *black/Afro-American/Negro/colored*, p. 224.

age/aged   For a construction like: He is a man *(age/aged)* 52, *aged* is preferable. *Age* is a noun and should not be used to modify another noun. You can avoid the whole issue with one of the smoother constructions: He is 52; He is a 52-year-old man, or he is a man 52 years old.

aggravate   Originally, *aggravate* meant only *to make more serious, to make worse* (He *aggravated* the situation. Eating mushrooms *aggravated* his dyspepsia). Now, it also has the meaning of *annoy* (Those kids have been *aggravating* me all day). Purists may frown at this more recent meaning, but it seems to be in general and acceptable use, as is the noun *aggravation*, which used to mean both *worsening* and *annoyance*.

agreement of pronouns, of verbs   Agreement of pronoun and antecedent is discussed on pp. 75–78. Agreement of verb and subject is covered on pp. 79–80.

agree to, agree with   One *agrees to* something and *agrees with* someone or a point of view:

He *agreed to* the plan.
He *agreed to* wait.
I *agree with* John.
He *agrees with* the idea of postponing our trip.

ain't   This contraction has yet to be used in polite society, especially in writing. But keep checking; it may make it someday.

alibi   Latin for *elsewhere*, it was originally used to denote defense that the person accused could not be guilty because he or she was somewhere else at the time the offense occurred, as in B-movie dialogue. "I got an *alibi*. The boys will all swear I was playing poker with them in Cleveland." *Alibi* has also been extended to mean an excuse of any kind, but this extension is not good usage. If an excuse other than *being somewhere else* is meant, use *excuse* rather than *alibi*.

alliteration   This term refers to the repetition of words all beginning with the same consonant sound. The sound focuses attention on a phrase.

Alliteration should not be strained, for then it becomes ludicrous, as it so often does in bush-league advertising with its shoddy phrases: *Krazy Kauffman's Kleen Kar Kastle* and *Mother Morelli's Marvelous Meatballs*.

If an alliterative phrase comes naturally at a time when it can focus attention on a point to be emphasized, use it whether writing or speaking. Don't be afraid of it as being too literate or arty for business or technical use, but never strain sweatingly to sew similar sounds side by side.

all of   When referring to a noun, it's best to omit the *of*.

> Poor: All *of* the accounts have been posted.
> Better: All *the* accounts have been posted.

Use the *of* when referring to a pronoun: *All of it* is gone; *All of us* enjoyed it.

all ready, already   *All ready* means *completely prepared* (The accounts are *all ready*). The single word *already* means *beforehand, by now, by that time* (I have *already* eaten).

all right/alright   *Alright* is still an unacceptable form for all written usage. Use the two words.

alternate, alternative   *Alternate* is an adjective. (With the same spelling, but a different pronunciation, it can be a verb, *alternāte*). *Alternative* is a noun. Don't use it as an adjective.

> Incorrect: Solar power offers an *alternative* energy source.
> Correct: Solar power offers an *alternate* energy source.
> Correct: Solar power is an *alternative* to other sources of energy.

At one time, *alternative* meant only the second of two. One could not correctly refer to a third *alternative*. That restriction has eroded and *alternative* has taken on the meaning of choice, and there may be as many *alternatives* as there are choices. If, however, you enjoy being a purist—

and there is much to recommend this devotion to the integrity of our language—use *alternative* for two and *choice* for more than two possibilities.

all together, altogether   *All together* means just what it says. *Altogether* is fully acceptable, but it has a different meaning: *completely, on the whole,* or *in total.*

> Review the files, but keep them *all together.*
> They were *all together* when I saw them.
> Were you *all together* at the meeting?

> I am not *altogether* pleased with our sales.
> *Altogether,* it wasn't a bad month.
> We have six products *altogether,* five consumer and one industrial item.

allusion, illusion   An *allusion* is *a casual reference, an indirect mention* (His *allusion* to our problems was in poor taste). An *illusion* is *a deceptive or misleading perception* or *concept* (He is under the *illusion* that we are going to hire him. Large sales volumes give the *illusion* of profitability).

alumnus/alumni; alumna/alumnae   *Alumnus* and its plural, *alumni,* refer to a male graduate or graduates. *Alumna* and its plural, *alumnae,* refer to a female graduate or graduates. When considered collectively, a mixed group of graduates of a coeducational school is referred to by the masculine plural, *alumni.* If this generic masculine is offensive, use the neuter English word *graduates.*
    Alumni is pronounced with a long *i* (the *i* in bite). *Alumnae* can end with either the long *a* sound (as in fate) or the long *e* sound (the *ee* in feet).

a.m., p.m., m.   These abbreviations are always written in lowercase. The abbreviation for *noon* is *m.* There is no abbreviation in common use for *midnight.* All these abbreviations should be used with times: *10 a.m., 5:16 p.m., 12:00 m.* They should not be used alone, especially in writing, to mean *morning* or *afternoon.*

among, between   Use *between* to speak of two; *among* to speak of more than two. There is a growing acceptance for the use of *between* to refer to more than two, but as *among* does the job nicely, why strain tradition.

amount, number   Use *amount* for things considered in bulk; *number* for things counted or considered individually.

> A large *amount* of gravel is required for the project.
> A *number* of typewriters have been stolen.

ampersand (&)   This sign (&), meaning *and*, should not be used in writing unless space-saving is essential. Some companies use it in their firm names. The sign is used with no comma preceding it.

Reagan & Kelliher, Inc.   *Devlin, Doucette & Kramer*

and (in infinitives)   An infinitive is the form of the verb with the word *to*. Infinitives are used as nouns, adjectives, and adverbs. See *infinitive*, p. 245. Sometimes in speaking and less often in writing, *and* is incorrectly substituted for *to*. This is unacceptable and must be avoided.

    Incorrect: Go *and* see it.
    Correct: Go *to* see it.

    Incorrect: Try *and* get it right.
    Correct: Try *to* get it right.

and etc.   *Et cetera* means *and the like*. *And etc.* is thus redundant and should be avoided. See *etc.*, p. 235.

and/or   This combination may be necessary in certain precise or legal uses, but a simple *or* will generally get the point across. *And/or* has an ominous tone and makes any piece of writing look like a legal document, and it should be avoided in favor of *or* or even the longer XXX *or* YYY, *or both*.

ante-, anti-   These prefixes have different meanings. *Anti-* means *against* or *opposed to*. *Ante-* means *before*.

antecedent   An antecedent is the word for which a pronoun stands (Give John *his* coat). *"His"* stands for *John*; thus, *John* is the antecedent of *his*. Pronouns should agree with their antecedents in person, number, and gender. See Chapter 10, "Problems with Pronouns," pp. 74–78.

antennas/antennae   *Antenna* always used to be given its Latin plural, *antennae*. At that time it referred to the *antennae* of insects and was infrequently used except by biologists. As the word became more widely used through the growth of electronics, it became a full-fledged English word pluralized by adding *s* (*antennas*). Today, *antennas* is the preferred plural when speaking of electronic *antennas*, but *antennae* remains the plural in biological use.

antonym   Antonyms are words that are the opposites or near opposites of each other. *Hot* is the antonym of *cold*. *Noisy* is the antonym of *quiet*; *profit* of *loss*.

a number, the number   The words *a number* are considered plural; *the number* is singular:

> *A number* of orders *are* in.
> *A number* of boats *have been* lost.
> *The number* of orders *is* increasing.
> *The number* of accidents *is* down.

anyone, any one   Use the one word *anyone* (*Anyone* can go), except where special emphasis is desired (*Any one* of the reasons would be sufficient).

any way, anyway, anyways   Use the two words to emphasize the *way* (We've tried all the ways we know, and *any way* seems wrong.) Use *anyway* when you would stress the first syllable in pronouncing it and when you want to stress the *any* concept in the word (There's no point in asking; they won't let us do it *anyway*). Avoid *anyways*, especially when writing. It's not standard and should not be used except possibly in the most informal conversation, and even then *anyway* is preferable.

any where, anywhere, anywheres   Use *anywhere* for almost all uses except for the rare occasion when you want to emphasize the *where* concept (We must be ready to provide field service any time, *any where*). Avoid *anywheres*; it's unacceptable.

anxious, eager   These words are often used interchangeably, but they should not be. *Anxious* means *full of worry, apprehensive of danger* (I'm *anxious* for his safety. I'm *anxious* about our sales figures for the next quarter). *Eager* means *earnest, impatiently looking forward to* (He's *eager* to begin). *Anxious* has the negative connotation of dread; eager, the positive connotation of anticipation. It's best not to use *anxious* in a positive sense.

> *Poor:*   We're *anxious* to begin work on your order.
> *Better:*   We're *eager* to begin work on your order.

The distinction between *eager* and *anxious* might be best seen in a father's comment to his wife at 3:30 in the morning when their 17-year-old daughter is two and a half hours late coming home from a date, "I'm getting anxious about Eloise, dear. I hope she's not too eager."

apostrophe   This punctuation mark is used to indicate letters left out in contractions, before an "s" to indicate possessive form of most singular nouns, and after an "s" to indicate possessive form of nouns that are made plural by adding "s." See Chapter 10, p. 98, for a complete discussion of the uses of the apostrophe.

appendix   This word may be pluralized as either *appendixes* or *appendices*, although *appendixes* is generally preferred when referring to supplementary material at the end of a book, report, proposal, or other document. *Appendixes* is the only acceptable plural for the anatomical *appendix*.

Appendixes are one of the most useful devices for the business or technical writer. Often, we are faced with the problem of a diverse audience for a document. You might, for instance, have to prepare a report or proposal that will be read and acted upon by many people from many fields with many different interests. How do you satisfy each of them without boring the whole readership with detail in which they are uninterested and which they lack the competence to understand? The most frequent and effective answer to this problem is to use appendixes. Use the body of the document to present the most significant information about each special interest area. Readers will understand their own areas better if they see it in the context of its relationship to other specialties. But put detailed or highly technical data in appropriate appendixes.

If, for instance, you were preparing a report on a proposed site for a new plant, you would have to include data on transportation and traffic, cost, engineering aspects of the site, legal considerations, work force availability, and a host of other important specialized subjects. Your readership would include generalists and specialists. The generalists would want a clear overall picture that would promote a sound decision. Specialists would want mountains of detail. The civil engineers, for instance, might want extensive information on the geology, topography, and soil conditions of the site. This would bore and distract most of the other readers, but the engineers would need this information. The same would apply to all of the other specialists. That's where appendixes would be most helpful. An appendix on engineering could give the required information to those interested in it and competent to understand it. Other readers would not get bogged down by it. They would avoid that appendix. And so for the other specialized sections.

When you're faced with a diverse readership, consider the appendix as a way to effectively solve your problem.

applicable   The preferred pronunciation accents the first syllable: AP-pli-ca-ble. The often heard a-PPLIC-a-ble creates syllables where none exist and is definitely second-rate.

appositive   See Chapter 10, "Comma" (use 3) on p. 87.

apt to/liable to/likely to   These three phrases originally had different meanings. Some of the distinctions have been lost over the years, and it is now permissible to use *apt to* and *likely to* to indicate either tendency or probability, with a slight edge being given to *likely to* when discussing probability. Thus, "He's *apt to* object" is acceptable, but "He's *likely to* object" is slightly better.

Liable to could also be used as a substitute for *apt to* or *likely to,* but it might better be reserved for phrases that indicate the possibility of incurring a legal or moral burden ("He's *liable to* be sent to jail for that," or "We're *liable to* be sued").

assent, ascent   These sound-alikes seldom cause trouble. Both are pronounced with the accent on the second syllable: ass-SENT. *Assent* as a noun or verb refers to agreement. *Ascent,* a noun, refers to movement upward.

as to   This phrase is cumbersome. Try to substitute a smoother word like *of, about,* or *for,* or recast the sentence to eliminate it.

at about   This contradictory phrase says *approximately precisely.* If you say, "I'll see you *at* one o'clock," you suggest a meeting at a precise time, and I wouldn't expect you at 12:40 or at 1:20. I'd look for you at 1:00. If, on the other hand, you say, "I'll see you *at about* one o'clock," I'll probably expect you sometime between 12:30 and 1:30. The phrase *at about* says both at the same time. Pick one or the other—*at* for precision, *about* for approximation.

athlete, athletic, athletics   These words aren't often misspelled, which is quite surprising when one considers how often they are mispronounced. The mispronunciation takes the form of an extra *a* to produce the offensive ATH-*a*-lete, ATH-*a*-let-ic. This extra *a* is never acceptable. The only acceptable pronunciations are ATH-lete, ath-LET-ic, and ath-LET-ics.

audio-visual aids   See Chapter 13.

auxiliary verbs   Verbs used with main verbs to form voices and tenses are called auxiliary verbs, *helping verbs.* The most common auxiliary verbs are parts of *be, have, do, can, may, must, ought:*

> I *did* put them back on your desk.
> We *are* going to need you.
> You *must* send it.
> I *may* go, or I *may* stay.
> I *have* prepared an abstract.
> It *has been* suggested that you resign.

averse, adverse   *Averse* means having a strong feeling of dislike, repugnance. *Adverse* means in opposition, unfavorable.

awful, awfully   These words most strictly mean *awe inspiring* ("How *awful* is our God"), and for years purists defended this as the only legitimate one. They lost. In all but the most formal writing, *awful* may be used to mean *extremely bad* or *unpleasant*. *Awful* and its derivatives should not, however, be used as intensives, as in: This is *awfully* good ice cream. He's an *awfully* good dancer.

a while, awhile   *Awhile* is an adverb meaning *for a short time* (Stay *awhile*). The two words *a while* are a noun and an article and should be used as the object of a preposition (Stay for *a while*.) or of a verb (I need *a while* to think).

Incorrect:	Stay *for* awhile. (as object of the preposition *for*)
Correct:	Stay awhile. (as an adverb)
Correct:	Stay *for* a while. (as object of the preposition *for*)
Incorrect:	I'll see you *in* awhile. (as object of the preposition *in*)
Correct:	I'll see you *in* a while. (as object of the preposition *in*)

B

bad, badly   Generally, *bad* is an adjective, and *badly* is an adverb. To describe how a person feels, use *bad* (He feels *bad* today). You'll sometimes see *badly* used in this sense (He feels *badly* today), and a few authorities may accept it, though all seem to agree that *bad* would be the better and grammatically more accurate choice.
   Badly should not be used to mean *very much*.

Poor:	I want *badly* to go.
Poor:	I want to go very *badly*.
Better:	I want *very much* to go.
	I want to go *very much*.
Poor:	I *very badly* want to meet him.
Better:	I want *very much* to meet him.

balance   This word should not be used to mean *rest* or *remainder* except in a bookkeeping sense.

Correct:	There is a *balance* of $48.12 in your account.
Incorrect:	We spent the *balance* of the day in his office.
Correct:	We spent the *rest* of the day in his office.

B.C., A.D.   See *A.D., B.C.,* p. 212.

being as/being as how/being that   Don't use these phrases for *since* or *because.* They are substandard for any use in business or technical writing or speech, including conversation.

because   See *reason is because,* p. 263.

been   Depending on your part of the country, this can be pronounced BIN or BEN. The long *e* sound that produces the sound of BEAN is chiefly British and is not in general U.S. usage, though it is acceptable here.

beside, besides   *Beside* means *next to. Besides* means *in addition to.*

> The book was *beside* the telephone on his desk. (next to)
> There were four other people *besides* me there. (in addition to)

between, among   See *among, between,* p. 218.

between you and me   This is the correct form. *Between* is a preposition, and its objects must be in the objective (accusative) case. *Between you and I* is incorrect in all uses and is, beyond that, pretentious. The same principle applies whenever *me* is the object of any preposition; thus, *for you and me, to you and me,* and *at you and me.*

black/Afro-American/colored/Negro   The word *black* as a noun or adjective to refer to black people is unlikely to offend anyone and is most likely to be preferred by most black people. *Colored* used to be a polite form, but is not now in favor. Though the NAACP (National Association for the Advancement of Colored People) retains *colored* in its name, the organization is generally referred to by its abbreviation, and many black people call it simply The National Association. *Negro* and *colored* may be used by older blacks out of habit, but younger and urban black people resent the terms. *Afro-American* is a term used to denote aspects of black culture having African origins, forms, or traditions. See *Afro-American,* p. 216.

blond/blonde   Strictly, these words are borrowed from French and therefore follow the rules for French. *Blond,* as a noun or adjective, refers to a male; *blonde,* to a female. In practical U.S. use, however, *blond* can be generally used regardless of gender.

both alike   The *both* in this phrase is superfluous.

> *Incorrect:*   The drawings are *both alike.*
>   *Correct:*   The drawings are *alike.*

brackets   See Chapter 10, p. 94.

bring, take   *Bring* indicates motion *toward* the speaker or writer; *take,* motion away.

> *Incorrect:*   *Take* those over here to me.
> *Correct:*   *Bring* those over here to me.

> *Incorrect:*   *Bring* this up to the president's office.
> *Correct:*   *Take* this up to the president's office.

broke   This is a harsh word to describe a harsh set of circumstances when it's used to refer to a lack of money. It's *nonstandard* and *informal* even in an up-to-date dictionary. In spite of that, I'd be forced to agree with L.M. Myers in his *Guide to American English* (Prentice-Hall) as he observes, "*Broke* may be slang, but it's better than 'financially embarrassed' or—well, what else would you say?"

bunch   This word is used to describe things that grow in a cluster (*bunch* of grapes) or that can be held or clutched together (*bunch* of carrots, *bunch* of keys). It's also used to describe a collection. Its use in this second sense may be questionable, and in writing you ought to choose some other collective. Informal speech may allow certain phrases—"He lost *a bunch* of money on that deal" or "There were *a bunch* of people there"—but those phrases would be best left out of business writing.

buoy   The preferred pronunciation is BOO-ee, but BOY is acceptable to landlubbers. I never heard a boatswain's mate call it anything but a BOO-ee, and for that term a Navy Chief Boatswain's Mate has to be the ultimate authority.

burst/bust   *Bust* (as a verb) seems to be coming into its own. It used to be regarded as a modern corruption, but lately it seems marginally acceptable in the United States. The principle parts of *burst* are *burst burst burst;* of *bust, bust busted busted.*

bus   The plural is *buses,* though *busses* is acceptable. The single or double *s* is optional for all forms: *bused* or *bussed, busing* or *bussing.*

C

calculate, guess, reckon   In those more restrictive days when English teachers determined the proprieties of usage, these words were condemned as synonyms for *think, suppose, expect*, and *anticipate*. Now, they are often used in speaking, to no one's horror or confusion. *Guess* has even worked its way into acceptable business writing. *Calculate* and *reckon* are regional forms when used as synonyms for *suppose* or *expect* and should be avoided in writing. They should also be avoided in speaking if they don't come naturally to the speaker and are used just to be folksy.

can, may   Keep these words separate in meaning. Use *can* to imply ability; *may*, to imply permission or possibility.

> I *can* be in your office by four o'clock. (ability)
> I *can* help you with your report. (ability)
> He *can* do it. (ability)
> I *may* be in your office by four o'clock. (possibility)
> I *may* help you with your report. (possibility)
> He *may* do it. (possibility or permission, depending on the context)
> You *may* take the afternoon off. (permission)

cannot/can not   There doesn't seem to be much difference in the meaning or acceptability of the two forms, so take your pick. *Can not* may have a little more emphasis in some situations, but the emphasis would be difficult to spot.

can't help but   Leave off the *but*.

capitalization   Capitalize:

- The first word of a sentence.
- Proper nouns and adjectives:
  Days of the week
  Names of months
  Names of people, companies, agencies, places, institutions
  Races (Caucasian, Negro, Amerind)
  Languages (German, Esperanto, English)
  Names of ships, airplanes, works of art
  Religions (Presbyterian, Islam, Seventh Day Adventist)
  Historical events (French Revolution, War of 1812)
  Documents (the Constitution, Declaration of Independence)
- The nominative of the first-person singular pronoun (I).
- Major words in the titles of writings, except one-syllable prepositions, coordinating conjunctions (and, but, for, or, nor, yet), and the articles *a, an,* and *the,* unless any of these is the first or last word in the title.

- The first word in a line of verse was traditionally capitalized. Many modern forms don't follow this practice, so if you're quoting, quote as written by the versifier. If you're writing verse, follow the form that pleases you.
- References to God (noun or pronoun). His attributes, or powers used to be capitalized in all cases. Modern usage is divided, even among the devout.
- General words, usually not capitalized, like *department, section, company,* and *government,* are capitalized when they are used as the short form of a proper name for an institution or section of an institution, particularly when they are preceded by the word *the:*

  The Department will close on Monday. (the Shipping Department)
  It follows Government policy. (the government of the United States or the government of a State or other political entity)
  He represented the view of the Administration. (the administration of a particular President or other official)
  The Company will provide transportation. (a particular company)

- If you use a common noun to refer to a particular person, place, thing, institution, event, or entity in a proper sense, capitalize.

  He fought in the *Revolution.*
  The event memorialized the *Founder.*

Don't capitalize:

- Seasons of the year (winter, summer, fall, spring) except for emphasis.
- Directions of the compass (north, southeast, south southwest). If you use a compass direction word to refer to a region, capitalize: The product should sell well in the *South* and the *Southwest,* but probably not in the *Northeast.*
- Proper nouns and adjectives that have become common nouns by losing their original association with the places or persons that originally gave them proper status: *paris green, brussels sprouts, tweed, sandwich, plaster of paris, roman type,* and *cheddar cheese.*

case   Case is normally not a problem in English as it is in other languages. Nouns and adjectives have no case distinctions (except for the possessive case of nouns). Personal pronouns are the only words that change form to indicate case.

Use the nominative case for a pronoun used as the subject of a sentence, as the predicate pronoun or complement, or as an appositive to either subject or predicate pronoun.

Use the objective case for direct and indirect objects of verbs, for objects of prepositions, and for appositives to any of these.

Use the possessive case to indicate ownership, possession, or attribution.

Case Forms of the Personal Pronouns

	Nominative	Possessive	Objective
1st person (sing.)	I	my, mine	me
(pl.)	we	our, ours	us
2nd person (sing.)	you	your, yours	you
(pl.)	you	your, yours	you
3rd person (sing.)	he	his	him
	she	her, hers	her
	it	its	it
(pl.)	they	their, theirs	them

cast, caste   *Caste* refers strictly to a Hindu social class. It may, by extension, be used to refer to any social class. Use *cast* for all other uses.

censor, censure, censer   A *censor* is one who takes a census or who examines something to suppress objectionable parts. As a verb, *to censor* is to examine something to suppress objectionable parts. *Censure* as a noun or verb suggests strong expression of disapproval. A *censer* is an incense burner.

chairman/chairwoman/chairlady/chairperson   Traditionally, *chairman* has been an acceptable form for reference to persons of either sex. *Chairwoman* has seen limited use to refer to presiding women. *Chairlady* has been, and is, regarded as unnecessary as is *chairgentleman*. With the advent of militant feminism and its insistence on the expurgation of "sexist" denominations, we have seen the birth of the term *chairperson* as a term for all presiding officers. The term was baptized if not born at the Democratic National Convention in 1972. So far it has seen little acceptance by the general public of either sex.

In the first edition of this book, published in 1974, I suggested that *chairperson* was a fad word and expressed the fear that that statement would probably come back to haunt me in the years to come. I still think that it's a fad word, one less in vogue now then it was in 1974, even though we have, since then, seen a few public works departments carry on their inventories *personhole covers*.

There is a better choice if you want to emphasize your lack of sexism. Refer to the presiding officer as the *chair*.

By the Grace of God, all of this will become a footnote in history. I say that because words and symbols are of primary importance only when reality is awry. Perhaps, in the near future, conditions will be such that women will justifiably feel that they have equality in all spheres. When they can feel that way, they—and those of us who respect their person-hood—will no longer be concerned with words and symbols.

check/cheque   Use *check* for all U.S. uses. *Cheque* is British usage.

Chinaman/Chinese   *Chinaman* is in the same class as *nigger, kike, wop,* and the like. Use *Chinese* as a noun or adjective, singular or plural. As a compound form, *Sino-* is sometimes used, as in *Sino*-American relations.

cite, site, sight   To *cite* is to refer to or to call attention to. *Site* is a place. *Sight,* of course, is vision.

clauses   A clause is a group of words with a subject and a predicate.

An independent (main, principal) clause is one that could be a sentence if it were written alone. Indeed, a simple sentence is one independent clause.

A dependent (subordinate) clause cannot stand alone as a sentence. Subordinate clauses function within sentences as nouns, adverbs, and adjectives. Subordinate clauses are joined to their sentences by subordinating conjunctions or by relative pronouns.

A simple sentence has one independent clause.

A complex sentence has one independent clause and one or more dependent clauses.

A compound sentence has two or more independent clauses. See also *comma fault,* p. 230.

A compound-complex sentence has two or more independent clauses and one or more dependent clauses.

See also *phrase,* p. 257.

clothes   This word can be pronounced without the *th* sound as CLOSE or with the *th* sound. Either is acceptable, but I'd give the edge to the pronunciation with the *th*.

collective nouns   These name a group considered as a single entity—words such as *committee, jury, team, crowd, group, band,* and *company.* Collective nouns are normally treated as singular, and they take a singular verb (The jury *is* considering its verdict). As in the example, collective nouns are represented by singular pronouns. If you want to stress the individuality of the members of the group use an individual rather than a collective noun for that emphasis (The *jurors are* in disagreement).

colloquial   This word comes from the Latin verb that means to speak together or to converse. Words and phrases designated as colloquial are words that are quite correctly used in conversation. They may also be used, without stigma, in writing or speaking other than in conversation. Our society today is stressing content rather than form, and though colloquialisms were once forbidden in formal (and that certainly includes business) writing, they are now fully acceptable, though your corporate counsel may try to keep them out of contracts and proposals. Everybody has to earn a living. When you use a colloquialism, though, make it one that you'd use in good conversation and be sure that it's one that your readers or listeners will understand. Liberalism in usage should not be taken as a license to confuse.

colon   See Chapter 10, p. 92.

column, columnist   Pronounced KOL-um and KOL-um-nist. There should never be a Y sound in this word: KOL-yum and KOL-yum-nist are unacceptable.

comma   See Chapter 10, pp. 87–90.

comma fault   A comma should never be used alone to join two independent clauses. When one is, it's called a *comma fault*.
     A clause is a group of words with a subject and a predicate. An independent clause is one that could be a sentence if it were written alone. Sometimes two or more independent clauses are contained within one sentence. That structure is called a compound sentence. One independent clause alone is called a simple sentence.
     There are three ways to separate the independent clauses of a compound sentence. One way is to divide the clauses into two sentences, and if your writing style tends to favor many long sentences, this would be a good practice.
     The second way is to separate the sentences with a semicolon:

> We called them at their Chicago Sales Office; they promised delivery by the end of the month.

The third (and most common) way to separate the clauses is with a comma and a coordinating conjunction:

We called them at their Chicago Sales Office, *and* they promised delivery by the end of the month.

A comma fault uses a comma alone to separate the clauses:

We called them at their Chicago Sales Office, they promised delivery by the end of the month.

See *comma*, pp. 87–90 and *semicolon*, pp. 90–92.

communication, communications   Use *communication* as a noun or adjective to refer to the process that is the subject of this book:

We need to improve *communication*.
We have solved a *communication* problem.
Good *communication* is important.

Don't refer to the process as *communications:*

Incorrect: *Communications* among specialists are poor.
  Correct: *Communication* among specialists is poor.

Communication can refer to the process and, as a singular and plural noun, it can mean *message* and *messages*.

I've had a *communication* from our lawyer.
I've had four *communications* from our lawyer.

Use the form with *s (communications)* only as a plural noun to mean *messages*. Does that mean that the Federal Communications Commission is misnamed? It does.

compared to/compare with   Compare one thing *to* another to show similarities. Compare one thing *with* another to show either differences or similarities.

complected/complexioned   Use *complexioned*.

complement, compliment   A *complement* is something used to *complete* something. A ship's *complement* is the *complete* crew. *Complementary* angles form a *complete* right angle. A *compliment* is a pat on the back or a word of praise or encouragement.

concerning   Unless it clearly doesn't fit, use *about*.

consensus   This means an agreement of opinion; thus, the phrase *consensus of opinion* is redundant. Leave off the *of opinion*.

continual, continuous   *Continual* means *regularly recurring. Continuous* means *without interruption or pause.*

contractions   These have always been acceptable in speech. Until recently, there was some prejudice against their use in business writing. That prejudice now seems out of date, and contractions are generally accepted for use in all forms of business writing.

cooperate together   How else could one cooperate? Leave off the *together.*

counsel, council, consul   As a verb, *to counsel* is *to give advice or to give assistance in problem-solving.* As a noun, *counsel* is one, particularly a lawyer, who counsels. *Council* is a deliberative body (city council). *Consul* refers to a foreign service officer.

counselor, counseling   Forms of counsel may be spelled with one *l* or two. The one-*l* spelling predominates in the United States; the two-*l* spelling in Britain. Thus, *counselor* or *counsellor, counseling* or *counselling.*

credible, credulous   *Credible* means *believable. Credulous* means *gullible.*

criteria/criterion   *Criterion* is the singular form; *criteria,* the plural. Don't use *criteria* to refer to a single standard or decision element. The Latin plural is the only acceptable form. Avoid *criterions.*

> *Incorrect:*   This *criteria* is not negotiable.
> *Correct:*   This *criterion* is not negotiable.
>   These *criteria* are not negotiable.

curriculum   May be pluralized *curricula* or *curriculums,* with the latter gaining in frequency and favor.

D

dangling modifiers   These are words and phrases that confuse and often amuse readers because their position in a sentence suggests improbabilities.

> Walking around the corner, the building came into view.

Now, it's obvious that a *person* and not the building was walking; therefore, this sentence should be rewritten as:

When I walked around the corner, I saw the building.

Other examples:

Incorrect: At the age of 45, his company moved to Cleveland.
Correct: When he was 45, his company moved to Cleveland.
Incorrect: When fully cooked, six people may be served.
Correct: When it is fully cooked, six people may be served.
Incorrect: After eating his lunch, the foreman sent him home.
Correct: After Joe finished his lunch, the foreman sent him home.

dash   See p. 93.

dates, form of   The conventional U.S. form for dates is *May 3, 1935.* Military and European form is *3 May 1935,* and this is gaining in frequency and acceptance in the United States, particularly in business.

datum/data   *Datum,* the traditional singular form of this word, is not in very wide use except in technical phrases like *datum line. Data* is fully acceptable as singular or plural. Just about any pronunciation of the first *a* is acceptable. Avoid, however, any pronunciation which adds an *r* sound to the end: *dater.*

dialogue, dialog   Acceptable as a noun, it shouldn't be used when *talk* would do. Never use it as a verb:

Incorrect: We *dialogued* with them.
Correct: We *talked* with them.

Either spelling is correct.

different from/different than   Use *different from* and *differently from.* To remember this, refer to the form with the verb. We would say, "This differs *from* that." We would never say, "This differs *than* that."

disinterested, uninterested   Use *disinterested* in the sense of *impartial; uninterested* in the sense of *not interested.*

disc/disk   *Disk* is the preferred U.S. spelling, particularly in the data-processing field *(disk memory). Disc* is chiefly British and European.

division of words   Don't divide words unless failure to do so would leave a distractingly long space at the end of a line. Divide words between syllables, but keep related parts of a word together. Use a dictionary when you're unsure of syllables.

dove/dived   *Dived* is the traditional past tense of *dive* and is always acceptable. *Dove* is quite common in speech, less common in writing. A generation ago it would have been universally condemned, but it seems to have become acceptable. The best advice is still to use *dived*.

due to   This phrase has been the subject of considerable controversy among language specialists for some time now. Rather than go into a technical discussion, let's leave it at this: Use *due to* anytime you'd like, anytime it seems to fit what you're trying to say. You'll make no error in doing so.

E

each   When the pronoun *each* is the subject of the sentence, it calls for a singular verb:

Each of the *departments has its* own budget.

And as you can see from the preceding sentence, a singular pronoun (in this case, *its*) refers to *each*.
   When *each* is used as an adjective to modify the subject, it has no effect on the number of the verb. The number of the verb is, as always, determined by the number of the subject.

The *departments each* set up *their* own budgets.

each and every   This use is trite and redundant. Use either *each* or *every*, but not both.

effect, affect   See *affect, effect*, p. 215.

e.g.   This is an abbreviation for the Latin *exempli gratia*, meaning for example. Today's writing and speaking, particularly in business, best avoids Latin phrases in favor of their more easily understood English equivalents. Use the English *for example* instead of *e.g.*, unless space is severely and imperatively restricted.

either   The normal U.S. pronunciation is EE-ther. EYE-ther is acceptable, but unless it comes easily to you, avoid it.

elder/eldest   Correct but not as widely used as *older* and *oldest*.

ellipsis   See p. 95.

emigrant, immigrant   Everyone who moves out of one country or region to another is both an *emigrant* and an *immigrant*. He *emigrates* from the country he left and *immigrates* to the country he goes to. My grandfather was an *emigrant* from Italy, an *immigrant* to the United States.

employee/employe   *Employee* has been the traditional spelling and remains the most frequent and acceptable. Over recent years *employe* has been gaining in popularity, and though acceptable, it's still likely to jar most readers.

en route   Instead of fooling around with the proper pronunciation and punctuation (as a foreign phrase, it should be italicized) use the English *on the way*.

enthused/enthusiastic   *Enthuse* is technically called a "back formation," a word formed in the belief that it must exist when actually it doesn't. The adjective *enthusiastic* and the noun *enthusiasm* sponsored the popular belief that there must be a verb form to describe this state, and *enthuse* was born—illegitimately. It has been around for some time now and has gained some popular acceptance. People who are otherwise literate speak and write of someone's *enthusing* or being *enthused*, though I've never heard anyone say, "I enthuse." Prefer *enthusiastic*.

> *Poor:*   He was *enthused at* (or over) the idea.
> *Better:*   He was *enthusiastic about* the idea.

Environment   Pronounce the *n*.

Esquire/Esq.   An archaic (at least in the United States) title often used (chiefly by lawyers, who seem to delight in it) following the name of a lawyer in an address. When it is used, omit *Mr.* or any other title:

> Tidal B. Henry, Jr., *Esq.*

etc.   Abbreviation for the Latin *et cetera (and the like)*. Its use is quite acceptable, but don't overdo it. Don't use it to cover a lack of information or to try to cover all possibilities. In those cases, get the information you should have. Use it to avoid writing a long and uninformative list. The *et* means *and;* so avoid *and etc.*

euphemism   A nice way of saying something unpleasant or unspeakable. By way of euphemism, *death* becomes a *passing on* or *a crossing over to the other side; syphillis* and *gonorrhea* become *social diseases;* and a wealthy *lunatic* becomes an *eccentric.* An *alcoholic* has a *drinking problem* for which his company *lets him go.*

In the Victorian era, ladies had *limbs* rather than *legs*—and in that era even tables had limbs, lest anyone should have to utter the forbidden sound: *leg.* Today, pornography becomes *adult entertainment.* The meeting of a professional society is preceded by a *reception* or *social hour* for the consumption of *refreshments* or *the beverage of your choice.*

There's nothing inherently wrong with euphemisms, but their use tends to cloud reality, obscure communication, and waste time.

everyone, everybody   As subjects, these words are singular and call for singular verbs, but they may take either singular or plural pronouns:

> *Everybody* is here.
> *Everybody* should go to the lobby and get *his* ticket (or *their* tickets).

ex-   As a prefix, it means former and is used to form hyphenated compounds with nouns: *ex-wife, ex-director, ex-President, ex-coach, ex-senator.* Its use alone to describe a former spouse is decidedly substandard. (My *ex* is suing me for alimony.)

exclamation point   See p. 86.

except, accept   See *accept, except,* p. 211.

expect   Used to mean *suppose,* it is chiefly British (*I expect* you'll require accommodations).

F

farther, further   The only form used as a verb is *further* (In an attempt *to further* the company's interests . . .). As adjective or adverb, these words may be used interchangeably, but the most common practice is to use *farther* for expressions of distance (Going *farther* down the road, we found. . . . He went *farther* west than anyone else) and *further* for expressions of degree or intensity (A *further* weakening of the market is expected. This research project goes *further* into the subject).

feedback   Fine as a technical term in electronics, acoustics, and their related disciplines. For human interaction use *response, reply,* or some similar term traditionally used to refer to human communication.

female   For most expressions referring to female people, it's best to use this word only as an adjective (ten *female* employees). For use as a noun, it's best to express the female concept in another noun, such as *woman:*

> *Poor:*   The *females* in the company were consulted.
> *Better:*   The *women* in the company were consulted.

fewer, less   Use *less* for expressions of bulk quantity (There's *less* in this tank. Use *less* sand in that mixture). Use *fewer* to refer to things that can be counted (We hired *fewer* employees this year than last. The box contains *fewer* nuts than bolts).

fiance/fiancee   These words follow the French rule; so use one *e* for a man and two *e*'s for a woman. These words used to be written with acute accents (*fiancé, fiancée*) even when used in English sentences, but that practice is just about at an end; the accents have disappeared, probably to the horror of the French. As the words have been adopted into English, they need not be italicized.

fine   In acceptable use as an expression of approval, as either an adjective or an adverb.

foreign words and phrases   They're fine for foreign languages but usually unnecessary, confusing, pretentious, or all three when used in English. There are some that may be justified, but few. They cause problems in spelling and pronunciation, so avoid them.

  If you must use them, italicize them if they are distinctly foreign words and have not been absorbed into English, as have resume, fiance, buffet, negligee, protege, matinee, and lingerie.

former/latter   Less frequently seen than they would have been a generation ago. Now, we would be more likely to say *first* and *last.*

fragment   A fragment is an incomplete sentence and, therefore, not a sentence, but a group of words presented and punctuated as a sentence. We frequently speak in fragments, but the absolute rule for writing is: Always use complete sentences; never write in fragments. That's the rule, and it's a good one. But you should feel free to violate it whenever you will improve clarity or emphasis by doing so. Don't take this as a license to fragment sentences whenever you'd like. Do so only when you are sure that a better expression of your ideas will result.

from, off   Use *from* for constructions like: I got it *from* the personnel manager.

> *Poor:*   I got it *off* Jim.
> *Better:*   I got it *from* Jim.
>
> *Poor:*   He got three hits *off* Guidry in the last game.
> *Better:*   He got three hits *from* Guidry in the last game.

-ful   When the adjective *full* is added to the end of a word, it drops one l: *cupful, spoonful, bucketful, dreadful,* and *sorrowful.*

G

gentlemen   Followed by a colon, this word is the traditional salutation for a letter with an "Attention" line in the address. To avoid addressing women by this term, use no salutation when you have an "Attention" line in the address.

gerund   The name given to the present participle (-*ing* form of the verb) when it's used as a noun. It may also be called a verbal noun or a participle.

> *Fishing* was his hobby. (subject of the sentence)
> He liked *fishing.* (object of the verb)
> He used his boat for *fishing.* (object of the preposition *for*)
> His hobby, *fishing,* was time-consuming. (appositive)
> He gave *fishing* his undivided attention. (indirect object of the verb)

As you can see from these examples, gerunds can do anything that nouns can do. But they can also do things that nouns can't do. Because a gerund is a verb form, it may take an object, and it is modified by an adverb:

> *Fishing* the *river* took most of the day.

In the preceding sentence, the gerund *fishing* is the subject of the sentence. *River* is the object of the gerund. (Fishing what? Fishing the *river.*)

> *Fishing carefully,* he took four trout.

In that sentence, the gerund *fishing* is properly modified by the adverb *carefully*. A noun would have been modified by an adjective, but it would be incorrect to say "Fishing careful, he took four trout."

A gerund along with its modifiers, if it has any, and its object, if it has one, and the object's modifiers is called a *gerund phrase*.

A gerund functions in a sentence as a noun does, but unlike a noun, it has two verb qualities: it may take a direct object, and it is modified by an adverb. But a gerund is not a verb, though it may look like one and, in some ways, acts like one. It can never be, by itself, the predicate of a sentence. Thus, the following is a fragment because it has no verb predicate:

Fishing the river carefully and for days at a time.

Sometimes the *ing* form of the verb is used, with an auxiliary verb as the predicate: "He *is fishing*." In that sentence, *is fishing* is the verb, the predicate of the sentence. It is not a gerund. The *ing* form of the verb is a gerund *only* when it is functioning as a noun.

Another principle of usage is associated with the gerund: a noun (especially if it is a singular noun referring to a person) that refers to a gerund and that comes immediately before it is usually in the possessive case:

Poor: The *company sending* me here wasn't my idea.
Better: The *company's sending* me here wasn't my idea.

Poor: *Me going* won't help anything.
Better: *My going* won't help anything.

This principle is a difficult one to capture in a few words. Many times the use of the possessive is optional, and we hear it omitted more and more often, especially in speaking. In spite of this, you would be well advised to use the possessive form whenever the gerund is the subject of the sentence and whenever you refer to a person's or an institution's accomplishments.

girl   Use this word only to refer to children. *Woman* is the preferred form for reference to any adult female person, regardless of her job. The use of *girl* to refer to an adult, particularly if a man uses the word, is seen as evidence of prejudice, and with some justification. There is a parallel between this and the black man's resentment of *boy*.

got   See *have got*, p. 240.

good/well   Usually, *good* is the adjective form; *well*, the adverb. But to refer to a state of health, *well* may be used as an adjective. (I feel *well*. She took her child to the *well*-baby clinic.)

In speaking of a person's health or state of feeling, we appropriately use *well* to refer to physical health and *good* to refer to outlook on life at that moment. I *feel well* suggests that I have no symptoms. I *feel good today* suggests that I'm ready to meet the world on even terms.

Once you're past the positive degree, the difference ceases to be important, for both *good* and *well* have *better* and *best* as their comparative and superlative degrees.

good-by/goodby/good-bye/goodbye   These forms are without difference in degree of acceptance. Take your pick. If you'd like to save a little space, eliminate the hyphens. The unhyphenated form is steadily gaining in frequency.

gray/grey   Either spelling is acceptable, with *gray* the more frequently seen.

guesstimate   Cute. Avoid it.

H

had ought   Eliminate the *had*, even in its contracted form: I *ought* to go rather than *I'd ought* to go.

half   Either *a half* or *half a* is acceptable. *A half* is considered to have a slight edge as the written form. In any case, spoken or written, don't use *a half a*.

hanged/hung   *Hung* is the past and past participle form of *hang* for all uses of that word save one: hanging as a form of execution or suicide. For that verb, meaning to *kill by hanging*, the past and past participle forms are *hanged*. (You are sentenced to be *hanged* by the neck until you are dead.) Things, then, are *hung*. People are *hanged*.

have got   Drop the *got*, especially in writing. For emphasis, use *must*.

haven't hardly   Better phrased as *have hardly*.

healthful, healthy   Climates are *healthful*; living things are *healthy*. Food is *healthful* or *health-giving*.

he and/or she   Our language has no third-person pronoun that can be used for persons of either sex. *It* is neuter and inappropriate for any person. So what do we do? There are three ways to handle the problem.

1.   The traditional generic masculine form. Use the masculine pronoun to refer to a noun that could be either a man or woman:

     A *supervisor* should organize *his* work and that of *his* department.
     Whoever we hire will have *his* hands full.
     His sons and daughters came and each stated *his* position.

     Until recently no one minded (well, no one said he or she minded) the generic masculine form. Today, you may find some consider it presumably "sexist."

2.   Use *he or she, his or her.*

     A *supervisor* should plan *his or her* work and that of *his or her* department.
     His sons and daughters came and each stated *his or her* position.

     That's equable and not likely to be challenged on grounds of bias, but it's cumbersome at best and wordy.

3.   Use the genderless plural.

     Supervisors should plan *their* work and that of *their* departments.
     His sons and daughters came and stated *their* positions.

height/heighth   Though it would seem to parallel *depth* and *width*, the word *heighth* exists only in nonstandard use. Use *height*.

High school/high-school/highschool   Any of these spellings is acceptable. *High school* is the most commonly seen, *highschool* is gaining ground, and *high-school*, like many other hyphenated forms, is declining in use.

homonyms   These are words of different meanings that are pronounced alike. Some are spelled alike: a tree's *bark* and a dog's *bark, rock* music and a mineral *rock*, a jet *plane* and a carpenter's *plane*. Others are spelled differently but pronounced alike: *hare* and *hair, bare* and *bear, alter* and *altar, piece* and *peace*. These words seldom, if ever, cause problems, as context makes their meaning clear. The only possible problems that might arise are those in spelling. If you're in doubt, check a good, current dictionary.

Honorable/Hon.   Used variously to dignify political figures and office holders. It may be abbreviated when the honored's first name or initials are used. It should not be used with a last name alone. Frequently preceded by the word *the*.

hopefully   This word can be correctly used, but it seldom is. If you know how to use it correctly, you need no help from this entry. If you don't have any idea why I've said it's seldom used correctly, you'd need more explanation than you'd care to take the time to read. Avoid the word.

> *Instead of:*   *Hopefully*, we'll finish today.
> *Say:*   We *hope* to finish today.
> *Or more devoutly:*   *God willing*, we'll finish today.

Anything but *hopefully*.

however   Usually a conjunctive adverb (transitional connective), but may be an adverb. When used as a transitional word, it is set off by commas. If it introduces an independent clause, it is preceded by a semicolon and followed by a comma.

> We'd like to extend you credit; *however*, our interest rate is higher than that which you specify. (introduces an independent clause)
> We can, *however*, allow you a thirty-day cash discount. (transitional word within a clause)

When *however* is used to mean *in whatever manner*, it is an adverb and is not set off by commas:

> *However* you do it, do it by Wednesday.
> Do it *however* you will.

human   This word has traditionally been regarded as an adjective only (*human* race, *human* being, *human* anatomy) and was forbidden to be used as a noun (We are all *humans*). In recent years it has been used more widely as a noun, but such use is often criticized. Best usage would still prefer *human* only as an adjective. For noun use, say *human being* or avoid the whole thing and say *person*.

I

ibid.   Abbreviation of the Latin *ibidem, in the same place*, it's used in footnotes to refer to the citation in the footnote immediately preceding. If footnote 1 refers to a given book, and footnote 2 refers to different pages in the same book, you might expect to see "*Ibid.*, pp. 402–406." for the second footnote. It saves writing out the citation again. Modern practice is moving away from Latin, so repeated citations are often written now, by repeating the author's name or the first word of the citation to be repeated, followed by the new page numbers. Thus, for repeated sources in immediate succession in footnotes, you could find either:

>¹William J. Gallagher, *Report Writing for Management* (Reading, Mas-sachusetts: Addison-Wesley Publishing Co., 1969), pp. 25–28.
>²*Ibid.*, pp. 37–45.

Or:

>²Gallagher, pp. 37–45.

If the second citation is identical to the first (same work, same page(s)), you can use the citation *Idem* (Latin, *the same*) alone or the words, *The same:*

>²*Idem.*

Or:

>²The same.

idea   We in New England and our friends in the South really should stop pronouncing this as IDEAR.

idiom   Most frequently, we use this word to refer to a conventional part of the language that differs from normal patterns. Literally analyzed, idioms have odd meanings, but idioms aren't used literally. The following are American idioms:

>make a date   bring him in on the idea   quote a price
>get out a press release   I'll make it up to you.   make a deal

These are clear, communicative phrases. Idioms are quite acceptable for business writing and speaking, and only a *stuffed shirt* would avoid them.

-ile   This ending on words like *juvenile, puerile, virile, fragile,* and *senile, etc.,* is variously pronounced in the United States as ILL or like ISLE, as in tropic *isle.* The British seem universally to prefer ISLE, but we Colonials will have to check a dictionary or otherwise select the predominant pro-nunciation for each *-ile* word.

immigrant, emigrant   See *emigrant/immigrant*, p. 235.

imminent   This word means *impending, likely to happen soon*. It's a neg-atively charged word. Pleasant things should never be referred to as *im-minent*. Only disasters, calamities, and misfortunes should be *imminent*. A layoff at the plant may be said to be *imminent*, but a pay raise is *coming soon*.

impact   Fully acceptable as a noun. Avoid it as a verb.

> *Incorrect:*   It will *impact* our sales.
> *Correct:*   It will *affect* our sales.

imply, infer   To *imply* is to implicitly suggest something, to say it indi-rectly:

> He didn't call Jim a crook to his face, but he *implied* that he had been taking kickbacks from salesmen.

To *infer* is just the opposite, in that in *inferring*, it is the listener or reader who apprehends a hidden or indirect meaning:

> From what he said, I *inferred* that we've lost the account.

Thus, the phrase "Are you inferring that . . ." in reference to what someone else is saying should be "Are you implying that. . . ."

in, into   *In* indicates location (He's *in* the plant *in* Chicago). *Into* indicates motion or direction (even of mood or condition):

> Put it *into* the box.
> He's going *into* a depression.

In informal usage, *in* is often substituted for *into:* Put it *in* the box.

incredible, incredulous   Incredible means *not believable*. Incredulous means *unbelieving, not believing*.

> Your story is *incredible*.
> He was *incredulous*.

indirect object   If a sentence states that someone or something gets the direct object, that which gets the direct object is the indirect object. This is easier to illustrate than to explain:

He sent *me* a new *hat.* (*Hat* is the direct object of the verb *sent;* the *hat* is what was sent. *Me* got the hat; *me* is the indirect object.)

The judge granted the *plaintiff* a *continuance.* (*Continuance* is the direct object of *granted;* the *continuance* is what was *granted.* The *plaintiff* got the *continuance; plaintiff* is the indirect object.)

indirect question   A question that is reported in a declarative sentence. The sentence speaks of the question, but it does not ask it:

He asked if we would meet our quota.

infinitive   The basic form of the verb, the infinitive usually includes the word *to.* The infinitive is a verb form, but it does not function as a verb. The infinitive functions as a noun, an adjective, or an adverb.

Noun: *To rise* in the company was his ambition. (Subject of the sentence. What was? *To rise* was.)

Adjective: The urge *to win* motivated him. (Modifies the noun *urge* by telling the nature of the *urge.*)

Adverb: He was swimming *to win.* (Modifies the verb *was swimming* by telling how he *was swimming* or perhaps why he *was swimming.*)

Though an infinitive functions as a noun, an adjective, or an adverb, it is none of these parts of speech. Unlike a noun, an infinitive is modified by an adverb; unlike a noun, adjective, or adverb, it can take an object:

He wanted to sell *successfully.* (Successfully, an adverb, modifies *to sell,* even though it is functioning as a noun, the object of the predicate verb *wanted.*)

To win the contest was his goal.
His goal was *to win* the contest.

(In both of these sentences, *contest* is the object of the infinitive *to win.*)

An infinitive with its objects, if any, and its modifiers is called an *infinitive phrase.*

Split infinitive. H. W. Fowler once observed that there are three kinds of people in the world: those who think they know what a split infinitive is, but don't; those who think they know what a split infinitive is, and do; and those who never heard of a split infinitive, "and these last are a happy lot."

Stay happy, if you can. If you are driven to know about split infinitives, see the entry of that title on p. 266.

input   Save this word for discussing machines. Don't use it to refer to people's ideas, suggestions, comments, or other contributions.

> Avoid: I'd like to have your *input* on that.
> In favor of: I'd like your *ideas* on that.
> or:
> I'd like your *comments* on that.
> or:
> I'd like your suggestions and *recommendations* on that.

inside of   This construction is fine if *inside* is a noun: the *inside* of my hat. If the two words are used together as a preposition, it's better to drop the *of*.

> Poor: The papers are *inside* of my briefcase.
> Better: The papers are *inside* my briefcase.
> Better still: The papers are *in* my briefcase.

intensives   Words used to add force or to emphasize, such as *very, extremely, too, much, terribly, awfully, quite,* and *rather*. They are so overused that they tend more to weaken than to strengthen meaning. Avoid them whenever possible.

inter-, intra-   *Inter-* means *between* or *among*. *Intra-* means within. Thus, *interstate commerce* is commerce between or among states. *Intrastate commerce* occurs within a given state.

interface   An acceptable technical term in the systems sciences, but don't use it as a substitute for *communicate, work with, cooperate, contact,* and *coordinate*.

> Avoid: We *interface* with the marketing group.
> In favor of: We *work with* (or *coordinate with*) the marketing group.
>
> Avoid: They *interface* with the customers.
> In favor of: They *communicate* with customers.
> or:
> They *deal* with customers.

italics   See p. 98.

it's, its   With the apostrophe, this word is a contracted form of *it is*. Without the apostrophe, it is the possessive third-person pronoun.

It's raining. (contraction)
Put the letter back in *its* file. (possessive)

It is I/It is me; It's I/It's me   *Me* is totally acceptable in this construction when speaking. As to writing, take your pick. It depends more on how you think your reader might react. Is he or she a self-styled Englishist who hasn't read of grammar and usage since school days? If so, opt *I;* otherwise, *me.*

The same for *it's her, him, us,* and *them.*

J

jargon   This word can mean two things. *Jargon* is frequently used to mean *trade talk* or *inside language,* words used by people in a trade or profession to communicate to their colleagues. In that sense it's verbal shorthand and quite acceptable for messages that stay within the knowledgeable group— but don't use jargon with outsiders.

Jargon also is used to mean what have recently been called *buzz words,* words used more to dazzle than to communicate precisely, words used ritually. This kind of *jargon* is a frequent sin of business and technical writers. Avoid it.

job   More than acceptable, in most cases it is preferable to *position.*

judgment/judgement   Take your pick. *Judgment* used to be listed as the preferred U.S. spelling, but so many of us could never keep it in mind that we are allowed the spelling with the *e.* I suppose that one should be consistent, but to celebrate this freedom in spelling I use both with equal frequency, though I suspect that by the time this manuscript reaches book form, some editor will have made me correctly consistent, probably without the *e.* (Yup! *ed.*) God bless anything that makes spelling easier!

K

kind, sort   These words are singular and call for singular verbs and singular demonstrative adjectives (*this, that;* not *these, those*).

kind of a, sort of a   Drop the *a.*

L

lady   Except to emphasize the gentility of the woman referred to (*She's a real lady*), *woman* is the best way to refer to any adult female person.

Latin   A splendid language for Latin scholars, dead Romans, and Catholics who are sure that their Church is rushing headlong to damnation by allowing the vernacular. Otherwise, don't use it. It used to be a class mark of the liberally educated to sprinkle their conversation and particularly their writing with Latin words and phrases. It was then, and most assuredly is now, an absurd idea. English is a rich language, richer by far than Latin, and with few exceptions, it is well to confine your expression to our native tongue.

last, latest   Last may mean *final* or *most recent*. *Latest* means only *most recent*.

last/latter   See *former, latter*, p. 237.

latter, former   See *former, latter*, p. 237.

lay, lie   In the sense of reclining, use *lie*. In the sense of placing, use *lay*. See p. 81 for principle parts.

leisure   Usually pronounced LEE-zhur in the United States, LEHZ-ure is also acceptable, but don't force it if it doesn't come naturally to you.

less, fewer   See *fewer, less*, p. 237.

like, as   *Like* is a preposition and should have a noun or a pronoun for its object:

> This coffee tastes *like* mud.
> He's a lot *like* you.
> This is a lot *like* our own product.

As is a conjunction and should be used to introduce a clause (a group of words with a subject and a predicate).

> They don't do it *as* we do.
> He doesn't plan his work *as* he should.
> *As* you know, we will introduce it next year *as* we planned.

If there's a verb in the group of words to be related to what comes before it, use *as*. The verb indicates that you're dealing with a clause.

loan   Formerly, this was in good standing as only a noun. Universal business practice accepts it as a verb as well.

We want to arrange a *loan.*
They'll *loan* us enough to cover our start-up costs.

Of course, *lend* is still acceptable as the verb form. There seems to be no preference between *lend* and *loan* as verbs. Take your pick.

long words   For most long words, there's a shorter substitute. For many short words, there's a longer version. Most people use the short words for speaking, but for some reason, many—far too many—business writers use long words when writing, even when shorter equivalents are available. In Chapter 3, there is a thorough discussion of this point (see pp. 9–12), but it can all be summed up by simply noting that it's a good idea to use short, simple words when they will do the job for you.

lot/lots   Your sixth-grade English teacher to the contrary, these words are quite acceptable in the senses of *many, a good deal,* and *quite a bit.* A *lot of* is in better and more frequent use, especially in writing, than is *lots of.*

lousy   Probably offensive, and best avoided, particularly in writing, except for the rare (very rare) occasion when its shock impact might serve to express the proper degradation

M

m.   As an abbreviation, this refers to *noon* (Latin *meridies*) only. There is no abbreviation for *midnight* in common use. Write *m.* in lower case. Because so many people will misunderstand this abbreviation, avoid it in favor of *noon.*

mad/angry   These words may be used synonymously. Earlier usage demanded that *mad* be reserved for *insane,* but general use, written and spoken, has effectively removed this prohibition.

madam/mesdames   A form of address roughly the equivalent of *Sir,* used for women of any marital state, *Mesdames* is the plural form. It is, of course, best to address the woman or women by name. Use these words only when you don't know the addressees' names.

majority   At least one more than a half. *Plurality* means simply more than the second greatest. If three candidates run for office and the outcome is: Candidate A, 42 votes; Candidate B, 37 votes; Candidate C, 21 votes, Candidate A may be said to have won with a *plurality,* but not with a *majority* of the votes cast.

may, can   See *can, may,* p. 226.

maybe   Written as a single word only when used in the sense of *perhaps.* As a verb form, it is written in two words.

medium/mediums/media   *Mediums* is the usual plural form. *Media,* the Latin form of the plural, is often seen in technical writing. *Media* is also generally used in the expressions "mass *media*" or "news *media,*" but it should be used only in the plural. Lately, there has been a tendency, particularly among advertising people, to use *media* in the singular, as in "Television is the best *media* for that market." An otherwise respected newscaster for one of the networks testified before a Senate committee: "Our *media* is being harassed."
For singular forms, use only *medium.*

Messrs.   The plural of Mr., *Messrs.* was formerly in wider use than it is now. If there are fewer than four men, repeat Mr. with each name:

> *Acceptable:*   Messrs. Smith, Miller, and White were present.
> *Better:*   Mr. Smith, Mr. Miller, and Mr. White were present.

As *Messrs.* is an abbreviation (for French *messieurs*), it should be written with a period.

metaphor, simile   Both metaphors and similes are comparisons. A simile uses the words *like* or *as:*

> He works like three men.
> That convention was like a two-week vacation.
> Their bottom line is as red as your eyes.

A metaphor implies a comparison without stating it as such:

> He is a dynamo.
> Frank is an ass.

Metaphors and similes are excellent uses of language, but they should not be strained. Metaphors should not be mixed; make one comparison at a time lest you produce something like: "We are drowning on the horns of a dilemma."

Miss, Mrs., Ms.   Traditionally, *Miss* and *Mrs.* were used depending on the marital status of the woman so titled. *Ms.* was a form developed some years ago to address (in writing; it was never spoken) a woman when the writer was unsure of her marital status. It means Miss or Mrs.

Recently, *Ms.* has become the feminists' rallying cry. If men are to be addressed as *Mr.*, regardless of their marital status, they suggest, why then should women be discriminated against by having their marital status blatantly advertised by their title. Thus, the feminists have insisted that not only they, but all other women as well, be universally and forever titled *Ms.* (pronounced MIZZ). Other women, however, have suggested that they prefer the traditional designations.

What, then, are we to do in this time of fad or transition? The best guide seems to be that we should address each woman as she prefers to be addressed. If in correspondence she signs herself as *Miss,* address her that way; if as *Mrs.*, address her that way; if as *Ms.*, address her that way. And if she signs without title, use *Ms.*

As to the spoken form, it will take some time to see what should be done. This spoken word MIZZ is too new to have established any general patterns. My own guess is that it is not likely to persist. MIZZ is an unpleasant sound. I'd have little objection to it if it fell just a little softer on the ear—but MIZZ!

momento   An unacceptable misuse of *memento.*

money, expressions of   Use figures. And there's no need, in most instances, to repeat the amount in words, with the numerals in parentheses following.

If you frequently write about foreign currencies, it might be useful to know that you can produce a reasonably good Pounds symbol by overstriking a capital L on your typewriter with a small f (£). A good Yen symbol is a capital Y overstruck with an equals sign (¥).

months, abbreviation of   The most commonly used abbreviations are:

January:	Jan.	April:	Apr.	October:	Oct.
February:	Feb.	August:	Aug.	November:	Nov.
March:	Mar.	September:	Sept.	December:	Dec.

May, June, and *July* are not usually abbreviated.

moral, morale   *Moral* means *ethical. Morale* is an extremely imprecise word that is somehow descriptive of *level of cheerfulness* or *willingness to do the job. Morale* is not a very useful word to describe human behavior or state of mind. Avoid it in favor of some other word more precisely related to the state you wish to describe.

most   Unacceptable as a short form of *almost*.

Mrs.   See *Miss, Mrs., Ms.*, p. 250.

Ms.   See *Miss, Mrs., Ms.*, p. 250.

muchly   Not acceptable. Use *much*.

N

naive/naïve   Pronounced nah-EEV, and usually written without the two dots (dieresis) over the *i*.

Negro   When used as a noun or adjective, *Negro* is always written with a capital *N*. If you use this word, be sure to pronounce it with a long *e* and a long *o* sound (NEE-gro). That *e* is sometimes carelessly (at least one hopes that it's only carelessness) pronounced with an *i* sound and the *o* with an *a* sound; the result *(Nigra)* is offensively close to *Nigger*. See also *black/Afro-American/colored/Negro*, p. 224.

neither   Usually NEE-ther, but NEYE-ther is acceptable if it comes naturally to you.

nohow   No way. This is never correct.

nominative case   See *case*, p. 227.

notorious, notoriety   These words are never complimentary. They mean *infamous* and *infamy*.

nuclear   Though it's often mispronounced NEWK-u-lar by many people who should know better, the only correct pronunciations are NOO-kle-ar or NYEW-kle-ar.

number   See also *amount, number* (p. 218) and *a number, the number*. Use words to represent numbers:

- At the beginning of a sentence.
- To save space *($34 million)*.
- For numerals one to ten, except for units of measure.

Don't use words followed by numerals in parentheses. Use either, but not both.

O

of   Often redundantly used with other prepositions in combinations such as *off of, inside of, outside of,* and *out of.*

It's also misused, more often in speaking than in writing, for *have:*

You should *of* seen it.	You should *have* seen it.
I would *of* gone.	I would *have* gone.

In speaking, this *"of"* construction may be a sloppy pronunciation of the contracted forms *would've, should've, could've.* These contractions are acceptable in speaking, but not in writing. If you do speak them, make sure that your pronunciation indicates the contraction instead of the incorrect form with *of.*

often   Best pronounced with the *t* silent.

O.K./OK   Fine except for the most formal of writings either with or without the periods. Occasionally spelled *okay,* but why?

one   As the indefinite personal pronoun, *one* is correct, but unfortunately it grates on the ears of many people. One should, therefore, use it temperately, as one shouldn't risk turning off one's listeners over a simple thing like a pronoun—should one?

one of those who   This and similar constructions are usually plural and take a plural verb:

He is *one of those people who are* always complaining.
It's *one of those books* that *are* hard to find.

on the part of   A cumbersome way of saying *by* or avoiding the possessive.

Poor:	mistakes *on the part of* management
Better:	mistakes *by* management
	management's mistakes

-or   Always the preferable U.S. spelling in business usage. Avoid the British *-our: labour, honour, glamour.*

orientate   A made-up word, the result of an attempt to turn the noun *orientation* into a verb. There's already a verb in good standing: *orient.*

> *Poor:*   She will *orientate* the new employees.
> *Good:*   She will *orient* the new employees.
>   or:
>   She will conduct the new employees' *orientation*.

ought   See *had ought*, p. 240.

over-   If a word contains *over* as a prefix, it should not be hyphenated: *overkill, overtime*.

P

paid/payed   Use *paid*.

pair   After a number, *pair* may be either singular or plural:

There are 40 *pair* (or *pairs*) of safety shoes in stock.

parentheses   See p. 93.

participle   Like the *gerund* and the *infinitive*, the participle is a verb form used as another part of speech. Participles are often used as adjectives. A participle may also be used as part of a phrasal verb.

There are two kinds of participles: *present participles* and *past participles*. The *present participle* is the *ing* form of the verb: *swimming, running, coming, going, selling,* and *buying.*

The *past participle* of a regular verb is the *ed* form of the verb: *drowned, hunted, soaked,* and *finished.* For an irregular verb, the past participle may take a different form, but it can easily be recognized. It is the form that you would use with *have* to make a phrasal verb (a verb consisting of more than one word: *will have been chosen, has gone*). Some irregular past participles are *burst, clung, drunk, forgotten, proven, sought, bought, taught, written,* and *stung.*

Either present or past participles may be used as adjectives:

The *finished* product will be expensive. (modifies the noun *product*)
The *drying* paint is tacky. (modifies the noun *paint*)

Although a participle may be used as an adjective, it retains two of its verb qualities: it may take an object, and it is modified by an adverb:

The man *chairing the panel* is from our Chicago office. (The participle *chairing* modifies the noun *man. Panel,* another noun, is the direct object of *chairing. Chairing* what? *Chairing the panel.*)

The man *ably chairing* the discussion is Jack Howell. (*Chairing* is modified by the adverb *ably.*)

A participle may be used with or without an object, with or without modifiers. If it has any of these, the combination of participle, object, and modifiers is called a *participial phrase.*

English verbs frequently add words to the main verb for changes in tense, voice, and mood. The result is a verb more than one word long. A more-than-one-word verb is called a *phrasal verb* or a *verb phrase.* The *past* and *present* participles are frequently elements in a phrasal verb:

I *am going to be* in Cleveland next week.
We *have finished* the plans.
It *could have been* ready a week ago.
They *are being told* about it now.
The plans *have been copied.*
We *will have been marketing* it for a year in November.

When the present participle is used as a noun, it is sometimes called a *gerund* (see *gerund,* pp. 238–239), and sometimes a participle, depending on who is naming it. A few years ago, it would always have been called a *gerund.* Lately, it has occurred to language specialists that it would be less confusing to eliminate the word *gerund* and to say that a present participle may be used as a noun or as an adjective.

particular   This word is often used in writing, and especially in speaking, in ways that add no meaning. Unless it is a modifier essential to clarity, leave it out.

Poor: We are limited by the *particular* testing date for this *particular* item.
Better: We are limited by the testing date for this item.

Poor: This *particular* pattern is not available.
Better: This pattern is not available.

parts of speech   There are seven basic parts of speech:

The main elements:

1.   *Nouns* are used as subjects, direct and indirect objects, objects of prepositions, predicate nouns, and as appositives to any of the other noun uses.

2.   *Pronouns* are used in place of nouns and may be used in any noun function.
3.   *Verbs* state action or condition. They are the predicates of clauses.

The modifiers:

4.   *Adjectives* modify (describe, limit, specify, point out) nouns and pronouns.
5.   *Adverbs* modify verbs, adjectives, and other adverbs.
     Conjunctive adverbs (words like *however, moreover, accordingly,* and *therefore*), also called *transitional connectives,* modify entire clauses.

The connectives:

6.   *Prepositions* join nouns and their modifiers to other words in the sentence.
7.   *Conjunctions* join words and groups of words:
     a. *Coordinating conjunctions* join elements of equal rank.
     b. *Subordinating conjunctions* introduce dependent clauses.

party   Lawyers use this word frequently. The rest of us need seldom use it in the sense of *person.*

passé   Best not used.

passed, past   *Passed* is a verb (the past tense and past participle of *pass.*) *Past* is a preposition, or an adjective, or an adverb.

passive voice   See Chapter 3, *Guide 3,* pp. 14–17.

per   A Latin word. Useful perhaps in Latin expressions (which should be avoided by writers in English). For most business uses, substitute *a:* four *a* week instead of four *per* week; seven *an* hour instead of seven *per* hour.

percent/per cent   Spell it as one word.

period   See pp. 85–86.

person   The persons of a pronoun refer to the speaker (first person), the person spoken to (second person), and the person spoken of (third person). See *case,* p. 227.

phone   Fully acceptable as a short form of *telephone*. It used to be written *'phone* to indicate that it is a contraction, but the apostrophe is no longer used.

photo   Fully acceptable as a short form of the noun *photograph*.

phrase   A group of related words without a subject and predicate. A group of related words containing a subject and a predicate is called a clause. See also the entries for *gerund, infinitive, participle,* and *preposition.*

plan to/plan on   Both are acceptable. *Plan to* is more firmly established.

plenty   Must be followed by *of*. Should not be used as an intensive.

> *Incorrect:*   They'll be *plenty* hungry when they get here.
> *Better:*   They'll be *very* hungry when they get here.

p.m.   See *a.m., p.m., m.,* p. 218.

podium   An elevated platform such as that used by an orchestra conductor. This word should not be used to refer to a *lectern*, the stand used to hold a speaker's notes. If you want a note stand, ask for a *lectern*. If you ask for a *podium*, one of these days someone will give you a *podium*, and then what will you do?

practical, practicable   *Practical* has the sense of *useful. Practicable* means *able to be put into practice.*

pre-   Followed by a hyphen when the root word to which it is joined begins with an *e* or any capital letter. Otherwise, there is no hyphen:

> pre-emerging, pre-eminent, pre-election, pre-Columbian
> prearrange, predestine, preoperative, preclude, presentation

predicate   The *simple predicate* of a clause or sentence is the verb that states the action or the condition of the subject. The *complete predicate* includes the *simple predicate* plus its modifiers, objects, and complements. Normally, when we speak of the predicate, we mean the *simple predicate.*
    A *compound predicate* is two or more verbs with the same subject:

> We *sell* and *service* the complete line.
> They *designed* and *built* it.
> He *interviews* and *hires* all new technicians.

prefer   Use *to* with prefer.

I *prefer* bourbon *to* Scotch.
They *prefer* direct-mail selling *to* magazine advertising.
Not: They *prefer* direct-mail selling *over* magazine advertising.

prefix   An element placed before a root word to form a new word with a new meaning. The more common prefixes are:

Prefix	Meaning	Example
a-	not	amoral
		asymmetrical
ante-	before	antecedent
anti-	against, opposed	anti-American
(ant-)		antagonistic
com-	with, together	combine
(con-)	with	confident
(cor-)		correlate
contra-	against	contrary
(counter-)	opposed to	counterclockwise
de-	down from	descend
	reversing	defuse, debark
dis-	negating	disinterest
	reversing	disavow, disown
dys-	harmful, bad	dysfunctional
ex-	out, out from	exit, excavate
	former	ex-husband
extra-	outside, beyond	extramarital
	the scope of	extraordinary
		extracurricular
hyper-	over	hyperventilate
	too (much)	hyperactive
hypo-	under	hypodermic
in-	in, into	inject, insert
	not	incapable, inactive
inter-	between, among	international
		intervene, intercom
iso-	same	isoceles, isobar,
		isothermal
mis-	wrong, bad	misuse
	not	mistrust
non-	not	nonpayment, nonentity
per-	through,	pervasive
	throughout	perennial

Prefix	Meaning	Example
post-	after	post-War, postpone
pre-	before, in front of, in advance	pre-War, prepayment pre-eminent, prevent
pro-	forward in favor of	propel, project proponent, pro-Nazi
re-	back, backwards again	reverse, revoke rewrite, reacquaint
sub-	beneath of lesser rank	submarine, subway subordinate, subaltern
super-	above of greater rank in the highest degree, greatest	superimpose superior, superinten- dent superman, superstate
syn-	together, with	synonym, synchronize
trans-	across	transcontinental
ultra-	beyond, greater, more	ultramodern
un-	not, reversing	uncouth, unload undo, unorganized

preposition, prepositional phrases   A *preposition* is a word that joins a noun and the noun's modifiers, if any, to another word in the sentence. It helps to show the relationship of the noun to the word to which it is joined. The *preposition*, the noun (called the *object of the preposition*), and the noun's modifiers, if any, are collectively called a *prepositional phrase*. The most commonly used prepositions are *at, by, for, from, of, on, to,* and *with*.

Prepositional phrases are used as adjectives to modify nouns and pronouns or as adverbs to modify verbs, adjectives, or other adverbs:

Adjective: The end *of the day* will be here soon. (modifies the noun *end*)
  Adverb: He is going *to Dallas*. (modifies the verb *is going*)

Those of us over 40, and many of you under 40, were probably taught never to end a sentence with a preposition. As many of us recall, the rule was "Never use a preposition to end a sentence with."

There was never any reason for that rule, and although it may still be taught in some schools, language specialists are universal in agreeing that the rule has no value. The linguist Mario Pei once observed that if we were to follow that rule, one of our favorite expressions would lose much of its emphasis. "What the hell are you up to?" he suggests, would be far less fiery if expressed, "Up to what the hell are you?" In a more serious vein, there seems to be little need to recast a sentence like "What are you complaining about?" to "About what are you complaining?" Indeed, there seems to be sound reason not to recast it. The preposition at the end of a sentence is a firmly established tradition in our language, and any rule that condemns it is not a useful rule and should be ignored.

The list that follows shows some of the more frequently used prepositions. But use this list carefully. A preposition is determined by its function in a sentence, not by its appearance on a list. Most prepositions can be also used as other parts of speech.

Since the founding of the company, he has been its treasurer.

In the preceding sentence, *since* is a preposition. Its object is the gerund or participle *founding*, which is acting as a noun. If that confuses you at all, see the entries for *gerund* (p. 238) and *participle* (p. 254). But in the following sentence, *since* is a conjunction introducing the dependent clause *Since it was the end of the day:*

Since it was the end of the day, they closed the plant.

A word like *before* could, depending on its function in the sentence, be a preposition, a conjunction, or an adverb:

    Preposition: Don't put the cart *before* the horse.
    Conjunction: *Before* I go, I'd like to see you in my office.
       Adverb: I've heard that *before*.

Now, with all that warning, here's a list of the more common prepositions:

Preposition	*Example of use*
about	Tell me about it.
above	It is above average.
according to	It was done according to specifications.
across	It's across the street.
after	See me after lunch.
against	You're all against me!
ahead of	He's years ahead of his time.
along	We'll build it along the river.
among	You're among friends.
around	The news is around town.

Preposition	Example of use
at	He's at home.
before	See me before lunch.
behind	We're behind schedule.
below	Your work is below standards.
between	This is between you and me.
by	This is done by the book.
down	Send it down the line.
during	He fell asleep during our presentation.
for	He did it for our price.
from	Take it from me.
in	It's in the bag.
inside	Meet me inside the gate.
in spite of	He hired him in spite of his age.
into	He processed it into the memory.
like	You look like my brother.
near	Put it near his desk.
of	He told us of your work.
off	That's off the record.
onto	We loaded it onto his truck.
over	That's over your budget.
past	This project is past the point of diminishing returns.
since	He has been treasurer since the establishment of the firm.
through	Put it through the process.
to	He went to Chicago.
under	It's under your feet.
until	We can wait until the end of the month.
up	Take it up the ladder.
with	He's with the boss now.
within	Make the decision within the limits of your authority.

principal, principle   Use *principal* in the sense of *first in rank* (school *principal*), or *sum of money* (*principal* and interest), or *main importance* (principal characters, the *principal* stockholders).

Use *principle* in the sense of a *rule,* a *maxim,* or *a guide to behavior* or *judgment:*

The *principles* of fluid dynamics
Principles of ethical conduct

principal parts of verbs   See pp. 80–81 for listing of the *principal parts* of the more troublesome verbs.

prior to   Use *before* instead of this stiff phrase.

process   Normally pronounced PROHS-es. PRŌ-ses is chiefly British.

profanity   It's an excellent idea to avoid profanity in all business writing or speaking. The odd *hell* or *damn* isn't likely to offend too many people, but some might regard it as out of place. Language saltier than *hell* or *damn* is quite likely to offend many men and women.
　　We frequently hear a speaker at a meeting say something like, "I'm glad the ladies aren't here tonight, or I'd have to leave out some of my best stories." That statement, and anything like it, is a bad idea. Many men are offended by profanity, obscenity, and the like—especially in a business setting. A story or expression that might be accepted at the bar after a meeting is likely to be inappropriate at the meeting.
　　Profanity seldom advances your cause, and it often works against it.

professor   May be abbreviated *Prof.* when full name or initials are used (*Prof. John Miller, Prof. J. R. Miller*), but it should be spelled out when the last name alone is used (*Professor Miller*).

pronouns   See *parts of speech*, p. 255 and *case*, p. 227.

proper nouns and adjectives   See *capitalization*, p. 226.

prophecy, prophesy   *Prophecy* is a noun; *prophesy* is a verb.

proved/proven   Either is acceptable as an adjective or when used in a verb phrase. *Proved* is the more-established form. *Proved* is the past tense of *prove.*

provided/providing   *Provided* is the preferable word to state *as a condition*. It would be better to avoid the word in favor of *if.*

punctuation   See Chapter 10, pp. 84–101.

Q

question mark   See p. 86.

questionnaire   Always spelled with two n's.

quotation marks   See pp. 95–98.

quote, quotation   *Quote* is only a verb. It should not be used as a noun. The noun is *quotation*.

> Poor: His report began with a *quote* from Shakespeare.
> Good: His report began with a *quotation* from Shakespeare.
>   or:
>   He *quoted* Shakespeare at the beginning of his report.

R

raise, rise   *Raise* is a *transitive verb*. Something is always *raised*. *Raising* is something which is always done to something else:

> He *raised* the window.
> He *raised* a family.
> He *raised* my salary.

Rise is an *intransitive verb*. Nothing is ever *rised*. Something *rises* of itself:

> He *rose* and had his breakfast.
> The bread *rose*.
> The Dow-Jones *rose* to a new high.

See also *transitive and intransitive verbs*, p. 271.

real/really   *Real* is acceptable in the sense of *genuine*, but not as an intensive in the sense of *very*. *Really* is fully acceptable as an intensive.

> Incorrect: I'm *real* hungry.   This is *real* good.
>   Better: I'm *very* hungry.   This is *very* good.
>   I'm *really* hungry.   This is *really* good.

realty   Pronounce it rée-uhl-tea, not réel-uh-tea. The same applies to realtor (rée-uhl-tor, not réel-uh-tor). Both words are pronounced as they are spelled.

reason is because   *Reason* and *because* both have the sense of *cause*. It's incorrect to use both in the same sentence. Prefer *reason is that*.

> Incorrect: The *reason* that we're late *is because* the car broke
>   down.
>   Correct: The reason we're late is *that* the car broke down.
>   We're late *because* the car broke down.

recess   See *adjourn/recess*, p. 213.

reference of pronouns   See *Problems with pronouns*, pp. 74–76.

regardless, irregardless   *Irregardless* is unacceptable for any use. Say *regardless*.

respectfully, respectively   *Respectfully* means *with respect*. *Respectively* means *in the order given*.

Reverend   This word should be used as a title for a clergyman, not as a substitute for *minister*.

>   *Incorrect:*   The *reverend* officiated at the service.
>   *Correct:*   Reverend John Reagan preached the sermon.
>   The *minister* officiated at the service.

right, very   *Right* in the sense of *very* (It was *right* expensive) is unacceptable for any use except the most informal of conversations and only then in some regions of the country.

S

said   As an adjective (. . . and shall convey the *said* parcel . . .), it's best left to lawyers. And they would improve their writing by not using it.

same   Don't use it as a pronoun. *Same* is an adjective.

>   *Incorrect:*   We agree to buy the land and then to lease the *same*
>   to . . . .
>   *Better:*   We agree to buy the land and then to lease *it* . . . .

seasons   Don't capitalize the names of the seasons of the year, except for emphasis.

semi-   Like *hemi-* and *demi-*, this prefix means *half (semicircle)*. Unlike the others, *semi-* can also mean *twice a (semimonthly, semiannually)* or *partially*, or *only partially (semireligious, semirefined, semiprofessional, semiconductor)*.

semicolon   See pp. 90–92.

set, sit   I *sit*, you *sit*, your dog *sits*, and Cambridge, Massachusetts *sits* on the Charles River; a judge *sits* on a case. But we *set* (place) things.

shall/should   As noted in the following entry, *shall* is a little-used future form (of the verb *to be*). *Should* has the sense of *oughtness*. *I ought to go* and *I should go* say about the same thing.

shall/will   The distinctions between these forms have practically disappeared from all but the most formal uses. *Will* is the most common choice for all constructions in business or technical writing. Some writers may prefer *shall* for special emphasis, but it's doubtful that it gives a sentence much punch.

sic   Latin for *thus*, it is used in brackets to indicate that an error in a direct quotation was part of the original source and that it is not the quoter's error. As it's a foreign word, it should always be italicized.

> "Bostin [*sic*] is the capital of Massachusetts."
> "Water freezes at 212°F. [*sic*] and boils at 212°F."
> "He was born in 1997 [*sic*] in Medfield."

Modern usage increasingly favors the substitution of English for Latin designations. *Thus* is beginning to take over from *sic*.

> "Bostin [*thus*] is the capital of Massachusetts."

Still other writers prefer to put the correction in brackets following the error:

> "Water freezes at 212°F. [*32°F.*] and boils at 212°F."

However you indicate an error, indicate it—don't correct it. It is never correct to change a direct quotation in any way—and that includes correcting it.

simile   See *metaphor, simile*, p. 250.

slow, slowly   *Slow* is the adjective (It's a *slow* day), but either form can be an adverb. *Drive slow* is as acceptable as *Drive slowly*. For other adverb uses, let your ear be your guide. If you're not sure which to use to modify a verb, say both aloud and choose the one that sounds better.

so . . . that   These two words form a single construction. There should not be a comma before *that* even if several words come between *so* and *that*:

He was so persuasive and so completely at ease that he soon had everyone else relaxed and ready to buy.

sooner . . . than/sooner . . . when   *Sooner . . . than* is the acceptable form:

Poor: He had no *sooner* fastened his seat belt *when* he remembered that he'd promised to call you.

Better: He had no *sooner* fastened his seat belt *than* he remembered that he'd promised to call you.

split infinitive   In Latin, *missere* means *to send*. In French, *vendre* means *to sell*. In Italian, *cantare* means *to sing*. All these words are infinitives, the basic form of the verb. In each of the languages mentioned, and in most other languages as well, the infinitive is one word. To translate a foreign infinitive into English takes two words: *to* plus the verb word. That seems to be the root of the split infinitive problem. Once upon a time, someone decided that the English infinitive should be like all the other infinitives, a single construction. This rule had nothing to do with the way the language was spoken. People have been splitting infinitives for years. Nonetheless, somebody made it a rule that English infinitives should not be split, that is, that no word should come between the *to* and the verb word.

According to this rule, it is incorrect to write or say:

We want *to* successfully *challenge* their domination of the institutional market.

Because *successfully* interrupts the infinitive, the rule says that sentence must be recast as:

We want *to challenge* their domination . . . successfully.

or:

We want *to challenge* successfully their domination. . . .

It's a matter of style and personal preference, I suppose, but to me the first version, that with the split infinitive, is a far better sentence.

Many infinitives in sentences are better unsplit:

I want *to* easily *repair* it.

That would be far better expressed as:

I want *to repair* it easily.

Just as the don't-split-an-infinitive rule is nonsensical, so would be an always-split-an-infinitive. The writer or speaker should decide which construction will most clearly express the idea to be communicated.

squinting modifier   A *squinting* modifier is one that could easily be understood as modifying what either comes before it or follows it:

> We told them *frequently* to call us. (Did we tell them frequently, or should they call us frequently?)
> He told the policemen *with his eyes bruised and cut* that he had been attacked. (Who had the facial damage? This sentence adds a confusing pronoun to the *squinting modifier*. The result is complete confusion.)
> He advised me *quietly* to report it. (*Advised* quietly or *report* quietly?)

Each of these sentences would make more sense if the squinting modifiers were properly placed:

> We *frequently* told them to call us.
> We told them to call us *frequently*.
> *With his eyes bruised and cut,* he told the policeman that he had been attacked.
> He *quietly* advised me to report it.
> He advised me to report it *quietly*.

As you read over your writing, check to see that modifiers clearly modify only one element of the sentence.

stationary, stationery   The *ery* spelling refers only to office supplies. Use *ary* in all other senses.

strata   The only acceptable plural for *stratum. Stratums* is substandard. May be pronounced with either a long or short *a*.

subjunctive mood   If you want to know the details of the subjunctive mood, to know what it is, when to use it, and what forms it takes, look elsewhere. Any explanation is very technical, very detailed, extremely imprecise, and often confusing. You don't need to know all about it because you use the subjunctive mood correctly almost all the time without even knowing that you're doing so. When you say, "If I were President," or "I recommend that new markets be developed," or "It is important that each manager prepare a new budget," you use the subjunctive mood. You've been doing it for years and correctly. Suffice it to say that (also a subjunctive). If you have a scholarly interest in our tongue or the sort of curiosity that gets you into trouble, consult some scholarly source.

suffixes   An element placed after a root word to form a new word with a new meaning. The more common suffixes are:

Suffix	Meaning	Used for	Example
-able (-ible)	able to be	adjectives	malleable, pourable flexible
	tending to		changeable
-al	like, resembling	adjectives	metaphorical
	related to		procedural, sensual
-ic	like, resembling	adjectives	spastic, cryptic
	tending to		romantic
-ive	like	adjectives	figurative, massive
	of the nature of		persuasive
-ar	like	adjectives	insular
-ine	like	adjectives	leonine, asinine
-less	without	adjectives	penniless, topless
-ly	like	adjectives adverbs	friendly, motherly acidly, quickly
-ate	to make, to do	verbs	activate, complicate
	related to	adjectives	sensate, inanimate
-ize	to make, to do	verbs	sterilize, finalize
	to act in the way suggested by the root word	verbs	economize
-en	to make to become	verbs	enliven, quicken sicken
-wise	in this way	adverb adjective	crosswise counterclockwise
-al	the act of	nouns	betrayal
-cy	the condition of	nouns	accuracy
-ity	the condition of	nouns	incongruity, senility
-ness	the condition of	nouns	miserliness
-ant	one who does	nouns	consultant, accountant
-ian	one who does	nouns	valedictorian, custodian
-ist	one who does or is	nouns	cellist, optimist
-or	one who does	nouns	orator, censor, executor
-ster	one who is or does	nouns	youngster, jokester

suite   Pronounced SWEET except in the furniture trade, where SUIT seems standard. No need to italicize this word. It's now a part of English.

sure   As an adverb (That's *sure* nice of you folks), it is substandard. As an adjective, it's in excellent standing (It's a *sure* thing. I'm *sure* he'll agree).

suspect, suspicion   *Suspicion* should not be used as a verb. *Suspect* is the verb.

> *Incorrect:*   I *suspicion* that we'll regret it.
> *Correct:*   I *suspect* that we'll regret it.

Suspect, with the accent on the first syllable (SUS-pect) can be a noun in the sense of: The police have four *suspects.*

swell

> *Miss Smith:*   There are two words that I never want you to use, class. One is "swell"; the other is "lousy."
> *Student:*   What are they, Miss Smith?

"Swell" has been faced with this sort of prohibition for some time now. But, it persists. Don't fight it—but keep it out of your more formal writing. It would do for many letters, but for few reports.

synonym   Words with approximately the same denotation, or definition, are called *synonyms. End, finish,* and *terminate* are synonyms, as are *buy* and *purchase.* That doesn't mean, however, that one word is as good as the other for any given use. In addition to denotation (definition), words have connotation, or associated meaning, that must be considered. *Stubborn* and *resolute* are synonyms, but they have different connotations.

Then, too, you must consider the readability of written words and the sound of spoken words. Will they be clear and familiar to your receivers? Do they represent your best style? Synonyms are not interchangeable.

T

that   If a sentence can be written as well without *that* as with it, eliminate *that.*

There is the book *that* I wanted to buy.

would be better written as:

There is the book I wanted to buy.

theater/theatre   Preferable American spelling is *theater*. The preferable pronunciation is THEEE-uh-ter. Theee-AY-ter and theee-ETER are regional.

there, their, they're   *Their* is the possessive pronoun (*Their* reports are here). *They're* is the contracted form of *they are*. Use *there* for all other constructions.

there is, there are   In these constructions, *there* is either an adverb of place to tell where someone or something is (*There* are your gloves), or it is what is variously called an *expletive* or an *anticipatory subject*. In either case, the true subject determines the number of the verb.

There is my glove.
There are my gloves.   (*There* as an adverb)

There is one cause.
There are many causes.   (*There* as an anticipatory subject)

they   Avoid the overgeneral *they*. Use *they* only when its antecedent is clear.

Poor: *They* have an index in this book.
Better: *There* is an index in this book.

Poor: *They* have had trouble with insecticides.
Better: *Insecticides* have caused problems.
    There have been problems with insecticides.

Poor: *They* say that our winters are getting warmer.
Better: Our *winters* are getting warmer.

till/until/'til   Both *till* and *until* are fully acceptable, but *'til* is not.

topic sentence   The key sentence in a paragraph; it states the main idea (topic). The other sentences in the paragraph (support sentences) give fullness of expression and clarity to the topic sentence.

toward/towards   One is as good as the other. Take your choice.

transition   The movement from concept to concept in written or oral expression. Transitions show the receiver the relationship of one idea to another. If, for example, we state:

A happened. B happened.

we have given our receiver two bits of information, but we have failed to show what one has to do with the other. The receiver must try to guess our meaning. That's poor communication. Those two statements might mean one of many things:

A happened as a result of B.
A caused B.
A and B happened.
A happened in spite of B.
A happened; however, B happened.
A happened and B happened, but one had nothing to do with the other.
A happened after B.
A happened before B.
A happened here; B happened there.

You know, or should know, what happened and what the relationship of the happenings was. Make sure that your receiver knows, too. Show the relationship.

transitive and intransitive verbs   A verb that takes an object is *transitive;* one that does not is *intransitive.* Many verbs can be either *transitive* or *intransitive;* they sometimes have objects and sometimes appear without them:

He *ran. Ran* is intransitive. No object.
He ran the company. Ran is transitive. *Company* is its object.

Some verbs are always transitive: *lay, set,* and *raise.* They must always have an object.
Other verbs are always intransitive: *lie, sit,* and *rise.* They never have an object.
The verb *to be* is always intransitive. It never has an object, but it and other *linking verbs* frequently have a *predicate adjective,* a *predicate noun,* or a *pronoun* as a *complement.* A *complement* is a word that completes the meaning of the subject-verb idea. (Harold is our *accountant.* I'm *hungry.* Is that *you?*)

try and   Don't use this as a substitute for *try to*. See also *and (in infinitives)*, p. 219.

-type   Constructions with *-type* as a suffix are substandard except on Damon Runyan's Broadway (My escort is a very *high-type* person.).

U

underlining   See *italics*, p. 98.

unique   Unique means *one of a kind*. It is an absolute and cannot be compared as *more unique, most unique. Unique* should not be used in the sense of *unusual*. If you must compare things in the degree to which they approach *uniqueness,* use *more nearly unique* and *most nearly unique*—or far better, call one *unusual,* another *more unusual,* and the strangest one in the bunch can be *most unusual.*

until   See *till/until/'til,* p. 270.

used to   It's always spelled this way, even though the *d* is usually not pronounced with any emphasis. It's there if you listen carefully to someone who pronounces it correctly, but you must keep a sharp ear tuned for it.

utilize/utilization   Cumbersome forms. Use *use* instead.

V

verbals   Verb forms used as other parts of speech. See also *infinitive,* p. 245; *gerund,* p. 238; and *participle,* p. 254.

very   An overworked intensive. Eliminate it unless you're sure it is essential to your meaning. Ninety percent of the *very's* in business writing can safely be eliminated without threat to meaning and with an improvement in readability.

viable   Unless you're a biologist, drop this word from your vocabulary. It has been deadened by misuse and overuse.

vice, vise   A *vice* is a bad habit or a matter of concern to the *Vice* Squad. A *vise* is a tool. The tool is sometimes spelled *vice,* but it would be better to stick with the *s* spelling for the tool. With the *c* spelling used for both meanings, you can write some embarrasingly misunderstood sentences, particularly if it's your *vise* that you're writing about.

viz.   An obsolete abbreviation (for the Latin *videlicet*) meaning *namely*. Avoid it, and if you come across it while reading aloud, say *namely* rather than *vizz*.

vs.   Abbreviation for the Latin *versus (against)*. It should be used in business only for legal citations *(Brown vs. Smith, U.S. vs. Jones Manufacturing)*. Pronounce either the full word *(versus)* or the abbreviation as VER-sus.

W

wait on, wait for   A waiter *waits on* his customers. One *waits for* someone or something to come or to happen.

weather, whether, wheather   *Weather* is studied by meteorologists. *Whether* is the word in phrases like *whether to go or not*. *Wheather* is a misspelling.

well   See *good/well*, p. 240.

where   Refers to location, but it should not be used instead of *that*.

> *Poor:*   I see *where* the price of our stock went up.
> *Better:*   I see *that* the price of our stock went up.
> *Better:*   I see the price of our stock went up.

while   Refers to duration. It is often, and incorrectly, used as a synonym for *although* or *though*. It can be confusing in that sense:

> *While* he was here, he could do nothing to solve the problem.

Does that mean "although he was here," or does it mean that "during the time he was here"?

Use *while* only for duration, and check sentences in which you use it to make sure that the meaning can't be confused with *although*. If it can be, recast the sentence.

will/shall   See *shall/will*, p. 265.

wire   Fully acceptable as a synonym for telegram or cablegram.

X

x-ray　Always hyphenated. May be capitalized or not, at your whim.

Y

you/one　*One* was the traditional form for use as an indefinite pronoun. *You* has gradually come into acceptable use as a substitute. Language changes. In this case it's regrettable that *one* is coming to be frowned upon as snotty. One would wish it were otherwise.

you all　Standard and fully acceptable for spoken uses in certain parts of the country, notably, but not exclusively, in the South. *You* is the preferable form, singular and plural, in writing.

your, you're　*Your* is the possessive pronoun. *You're* is the contracted form of *you are.*

Appendix
Letter Conventions
and Forms

The date.

Don't abbreviate the month in the date of a letter. The date may be written in either of two ways:

Month, day, comma, year: July 6, 198X
Day, month, year: 6 July 198X

The first of these forms is the more familiar in the United States. The second is more widely used in Europe, but it has also been used in the United States, and is gaining in use and popularity.

Names.

Don't use initials or abbreviations unless the person addressed customarily signs that way. If someone signs with his full name, for example, *John L. Mitchell*, don't address him as *J. L. Mitchell*.

Titles.

In addressing someone by title, use a title only once.

Incorrect: Dr. John J. Alworth, M.D.
Correct: Dr. John J. Alworth, or John J. Alworth, M.D.

Zip code.
The zip code follows the name of the state and is separated from it with a single space. No comma is used:

Medfield, MA 02052

Attention line.
Avoid this if at all possible. Perhaps you may have to use it to address a proposal or invoice or other quasi-legal document. Other than that, address the person to whom you're writing.

Instead of:	*Use:*
Mercy Hospital	Dr. Anne Prospect
27 Central Street	Mercy Hospital
Medvale, MA 02020	27 Central Street
Attn: Dr. Anne Prospect	Medvale, MA 02020

The attention line, according to still widely followed tradition, requires Gentlemen: or Mesdames: as the salutation. Avoid these terms. If you do use an *Attention line*, eliminate the salutation entirely and put the first paragraph two spaces below the inside address.

LETTER FORMS

Any of the following four forms may be used for business correspondence:

1. The *Blocked Form* is the most common today.
2. The *Alternate Blocked Form* is new, but is gaining acceptance—slowly
3. The *Conventional Indented Form* is on its way out, though it's still commonly seen.
4. The *Simplified Letter* was an interesting experiment that was introduced before its time. You'll see it rarely, but it may appeal to the pioneer in you.

The following sample letters illustrate these four forms and explain them.

1. Blocked form.

6 July 198X

Mr. Harold Miller
Miller Associates
275 Arnold Avenue
Medvale, MA 02055

Reference: Your Purchase Order 2345

Dear Mr. Miller:

This is a sample of the blocked form of a business letter. It is becoming more widely used for a number of reasons. First, it is easier to type, as the typist does not have to use any tab stops. Second, it presents a neat, businesslike appearance.

The date form used above is optional. You could use the standard form, with the day following the month, but this use saves a comma and separates the numbers.

The reference line puts reference information in an easily accessible spot, allowing you to begin your letter with a reader-centered opening instead of the usual "Reference is made to your purchase order." Use the reference line as needed for references of any kind. If you don't want to refer to anything, eliminate the reference line.

Sometimes, you'll see a subject line in place of the reference line. This focuses the reader's attention on the subject, and it can be useful for filing. But like the reference line, the subject line is optional and can be omitted.

> If you have to refer to a long quoted passage (three lines or more), you can indent it, as this subparagraph is indented, to indicate that it is a quotation. If this had been a quotation, the preceding paragraph would have ended with a colon.

If the quotation is longer than one paragraph, double space between the paragraphs. When using indentation to indicate a direct quotation, don't use quotation marks.

After a quotation, return to the normal margin. The quotation is the only reason for indenting anything in this letter form.

Yours very truly,

John L. Michaels
Sales Manager

2. Alternate blocked form.

6 July 198X

Mr. Harold Miller
Miller Associates
275 Arnold Avenue
Medvale, MA 02055

This, Mr. Miller, is an alternate form of the blocked business letter. It is like the blocked form in all respects except two. It has no salutation and no complimentary close.

In place of the salutation, the writer addresses the reader in the first sentence of the letter. There is no complimentary close, nor is anything substituted for it. Some people object to these omissions because they are so different from what they are used to seeing. You'll have to decide which form is more acceptable to you and to your readers.

This letter used no reference or subject lines. They could be part of this form; however, if used, they would be placed two spaces below the inside address. Two spaces would follow the reference or subject line.

The indented paragraph could also be used in this form to indicate a quotation.

This form is not too widely seen because of its departure from the salutation and complimentary close conventions, but it is gaining in acceptance.

John L. Michaels
Sales Manager

3. Conventional indented form.

July 6, 198X

Mr. Harold Miller
Miller Associates
275 Arnold Avenue
Medvale, MA 02055

Dear Mr. Miller:

This letter is the traditional form of a business letter. It is the one that most people are used to seeing, but that seems to be its only grace. The tab stops required for the date, the complimentary close, the signature, and each paragraph, do little to improve the appearance of the letter, and they do take extra time and space.

If you're willing to expend that time and space, there's really nothing wrong with this form of letter. A reference line could be used with this letter. It would be placed two spaces below and two spaces above the salutation.

Sometimes, this form is presented with double spacing to make a short letter look longer. Though there's nothing wrong with double spacing, I would have to question the philosophy that holds that there's something wrong with a short letter. A short letter is refreshing to most readers. It stands out from the rest of the pile in the in basket. If a letter is short, simply space it in the middle of the page to avoid the top-heavy look of one that's entirely at the top half of the paper.

Yours very truly,

John L. Miller
Sales Manager

4. Simplified letter.

July 6, 198X

Mr. Harold Miller
Miller Associates
275 Arnold Avenue
Medvale, MA 02055

SIMPLIFIED LETTER

This form, though it looks new, was first introduced in 1947 by the National Office Management Association (now called the Administrative Management Society).

It's the basis for the Alternate Blocked Form. It eliminates the salutation and the closing. It is in blocked form and requires no tab stops or indentation.

You'll notice two main differences between this form and the Alternate Blocked Form: the SUBJECT LINE and the SIGNATURE and TITLE LINES. Both are typed as all in capitals. The SUBJECT line eliminates the word "subject" and presents the subject as though it were a title of the letter. The signature line is also typed in all capitals, and the writer's title follows on the same line, separated from the name by a spaced hyphen.

JOHN L. MICHAELS – SALES MANAGER

INDEX